The Future of
Competitive Strategy

Management on the Cutting Edge

Robert Holland, series editor
Published in cooperation with *MIT Sloan Management Review*

The Future of Competitive Strategy

Unleashing the Power of Data and
Digital Ecosystems

Mohan Subramaniam

The MIT Press
Cambridge, Massachusetts
London, England

The MIT Press would like to thank the anonymous peer reviewers who provided comments on drafts of this book. The generous work of academic experts is essential for establishing the authority and quality of our publications. We acknowledge with gratitude the contributions of these otherwise uncredited readers.

This book was set in ITC Stone Serif Std and ITC Stone Sans Std by New Best-set Typesetters Ltd. Printed and bound in the United States of America.

Library of Congress Cataloging-in-Publication Data

Names: Subramaniam, Mohan, author.
Title: The future of competitive strategy : unleashing the power of data and digital
   ecosystems / Mohan Subramaniam. Management on the cutting edge | Includes
   bibliographical references and index. | Digital media. | Competition.
Description: Cambridge, Massachusetts : The MIT Press, [2022] | Series:
Identifiers: LCCN 2021033927 | ISBN 9780262046992 (hardcover)
Subjects: LCSH: Strategic planning—Methodology. | Digital communications.
Classification: LCC HD30.28 .S85 2022 | DDC 658.4/012—dc23/eng/20211015
LC record available at https://lccn.loc.gov/2021033927

10 9 8 7 6 5 4 3 2

Contents

Series Foreword

The world does not lack for management ideas. Thousands of research-ers, practitioners, and other experts produce tens of thousands of arti-cles, books, papers, posts, and podcasts each year. But only a scant few promise to truly move the needle on practice, and fewer still dare to reach into the future of what management will become. It is this rare breed of idea—meaningful to practice, grounded in evidence, and *built for the future*—that we seek to present in this series.

Robert Holland
Managing Director
MIT Sloan Management Review

Preface

My association with the field of competitive strategy began over thirty years back when I started my doctoral studies. Industrial organizational economics then had a significant influence on this field. It helped frame competitive strategy in the context of a firm's industry. Industry characteristics influence a firm's profitability; hence it made sense for firms to compete in ways that best marshalled industry forces to their advantage. This perspective offered elegant conceptual frameworks and strong empirical anchors for academics. For practitioners and a vast majority of businesses operating with value-chain-driven business models, this perspective also offered pragmatic approaches for businesses to position themselves within their respective industries and clear guidelines to gain competitive advantage.

By the turn of this century, new technologies began to grab our attention. The power of software became apparent. The internet started changing business processes. We saw exponential advances in digital connectivity and the emergence of digital platforms. Businesses, especially technology companies, started seeing their world around them as ecosystems rather than industries.

Observing these trends, I began to wonder: what would competitive strategy anchored on *ecosystems* rather than industries look like? Ideas then were fuzzy. But the desire and objectives were clear: first, to develop new frameworks for competitive strategy that gave ecosystems the same depth and rigor as prevailing frameworks did for industries; second, to make these frameworks relevant to a vast majority of industrial firms competing with value-chain business models—not just to new technology firms that operated with platform-based business models.

In October 2014, I happened to reconnect with Bala Iyer at a social gathering at a common friend's place. I knew Bala from the time he was a newly minted faculty member in the information systems department at Boston University, and I was graduating from my doctoral program in strategic management from the same school. By 2014, he was at Babson, and I was at Boston College. Our conversation turned to ecosystems. There was enough common interest to conclude that we must take our initial conversations further.

We started meeting two to three times a week; our discussions would last for hours. He came from the technology angle, while I offered my strategy perspective. Early thoughts coalesced around how digital ecosystems could be built on the foundations of APIs (application program interfaces). APIs that allow software programs to talk to one another were then well-known to the technology world. For the industrial world, however, their potential to help create new ecosystems were not as obvious. We published a few articles on the strategic significance of APIs to industrial firms.

Bala tragically passed away in his prime, a few years after we started working together. He left behind for me precious seeds of insight that I could grow and nurture.

Around that time, I was also conducting executive education workshops around the world. These workshops gave me the opportunity to present my new thinking to seasoned executives in the digital space and an invaluable forum to expand and refine my ideas. The key elements of a digital ecosystem framework for competitive strategy started taking shape.

Since I started this work, digital forces have continued to gather strength. Sensors and the Internet of Things (IoT) are now ubiquitous in the industrial world. The power of data is obvious to all. The need to shift from an industrial mindset to a digital mindset has never been more urgent. The future of competitive strategy, in other words, has arrived.

This book lays the foundation for a digital future of competitive strategy. I hope you enjoy reading it as much as I enjoyed writing it.

Introduction

"The world's most valuable resource is no longer oil but data," proclaimed the May 6, 2017, lead article of the *Economist*.[1] The article drew attention to a handful of digital titans that have cornered most of the value from this resource, such as Amazon, Google, Apple, and Facebook. These digital titans, which dominate our economy with their digital platform–driven business models, have indeed displaced such long-standing industrial titans as Exxon, General Motors, and Boeing from their erstwhile perch of being among the most valuable companies in the world. This upending of the business value order should make many CEOs of legacy firms—anchored on value chain–driven business models, and with rich histories in the industrial world—ask, Why can't *we* benefit from data's newfound potential? What should *we* do to unlock the value of data?

A vast majority of legacy firms have yet to grasp the full scope of the value that data can unlock for their businesses. A 2019 McKinsey Global Institute report, for instance, highlights that modern digital technologies can help firms add $13 trillion to global GDP by 2030. Yet it also finds that "the gap to the digital frontier remains large across industries."[2] The institute's analysis suggests that most firms have yet to establish strategies to benefit from the new opportunities that lie ahead. For decades, firms derived their competitive advantage from how they produced and sold their products[3] within their industries. They now additionally need to draw competitive advantage from data—data their products can generate with the help of modern technologies, data they can harness in the digital ecosystems evolving around them.

Meeting this challenge requires three key inputs: first, a new understanding of how digital technologies have transformed prevailing ways of utilizing data; second, a fresh comprehension of business environments as digital ecosystems; and third, new mindsets and frameworks for a strategy that builds a data-driven advantage for competing in digital ecosystems.

The purpose of this book is to provide insights into how firms can draw competitive advantage from data. It draws attention to the new competitive dynamics of the modern digital world and explains how a firm can establish an advantage in it using its own or others' data. The book serves as a guide for firms to shape their digital transformation journeys and to envision and execute their modern-day digital strategies. This introduction explores the foundational concepts and lays the groundwork for subsequent chapters.

The Ford Motor Story

To get some grasp of the task ahead, let's consider some of Ford Motor Company's new initiatives as it adapts to a changing business landscape. A doyen of the industrial era and one of the original champions of the automotive industry, Ford in 2018 pledged $11 billion toward its digital transformation efforts, planned for a ten-year span.[4] One of the underlying features of its digital initiatives is an expansive adoption of sensors installed in Ford vehicles that generate data from a vast array of sources. Sensors that detect and capture in real time the status of engine performance, braking performance, tire pressure, road conditions, and air quality are some examples. Ford's sensors can send data updates at rates of up to fifty times per second. In one hour of driving, they generate around 25 gigabytes of data.[5]

With these data, Ford is able to offer several new "smart" car features. Cars can detect and alert drivers to other vehicles in blind spots. They help drivers stay in their lanes. They automatically brake before imminent collisions. They adapt to speed limits (with the driver's consent) and decelerate when detecting slowing traffic ahead. Electric cars provide drivers with information on the current and projected state of charge, along with the amount of charge time necessary for any planned distance. At charging stations, these cars alert users if the charging stops unexpectedly owing to a power outage, plug removal, or similar event. Cars car even map routes that ensure adequate charge for a journey.

Ford also channels data through its in-vehicle communications system, called SYNC, and an array of apps available through its app store, connected via a user's smartphone. Beyond taking a driver from point A to point B, Ford's apps offer services that resonate with the driver's lifestyle during the ride. One such example is an app that permits ordering Starbucks coffee through Alexa.[6] By assessing the real-time location, weather, and traffic data, the car predicts the precise time that Starbucks should expect the driver, ensuring prompt availability for a drink pickup, without the driver needing to wait in line. In the meantime, Ford's MyPass app automatically completes the purchase through a connected bank. Such features make Ford's modern cars operate as "smart phones on wheels."[7]

Yet Ford also recognizes that these initiatives are just a start. Many more milestones lie ahead in its digital transformation journey. Ford is working to vastly expand its "smart" driver-assist features to make its cars fully autonomous. It plans to achieve 100 percent "uptime" in commercial fleets, with each car predicting component failures and scheduling repairs while also prearranging for requisite spare parts availability.[8] Another of Ford's goals is to expand its app-based services beyond, say, ordering coffee with new offerings, such as helping drivers find empty parking spots or proposing alternative routes when drivers are stuck in traffic jams.

Key Takeaways and Emerging Questions

Ford's example offers some useful takeaways for other firms. Not every firm will want or need to invest billions in the coming decade. Yet every product can interact with users in new ways through data. Product-generated data can open new business opportunities for every firm. And, with the scope of these opportunities still expanding, data becomes a fountainhead for new initiatives for all firms to create value.

These takeaways, however, also raise some important and broader questions. What, for instance, underlies the ability of data to generate new value-creating opportunities? How can firms envision and maximize the scope of these opportunities? How can firms establish competitive advantage when contending for them?

To answer such questions, firms need first to appreciate some key tenets regarding how they can effectively generate and steer digital initiatives. Three such tenets, discussed next, provide a glimpse of what is at stake for every legacy firm aspiring to compete in the modern digital world. These tenets also present the foundational concepts for a modern-day digital competitive strategy that the book elaborates on in subsequent chapters.

Tenet 1: Recognize the New Potential of Data

Using data is not per se a novel concept. Most firms possess data on their products, markets, and operations. They analyze it for insights and decision-making. Based on analyses of sales data, for instance, Ford knows which of its cars are more popular, in what geographies, and with which specific dealers. Ford routinely uses such insights for product development, capacity planning, and marketing. These are long-established practices in legacy firms. What is different today is that modern digital technologies allow data to be used in far more expansive ways.

Interactive Data

Modern data is shifting its emphasis from being *episodic* to *interactive*. Episodic data is generated by discrete events, such as the shipment of a component from a supplier, the production or sale of a product. Interactive data, on the other hand, is streamed by continuously tracking asset performance and product-user exchanges through sensors and the Internet of Things (IoT). Continuous tracking of assets and their operational parameters can boost productivity. For example, sensors that track and maintain temperature levels in the right range while super heating molten steel, improve production quality and yield. Sensors embedded within products, in addition can drive revolutionary user experiences.

Many of Ford's new features, such as lane change assists, automatic braking, alerts for the car's charging status, or apps to order coffee, are based on real-time insights—and feasible only through using interactive data. Similarly, GE's jet engines interact with pilots during flight to help them optimize fuel consumption. They do so by tapping interactive data when the jet engine is in use, such as data on headwinds, tailwinds, turbulence, and the plane's elevation. Babolat's tennis rackets capture interactive data that can track a player's skills and recommend ways for improvements. Tempur Sealy International's mattresses interact with users, helping them change body positions to improve their sleep quality. The company achieves this by using real-time data on heart rates, breathing patterns, and body movements.[9]

Legacy firms can also use web- or app-based sensors to capture interactive data. With the help of such data, for example, the *Washington Post* recommends journalistic stories that may particularly interest readers as they browse for news on the company's website. Bank of America's app, named Erica, interacts with its users, tracking spending behavior to enable features such as refund confirmations from vendors, analysis of weekly spending, or reminders of bill payments due. Allstate Insurance's app-based sensors help users adopt safer driving habits. This is because of interactive data obtained during driving. In sum, legacy firms can adopt several sensor-driven approaches to capture interactive data (see figure 0.1)

Real-Time and After-the-Fact Data: New Kinds of Insights

Real-time data from product-user interactions eventually turn into after-the-fact data that can be analyzed to generate retrospective insights. But these after-the-fact insights, when derived from accumulated sensor data, have some noteworthy attributes. To begin with, sensor data

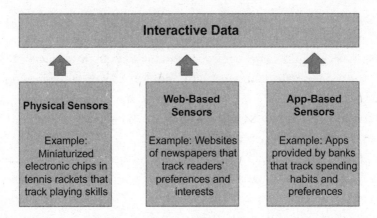

Figure 0.1
Sensors generate interactive data. *Note:* Digital platforms, such as Amazon or Uber, typically use only web-based or app-based sensors. Legacy firms can use web-based, app-based, and physical sensors.

help firms pinpoint the subjects for which they wish to develop after-the-fact insights. Here we may consider two such subjects from the Ford example: car components, such as engines, and drivers. Ford creates distinct profiles for each engine by accumulating data separately from hundreds of sensors in the engine. Similarly, it aggregates data from several sensors to develop profiles for each individual driver. This allows Ford to analyze the performance of each engine individually to (among other things) predict when it is likely to fail. It also allows Ford to understand several attributes of every individual driver, such as how frequently the driver charges the electric car, or how safely she drives. The more widespread the adoption of sensor-equipped products, the more subjects a firm can build after-the-fact insights on.

The accumulating sensor data also help companies develop intricate insights for each profile. Caterpillar knows whether its customers use their motor graders to move heavy dirt or lighter gravel. Sleep Number mattresses know how well you sleep each night. Allstate knows how safely a subscriber to its services is driving. Nike, similarly, could know whether a running shoe customer uses a shoe primarily for running or walking.

As sensors continue providing real-time data, they help firms further refine and generate finer-grained product and user profiles. The consequent deep insights set up a foundation for firms to offer more customized product features, new experiences for customers, and fresh opportunities to create value. Caterpillar, for example, developed a new design of its motor grader to more effectively move gravel rather than dirt, reducing its costs of production, offering a more competitive price, and improving margins. Sleep Number Corporation offers new wellness services anchored on getting better sleep. Allstate can offer customized and more attractive premiums for safer drivers. Nike, similarly, can offer a different shoe that more precisely suits the customer's mix of walking and running preferences.

Modern Digital Technologies Expand the Role of Data

The kinds of insights firms can now derive from interactive data point to a transformation in the conventional purpose of products. Products are no longer meant just to deliver a functionality, build a brand, or generate revenue. Instead, products are a significant conduit to generate data that serve as wellsprings for new customer experiences. Relatedly, businesses will also observe a reversal in the roles of data and products. The prevailing role of data is to support products. Now, rather than data supporting products, products support data—because products become conduits for new kinds of product-user interaction data empowered by modern digital technologies such as sensors and the IoT. With this role reversal, products are not the only revenue generators for legacy firms. Data too become a significant revenue generator. As modern technologies transform data's key characteristics, data are assuming an expanded role in today's corporations (see tables 0.1 and 0.2).

Moreover, products are not the only source of interactive data. A variety of different sources can generate interactive data through sensors. Such data can come from suppliers, from assets, from different processes (such as assembly, manufacturing, bank loan applications, insurance claims), from logistical services, from retail shelves, and so

Table 0.1

Transforming characteristics of data

Prevailing Characteristics	New Characteristics
• Episodic: generated through discrete events (e.g., every time a product—say, a mattress—is sold)	• Interactive: generated through ongoing interactions (e.g., continuous streaming of heart rates and breathing patterns to assess quality of sleep from sensors in the mattress)
• Stored in aggregate form (e.g., aggregate revenues from different mattress types, retail channels, or geographies)	• Stored to create individual profiles (e.g., how restfully an individual sleeps over time)
• Value extraction mostly from after-the-fact analysis of stored data (e.g., why sales are up or down for a particular mattress model, in a particular retail channel or geography)	• Value extraction from both real-time aspects of interactive data and stored data (e.g., improving rest as user sleeps using real-time data and understanding sleep patterns through analysis of archived data)

on. Such data can be merged with a firm's traditional databases and with alternative sources of data such as social media.

A host of other advances in technology further elevate what firms can do with such emerging pools of data and by combining real-time and accumulated after-the-fact data. The latest cloud technologies allow firms to maintain vast repositories of profiles and ongoing real-time data sourcing for each sensing unit. Technologies such as artificial intelligence (AI), machine learning, and data analytics further amplify insight-building processes for each profile.[10] Firms can also share select facets of real-time data across various connected assets linked through the IoT. With connected parking lots, for example, Ford can, with the driver's permission, share a car's location data to guide a driver to an empty parking spot. Moreover, while sensing units communicate with one another with real-time data, their communications can be shaped based on intelligence garnered through its accumulated data. Babolat can use its accumulated data on a tennis player's skill level acquired from its users' connected tennis rackets to match the player to other players with similar skills or appropriate coaches. Estimates range from

Table 0.2
The expanding role of data

Examples	Prevailing Role of Data	New Role of Data
A mattress company	• Streamline inputs from suppliers • Optimize production scheduling, inventory, and distribution logistics • Shape product design • Tailor marketing and sales efforts to customer needs	• Track mattress-user interactions to monitor quality of sleep (through sensors) • Improve quality of sleep, making mattresses adapt in real time to sleep data • Improve quality of sleep by sharing real-time sleep data with external objects in the room (e.g., lights, soothing music) • Generate new data-driven services and revenue streams by making mattresses a health and wellness product
An insurance company	• Assess risks in populations (e.g., populations of homes for home insurance) • Price profitable and competitive policies • Improve efficiencies in processing claims post-damage • Generate effective marketing campaigns tailored to different market segments to increase population base, mitigate customer churn, and reduce average risks	• Monitor individual risks (e.g., individual homes through sensors) • Predict damage (e.g., the likelihood of frozen pipes) • Avert damage through alerts (e.g., by asking homeowners to run hot water through their pipes before they freeze) • Provide post-damage services (e.g., sending repair crews if damage is not averted) • Reposition the insurance business from compensating damage to preventing and servicing damage through new data-driven services and revenue streams

30 to 50 billion such connected assets in the coming years, creating vast opportunities to unlock the value of data for competitive advantage.[11]

Tenet 2: Comprehend Emerging Digital Ecosystems

To unlock data's new potential, a firm needs a network of data recipients to share data with. Some of these recipients are internal to a firm's value chain. Sensor data on any specific component in Ford's cars, for instance, are shared with recipients such as software design departments, AI centers, units coordinating digital services, warehouses that stock spare parts, and service dealers—all part of Ford's organization. These recipients can coordinate their activities to deliver new digital value propositions, such as predictive maintenance services. Other recipients of sensor data are external to a firm's value chains. Amazon (through its Alexa smart speaker), Starbucks, banks, and app providers for weather or traffic are examples of data recipients that coordinate their roles to effect Ford's coffee service described earlier. A network of data generators and recipients constitutes a firm's digital ecosystem. For legacy firms, such a network has two components: one, internal to its value chains consists of its *production ecosystems*; the other, external to its value chains, consists of its *consumption ecosystems*.[12]

Production Ecosystems
Production ecosystems arise from digital linkages between and among various entities, assets, and activities within a company involved in producing and selling products, including suppliers, R&D, manufacturing, assembly, and distribution channels. These linkages are possible because of sensor-equipped and IoT-enabled connectivity across the company's value chain activities. Production ecosystems thus provide an internal avenue for a firm to unlock the value of data. By establishing a sensory network within its supply chains, for example, firms achieve tighter inventory coordination based on the real-time status of inventory usage. With sensors in their smart factories, firms can further enhance operational efficiencies by synchronizing how machines,

robots, or production and assembly units communicate to streamline workflows.

With sensors in their products, production ecosystems help unlock new value by channeling product-generated data to drive new product performance–related features and services. This is possible when products adapt their attributes to individual customers' usage data. In addition, the outcomes of such services can be tracked, improved on, and displayed in the form of tangible metrics. GE introduced "outcome-based" services for its aircraft engines based on assurances of reduced fuel costs as pilots followed the engines' guidance when flying. GE's revenues from these services are in addition to those derived from its traditional jet engine sales.

Other firms can take a similar tack through offering smart products that adapt to customer usage data and improve product outcomes. For example, Oral-B's smart toothbrushes improve users' brushing habits by tracking and displaying brushing outcomes on smartphone apps. Caterpillar reduces the downtimes of its machines on construction sites based on sensors that monitor real-time usage and wear and tear. These are examples of how firms can unlock new value from their production ecosystems. R&D, product development, marketing, sales, and after-sales service units—when they are digitally connected to receive, analyze, generate, share, and react to sensor data—can deliver such value. The more widespread and intricate a firm's sensory network is across such units, the larger its production ecosystems.

Consumption Ecosystems

Consumption ecosystems differ from production ecosystems by focusing on connections external to their value chains. Consumption ecosystems stem from a network of external entities that complement a product's sensor-derived data. A retailer like Starbucks that offers coffee services to a driver based on data transmitted from sensors in a car is an example of a complement. A parking spot that digitally signals a car that it is empty and available is another example. Unlike the units and entities in its value chain, a firm does not directly control this network.

This network of independent entities also expands as more assets get digitally connected. Ford's consumption ecosystems, for example, expand when more retailers (in addition to Starbucks) or more assets (such as parking lots) are able to digitally complement its sensor data.

For a vast majority of firms, consumption ecosystems did not exist before modern advances in data and digital connectivity. An example here is the new consumption ecosystems developing around a light bulb when embedded with sensors. "Smart bulbs" contain sensors to collect data on such conditions as motion, the location of objects, and sound. Data on these conditions open up new opportunities for different parties to create value. Consumption ecosystems can emerge in a number of domains depending on the data the smart bulb generates and the third parties it attracts. Take motion, for example. By sensing motion in homes that are supposed to be empty, the sensor in a smart bulb can initiate a security services ecosystem of alarms and mobile apps. By sensing and tracking inventory in warehouses, it creates an ecosystem of entities that improves logistics. By sensing gunshots, it generates an ecosystem of camera feeds, 911 operators, and ambulances to improve street safety. Consumption ecosystems provide new avenues for traditional firms to expand into. They provide new ways to unlock the value of data.

Consumption Ecosystems and Digital Platforms

Unlike production ecosystems, which provide an internal avenue to unlocking value, consumption ecosystems offer an external avenue. To derive value from this avenue, however, a firm must orchestrate data-enabled exchanges across complementary entities. In other words, it has to operate as a digital platform. Cimcon, a Boston-based startup that developed the gunshot-sensing smart bulb, runs a platform connecting objects such as cameras and entities such as police and ambulance services and hospitals.[13] Ford's coffee service is enabled through a platform orchestrating data exchanges among the car driver, Alexa, Starbucks, various app developers, and banks. Although the idea is new for products,[14] the approach follows many established digital platforms that orchestrate exchanges among various third parties. Facebook, for example, orchestrates news- and information-sharing among friends and groups. Uber, the ridesharing platform, orchestrates exchanges between drivers and riders.

Ecosystems Run on Data

Data thus are the common thread running through digital ecosystems, whether they are the production kind or the consumption kind. Data are harnessed within digitally connected value chains in production ecosystems and through digitally connected complementary entities in consumption ecosystems. Both approaches expand a firm's competitive scope beyond products to the data generated by products. Both engender new opportunities for a firm to transform its interactions with customers. Taken together, they help a firm envision the full scope of its data's potential. However, it is important to analyze the ecosystem types separately as they require different business models—value chains versus platforms—that demand very different capabilities. Recognizing their differences also helps a firm envision more strategic options and consider a wider set of approaches to shaping its digital strategy.

Digital ecosystems understood as a combination of production and consumption ecosystems are thus at the crux of how a legacy firm deploys its data to shape its digital competitive strategy. Digital ecosystems represent the most significant force empowering firms to unlock the full potential of the data they acquire. How a legacy firm constructs and engages with its digital ecosystems significantly influences how effectively it can harness the power of data for a digital strategy.

Data and Digital Ecosystems Drive Digital Transformation

Depending on the kind of data a legacy firm elects to generate and the type of digital ecosystems it chooses to deploy, the firm can unlock the value of data in four progressive tiers.[15] Advancing through these tiers, the legacy firm will also confront increasing challenges to transforming its prevailing business models. In other words, these four tiers correspond to four echelons of digital transformation (see figure 0.2).

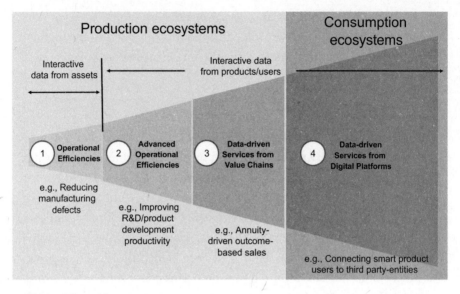

Figure 0.2
Four tiers of digital transformation.

Tier 1 in figure 0.2 entails leveraging sensor- or IoT-based interactive data from assets and machines in the value chain to improve value chain efficiencies. For example, Ford uses automated vision-based inspection of paint jobs in its plants (through sensors, the IoT, augmented reality, or virtual reality and AI) to improve detection of defects in its cars.

Tier 2 entails leveraging interactive data from product users to further advance value chain activity efficiencies. An example is Caterpillar designing a new, cost-efficient motor grader that more effectively moves gravel rather than dirt, based on insights developed from product-user interactive data. Using interactive data from product users as opposed to its assets poses greater challenges. In tier 2 a firm also expands the scope of its efficiency gains beyond asset utilization to broader processes such as R&D and product development.

Tier 3 entails leveraging interactive data from product users to generate new data-driven services. An example is GE using product-user interactive data to improve fuel efficiencies and appropriating a part of the cost savings of airline companies through new annuities from "outcome-based" revenues. Firms go beyond using data for efficiency gains to new ways of generating revenue. This requires making even more significant changes to prevailing business models compared to the earlier two tiers.

Finally, Tier 4 entails extending product or value chains into digital platforms by using interactive data acquired from product users to connect users to third-party entities. An example is Peloton that uses interactive data from its exercise equipment to create a community of users and to match individual users with suitable trainers. This is the most challenging tier for industrial-era legacy firms operating with value-chain–driven business models and little experience with digital platforms.

The first three tiers entail the deployment of production ecosystems. The fourth tier entails the deployment of consumption ecosystems. Subsequent chapters of this book elaborate on how legacy firms can move through these four tiers by amplifying the value of data acquired through their digital ecosystems.

The conception of digital ecosystems as a combination of production and consumption ecosystems is the central frame of this book's discussion. Digital ecosystems that are tailored to the needs of legacy firms critically underpin such firms' digital competitive strategies and are the cornerstone of the ideas introduced in this book.

Tenet 3: Develop New Mindsets for a Digital Strategy

A digital competitive strategy is a set of choices that a firm employs to build competitive advantage by harnessing data in its digital ecosystems. Such a strategy differs from traditional competitive strategy, which is rooted in building advantage through products within a firm's industry. Shifting the competitive focus to data and digital ecosystems also requires revisiting and reconfiguring many of the foundational premises associated with products and industries.

The Foundational Premises of Traditional Competitive Strategy

For firms competing with products, framing business environments as industries is helpful. A key premise is that competitive advantage stems from industry attributes; consequently, competitive strategy is about leveraging those attributes for advantage. Popularized by Michael Porter in the 1980s through his Five Forces framework,[16] this perspective helps firms identify key levers they can use to influence industry attributes, build competitive advantage, and earn above-average returns. To harness the strengths of their products, firms find ways to build asymmetric power over buyers, suppliers, and substitutes within their industry. They find ways to blunt the strengths of industry rivals that offer competing products. They further leverage industry attributes such as scale (e.g., large fixed-cost requirements, high investments in manufacturing capacity or advertising) to limit entry to a few incumbents, and consequently enjoy a dominant market share. Firms build capabilities to do so through their value chains and its underlying array of interdependent activities by which they produce and sell their products.

Foundational Premises of Digital Competitive Strategy

When firms compete with product-generated data, the foundational premises of traditional competitive strategy change. To begin with, harnessing the strengths of data requires a network of data recipients. In a world where exchanges of data and analysis of what that data means for companies, customers, and collaborators, the amount of manufacturing capacity (or the number of vacant hotel rooms or the square footage of retail floor space) that one firm has is suddenly less important. What matters more is the data on those assets, and how others who derive value from those data connect to it all. For legacy firms aspiring to compete with a modern-day digital strategy, digital ecosystems, not industries, thus become the primary source of, and the ground on which to seek, competitive advantage. For such firms, it no longer pays to focus only on the attributes of industries in developing an edge over traditional rivals. Instead, the strategy shifts to leveraging the attributes of digital ecosystems for competitive advantage. Digital ecosystems displace industries as a firm's principal business environment and competitive arena.

The Need for New Mindsets

Consider how this change from traditional strategy to digital strategy plays out for Ford as it plans to offer self-driving fleets in the coming years with fully autonomous cars.[17] Ford anticipates future customers preferring subscription-based services for car usage over car ownership. For example, a user could opt for a service whereby an autonomous car arrives when needed, is aware of the user's schedules, plans itineraries for different destinations, and is able to customize offerings for a variety of lifestyle needs, such as stops at favorite coffee shops or stores or tuning in to personalized news, videos, or music during the ride.

In such a scenario, the data management attributes of cars become more important than their physical attributes. Users may not care as much about which particular brand or model of a car arrives for their ride, instead valuing more the data-driven services offered by the ride. Consequently, the digital ecosystems that provide Ford the opportunities and strengths to offer such data-driven services become more important than the attributes of its traditional industry. Indeed, the boundaries of such digital ecosystems—encompassing all the entities that can generate and share data for the car's new data-driven services— transcend the boundaries of the traditional automobile industry.

Furthermore, competing in digital ecosystems changes many underlying premises associated with competing in industries. Rivals now are firms that have similar access to data, not just firms that offer similar products. Ford encounters new rivals such as Waymo, the self-driving car technology firm launched by Google parent Alphabet, and Uber, which compete with similar access to data and with different capabilities of managing data-driven services. Many of Ford's traditional industry rivals, if they continue offering just products, lose their competitive relevance.

With a shift in its competitive focus to data-driven services, Ford now needs new capabilities to manage digital platforms. Its prevailing value chain capabilities of producing and selling cars take a back seat. Ford needs to attract new customers who participate on its platforms by providing sensor data. This will require Ford to change its prevailing marketing tactic, which specialized in attracting customers to buy Ford cars. Ford must reckon with the fact that its new digital rivals may give away their platform services for free, to attract platform users and acquire their data. Ford's prevailing business models are not set up to do any of these things.

Digital titans commonly give away many platform services without charging for them because they understand the role and importance of network effects.[18] Their platforms become more attractive as more customers participate. Network effects are a hallmark of the new digital world, though they were noticed in the old industrial world too. For instance, typewriters with the QWERTY keyboard format benefited when a growing network of QWERTY users locked out alternative keyboard formats.[19] Such benefits, however, were relevant only to a few products and were observed just in select industries, termed "network industries."[20] Today, as legacy products become sensor-equipped and generate interactive data just as many digital platforms do, network effects are becoming far more pervasive and a crucial source of advantage across a wide spectrum of businesses. To operationalize its digital strategy, Ford too must build such network effects through its platforms. Network effect advantages grow exponentially, and the result is often a winner-take-all competitive scenario.[21] If Ford is successful, these network effects will eventually establish more formidable barriers to entry for new rivals with competing data-driven ride services than the sort of barriers Ford's prevailing manufacturing scale of operations posed. Table 0.3 summarizes these ideas.

Charting a Path Forward in the New Digital World

As firms shift their emphasis from products to data, they will face challenges similar to those Ford is facing. They will need to find fresh approaches to compete in the digital ecosystems emerging around them. The rise of digital ecosystems does not mean, however, that

Table 0.3
Evolution of concepts and the need to change strategic mindsets

Concept Domain	Traditional Competitive Strategy Premises	Modern-Day Digital Strategy Premises
Competitive Instrument	Product	Data
Business environment	Industry	Digital ecosystems
Capability repositories	Value chains	Smart value chains and digital platforms
Barriers to competition	Scale	Network effects
Value provided by customers	Buy products	Buy products and provide interactive data
Competitors	Product rivals	Data rivals

prevailing industry concepts lose all relevance. These concepts help firms maintain their product-based strengths. They are important. They provide a base for firms to build the new resources required to compete in digital ecosystems. These prevailing strengths also can help firms pivot into new positions of strength. Ford's brand and large customer base, for example, can be turned to help develop popular platforms with strong network effects. While this book is primarily about digital competitive strategy, it also reviews some key concepts of traditional competitive strategy to underscore both their differences and their interdependence. Going forward, firms will have to balance their traditional strengths and ways of thinking with fresh ones as they find ways to adapt to their unique competitive contexts.

This book provides the information firms will need to chart such a path forward. Through these chapters a reader will receive answers to many questions: How should firms build new data reserves? How do they entice customers to provide interactive data? How do they build new digital ecosystems that are best suited for their business? How do they retain their prevailing product strengths even as they search for new sources of value in their digital ecosystems? What strategy should firms adopt to harness data in their production ecosystems? What strategy should they adopt in their consumption ecosystems? How can firms extend their products into platforms? How should they compete

Figure 0.3
The data to digital strategy journey.

with these platforms? How do they recognize new competitors in their digital ecosystems? What new capabilities should they build? Finally, how can they select an approach that helps them establish a competitive advantage through the interactive data acquired in their digital ecosystems?

Core Focus and Structure of the Book

The core focus of this book is on how legacy firms can unlock new value from data through their digital ecosystems to execute a digital competitive strategy. All the chapters of this book rally around this core theme. Their ideas are anchored on a central framework of digital ecosystems, introduced here as a combination of production and consumption ecosystems. These digital ecosystems are specially intended for legacy firms to unlock new value from data; and, they are different from the digital ecosystems of the digital titans many of us are familiar with. The digital ecosystems framework offered in this book, enables legacy firms to retain their prevailing product-driven strengths, yet also find new value from data. All in all, this book is a novel "data to digital strategy" journey highlighting along the way four key digital enablers—ecosystems, customers, competitors and capabilities—and how to harness each of them for competitive advantage and growth (see figure 0.3 and table 0.4).

Table 0.4
The outline for this book

Introduction	Core idea of the book	Why harnessing data in digital ecosystems is the new source of competitive advantage
Chapter 1	Lessons from the digital titans	How traditional firms can learn to harness the power of data as the digital titans do
Chapter 2	APIs: the ecosystem glue	How APIs offer the foundations for a digital ecosystem strategy
Chapter 3	Digital ecosystems	How *legacy* firms should view their digital ecosystems: What are production and consumption ecosystems? How are they different, yet connected? Why are they significant underpinnings for a *legacy* firm's digital competitive strategy?
Chapter 4	Production ecosystems	How to unlock the value of data in production ecosystems
Chapter 5	Consumption ecosystems	How to unlock the value of data in consumption ecosystems: What are tethered digital platforms?
Chapter 6	Digital customers	Who are digital customers? How are they different from *legacy* customers? How do firms build a digital customer base?
Chapter 7	Digital competitors	Who are digital competitors? How are they different from current rivals in your industry? How do you recognize them? How do you assess their threats?
Chapter 8	Digital capabilities	What are digital capabilities? How are they different from prevailing industrial era capabilities? How do you build them?
Chapter 9	Looming societal concerns around data	How should *legacy* firms manage rising societal concerns around data privacy and data-driven competitive advantage?
Chapter 10	Digital competitive strategy	What is your digital competitive strategy? How do you find one optimal for you? How do you plan to execute one?

Digital ecosystems amplify the power of data and provide different options for legacy firms to unlock data's value. Digital customers provide product-user interactive data, crucial for legacy firms to offer new revenue-enhancing, data-driven services. Digital competitors compete with access to similar data. They are different from competitors competing with similar products that legacy firms are familiar with. Reckoning how to confront digital competitors is a critical part of an effective digital strategy. And finally, legacy firms need new digital capabilities to unlock the value of data and chart new frontiers with a digital competitive strategy.

Chapters 1 and 2 elaborate on how firms can build strong data reserves and improve their proficiencies at harnessing data. Chapter 1 starts this discussion by detailing what legacy firms can learn from the digital titans about harnessing the power of data. The chapter reveals the inner workings of the digital titans and how they have developed their prowess at unlocking the power of data through their digital platforms. The chapter highlights the specific ways legacy firms can apply these insights to their businesses to craft a digital strategy.

Chapter 2 describes application program interfaces (APIs), or tools that enable different software programs to communicate with one another. APIs can weave a diverse range of software programs together, share data across a multitude of firms, and establish intricate instructions on how firms transact with data. As a result, they have enabled unprecedented collaboration among firms for value cocreation and are today the force behind the emergence and growth of digital ecosystems. This chapter highlights how the digital titans use APIs. It also suggests how their best practices can be applied by legacy firms to build a foundation for their digital ecosystem strategy.

Chapters 3, 4, and 5 delve into the workings of digital ecosystems and how companies can best leverage them to unlock the value of data. Chapter 3 elaborates on the central framework of this book, presenting digital ecosystems as a combination of production and consumption ecosystems. It explains through various examples how a legacy firm can construct and engage with production and consumption ecosystems.

It analyzes the differences between production and consumption eco-systems. It cautions firms that their strong familiarity with their value chains may bias their perspective and limit them to taking advantage only of production ecosystems–related opportunities. The chapter reveals how recognizing consumption ecosystems as an added facet of digital ecosystems helps legacy firms avoid such traps and open new value-creating avenues.

Chapter 4 elaborates on production ecosystems, delineating through a variety of examples how firms can use their production ecosystems to enhance operational efficiencies and offer new data-driven services. It distinguishes between the value created by using production ecosys-tems for operational efficiency gains versus using them for new data-driven services. This chapter provides several examples of how legacy firms can go about executing these options.

Chapter 5 similarly elaborates on how consumption ecosystems help generate new data-driven services. This chapter also introduces the novel concept of "tethered digital platforms," whereby legacy firms can extend their current products into platforms. The chapter elaborates on the contingencies that determine when, why, and how products can extend into platforms and the kinds of approaches legacy firms can adopt if a platform is a feasible option for them. A tethered platform strategy is another important element of a firm's digital ecosystem strategy.

Chapter 6 introduces the concept of digital customers, or custom-ers who provide sensor data as they use or interact with a firm's prod-ucts. The chapter highlights why these customers are different from a firm's legacy customers and their significance to the firm as it seeks to develop a digital strategy. The chapter also discusses various approaches by which firms can build a base of digital customers and expand the scope of sensor data firms can acquire from them.

Chapter 7 introduces the concept of digital competitors, or com-petitors that have similar access to data. The chapter develops an understanding of how firms can anticipate and identify their digital competitors, discusses the nature of competitive dynamics with them, and explains how a firm can assess its relative strengths vis-à-vis these competitors. The chapter also discusses how a legacy firm can contend with digital competitors when crafting its digital ecosystem strategy.

Chapter 8 discusses new digital capabilities required to compete with data in digital ecosystems. It elaborates on the capabilities needed to unlock the value of data from production and consumption ecosystems. It discusses how legacy firms can fuse new digital capabilities with their prevailing capabilities as they craft their digital competitive strategy.

Chapter 9 discusses some of the challenges associated with data and data sharing in a world where privacy and security are of increasing concern. It offers some guidance for legacy firms to balance the value they can derive from sharing data with the negative externalities of doing so.

Chapter 10 puts all these insights together to offer a holistic view of what it takes to establish a data-driven digital competitive strategy. It also offers an action plan for legacy firms to develop and execute a digital competitive strategy.

This Book's Vision

In 1960, Professor Ted Levitt of the Harvard Business School published an influential paper titled "Marketing Myopia."[22] He noted that when firms focus solely on their prevailing products, they often lose sight of the changing needs of their customers. Firms focused on making buggy whips, for instance, failed to see their customers shifting from horse carriages to other forms of transportation. To avoid such myopia, he implored firms to ask the question, "What business are we in?" For the classic example, if the buggy whip company had asked the relevant question—"Are we in the buggy whip business or in the transportation business?"—it might have avoided being disrupted. It might have moved to sell products more suited for customers who were using new means of transportation other than horse carriages.

The notion of "business" soon became synonymous with "industry." Even Levitt's original article intersperses the terms "business" and "industry" frequently. Not surprisingly, his famous question more commonly was paraphrased as: "What *industry* are we in?" And a related follow-up question, implicit in this line of thinking, was: "How should we adapt our *products* to changing trends in our industry?" The buggy whip firm, following this rationale, would have tried to adapt its products to changing trends in the transportation industry.

In the modern digital world, Levitt's advice still rings true. "What business are we in?" is still a relevant question. Yet the ways in which that question can now be interpreted have changed. Modern-day myopia has changed from *marketing* myopia to *digital* myopia. Digital myopia stems from firms' continued insistence on relying on products and industries for competitive advantage. It occurs when firms fail to see a shift in customer preferences from regular products to new data-driven services and digital experiences. It happens when firms fail to see the new value they could generate from data through digital ecosystems, and how such new value could expand their business horizons.

This book aspires to expand the strategic vision of readers and help them overcome the common trap of digital myopia. If you are among the many executives today looking for fresh insights into how to unleash more value from data and revitalize traditional business models, you should read this book. If you are looking for ways to empower your products to offer richer customer experiences, you should read this book. If you are looking to expand your competitive arena beyond conventional industry boundaries into new digital ecosystems, you should read this book. And if you are looking to build new digital capabilities to compete with a winning digital strategy in the modern era, you should read this book.

1 Building Data Powerhouses: What Can We Learn from the Digital Titans?

In January 2020, at the start of a new decade, seven of the ten most valued companies in the world were digital titans. The aggregate valuation of five of them—Apple, Microsoft, Google, Facebook, and Amazon—surpassed $5 trillion. Together, they accounted for around 20 percent of the market value of the entire S&P 500 companies. They also remained poised to further entrench their dominance in the coming years.[1] What was the most significant factor behind their rise? Their prowess in benefiting from data.[2]

The ascent of these companies was made possible by the widespread use of the internet. They first used the internet and software to develop digital platforms. Subsequently they used their digital platforms to unlock unprecedented power from data. Although Apple and Microsoft predate the internet, they too established their dominance using the internet and through their digital platforms. Unlike the others, Apple used its products, such as smartphones, tablets, and laptops, to establish itself. Yet its digital platforms such as iOS played a major role in its ascent. Several other companies have also become known for their meteoric rise using digital platforms. Airbnb, Uber, Alibaba, Tencent, Baidu, Netflix, eBay, and Groupon are some well-known examples. A common attribute they all share: their digital platforms have transformed prevailing practices of utilizing data with new innovative approaches.

It's important to understand—in fact, it's the reason for this book—that legacy firms too can adopt these approaches. Modern technologies such as sensors, the Internet of Things (IoT), and artificial intelligence (AI) make it possible to emulate how the digital titans use their data for advantage. Legacy firms can also evolve into formidable data power-houses. For them to do so, however, it is helpful first to understand the inner workings of digital platforms.

Platforms

Platforms connect and facilitate exchanges among multiple users. While the term is mostly associated with such digital titans as Amazon, Airbnb, or Uber, physical platforms have existed for centuries. Market-places that facilitate traders and people gathering and exchanging provisions, livestock, and other goods for money have existed for more than five thousand years. Modern-day shopping malls function as platforms by similarly connecting merchants with consumers.[3] Exchanges on such physical platforms take place at physical locations where participants are in physical proximity.

The arrival of the internet removed the need for participants to share a common physical location to trade. Exchanges between book publishers and buyers or between music producers and listeners can be conducted without physical stores (for example, on Amazon's and Apple's platforms), exchanges between sources and seekers of information can be achieved without libraries (for example, by using Google's search engine), and exchanges between friends wanting to socialize can be undertaken without sharing a physical presence (as on Facebook).[4] In each of these cases, the data in the exchange can be transacted over the internet with the help of software and without the need for participants to share a common physical space. With such data on a movie title and a user's movie selection, for example, Netflix facilitates a movie rental exchange using software over the internet. A renter does not need to visit a physical store for this exchange to take place.

The Rise of Digital Platforms: The Enabling Role of Data

The initial competitive impact of digital platforms was felt by legacy businesses that conducted physical exchanges in physical locations.

Netflix dethroned Blockbuster as the leading video rental retailer; Amazon's initial foray into online book retailing was an assault on Barnes & Noble's brick-and-mortar stores and market status. Two kinds of advantages contributed to Amazon's competitive impact: a long tail advantage and a networks effects advantage. These advantages arose from the fact that exchanges could be made without the participants in the exchange needing to share physical space. By making it possible to conduct digital exchanges, data also made it possible for firms to avail themselves of these advantages. Each of these two advantages is explained further below using examples of companies that became household names. Because we are tracing the rise of digital platforms from their early origins, some of the examples may appear familiar. However, the objective is to use these familiar examples to derive a few fundamental concepts that ensuing chapters will build on to introduce new frameworks.

The Long Tail Advantage

The long tail is a part of a statistical distribution of items for sale, wherein lesser-known and unpopular items of a population far outnumber the popular items.[5] In movies or music, for example, there are only a few popular hits; a large majority of the movies and songs that are produced barely get known. The smaller set of popular items represents the "head" of the distribution while the larger number of less popular items represent the "long tail" of the distribution (see figure 1.1).

In traditional market settings, constraints associated with the need for a common physical space limit the scope of physical exchanges to a narrow set of popular items. Physical platforms thus mostly benefit from a limited head—the most popular items on the left of the distribution curve. However, those constraints do not apply when exchange participants do not need to share a common physical space. Consequently, digital platforms benefit not just from popular items but from a much broader set of lesser-known items, represented by the long tail, shown in light gray on the curve in figure 1.1. Digital platforms thereby get a long tail advantage.[6]

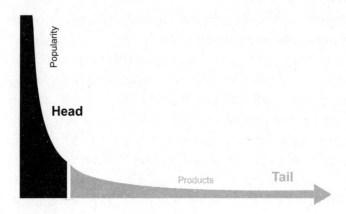

Figure 1.1
The long tail.

Let's consider how Netflix leveraged this advantage when competing with Blockbuster as it entered the video rental market. Both Netflix and Blockbuster facilitated exchanges between movie producers and renters. For Blockbuster, physical exchanges took place in thousands of stores spread across the country. Because of the space constraints in each of those stores, Blockbuster's business model focused on a narrow range of popular titles; it relied on "blockbuster" titles that renters were most likely to choose when browsing in the store. (Stores typically carried multiple copies of popular movies.) For Netflix, initially, the data-driven exchanges of DVDs took place over the internet through its website and software. The renter chose a DVD over the internet, without having to visit a store. The chosen DVD was shipped using postal services from one of around fifty large warehouses that could store millions of DVDs without the kind of space constraints Blockbuster's stores had (Blockbuster once had more than eight thousand stores in prime commercial locations). Netflix could hence offer a wide range of titles, not only popular ones but thousands of other lesser-known titles. This gave Netflix a long tail advantage over Blockbuster.

Netflix further strengthened its long tail advantage with other aspects of its strategy. One such aspect was to price its services using a subscription model. Because of monthly subscriptions, Netflix was not dependent on every title being rented for its revenue. It could afford to keep thousands of idle titles that had little chance of being rented. In contrast, Blockbuster realized revenue only when a movie was rented from its store. Consequently, unrented titles occupying expensive shelf space mattered to the company. This made Blockbuster further dependent only on popular titles, or the head of the video rental curve.

Another aspect of Netflix's strategy entailed using a software-based recommendation engine to "push" obscure titles, rather than just rely on the "pull" of popular titles, as Blockbuster needed to (more on this later in the chapter). All in all, its robust long tail advantage over Blockbuster helped Netflix gain ground in the video rental market.

The Network Effects Advantage

With data as an enabler and without the need for a common physical space to facilitate exchanges, digital platforms also had fewer constraints on the number of users they could invite onto their platforms. As more users joined, the platforms became more attractive to each individual user, an attribute known as a network effects advantage.[7] Netflix could invite movie producers to offer content on its digital platforms, irrespective of their popularity. Netflix could also expand its subscription base of renters because of the reach of the internet. It added subscribers even from small and remote towns with thin populations and a low likelihood of renting. Such places were infeasible for Blockbuster to establish viable physical stores in. Movie producers were motivated to offer more content as more renters subscribed to Netflix's platform; renters benefited as more movie producers offered content.

Such network effects are an intrinsic aspect of successful digital platforms. This is because millions of users can be connected through data- and software-driven exchanges in ways that physical space–driven exchanges cannot. Two kinds of network effects advantages are of note: direct and indirect. These types of advantages depend on the *groups* of users the platform attracts. The term "groups of users" refers to clusters of similar users. Movie producers, for example, constitute one group of users on Netflix; renters constitute another group.

A *direct network effects* advantage occurs when a user experiences more value with more of the same group of users on a platform. Facebook is more valuable to each "friend" as they are more likely to find other "friends" on this platform. Document users similarly find more value in using Microsoft Word because they are more likely to find users who also use Microsoft Word, making sharing documents and collaborating much easier.

An *indirect network effects* advantage arises when one group of users benefits from other groups of users on the platform. Facebook friends, for example benefit when more app developers offer their services on the platform (such as Spotify music streams or Zynga games). Apple's iOS and Google's Android provide their users access to millions of app developers and reciprocally provide app developers with access to millions of user, in this way building a significant indirect network advantage.

As digital platforms grow in size, their network effects advantage intensifies. This advantage, however, is different from the size-related advantages that their legacy firm rivals enjoy. Traditional size advantages come from supply economies of scale,[8] where efficiency benefits stem from supplying large volumes. Supplying large volumes of DVD rentals through thousands of stores, for example, lowered Blockbuster's unit advertising costs compared to those of smaller DVD rental chains. Large DVD purchase volumes also helped Blockbuster negotiate lower procurement costs of movie titles with producers.

In contrast, network effects advantages arise from demand economies of scale.[9] These advantages increase with increasing demand as efficiency benefits come from large networks of users. Networks increase value because of interdependence in consumer demand or when product adoption decisions of any one consumer are influenced by the decisions of other consumers in the network.[10] In other words, the more people who are part of a given network, the more attractive the network is to join. The larger the number of users, the more dominant is the networks effects advantage. What is notable about Facebook's advantage, for example, is not its supply-side economies of scale, such as from its underlying platform technology, but its demand-side economies of scale because of its formidable network of users. Some digital platforms, however, can enjoy both supply and demand economies of scale. Amazon's size not only helps it maintain low procurement costs, similar to those of Barnes & Noble (because of supply-side economies of scale), but in addition provides a network effects advantage (because of demand-side economies of scale) that Barnes & Noble lacks in its brick-and-mortar business mode.

Early Advantages of Digital Platforms and the Enabling Role of Data

As data-driven transactions enabled large varieties and numbers of users to connect, digital platforms enjoyed long tail and network effects advantages. When they first emerged, digital platforms did not dramatically affect how firms produced goods and services. Instead they influenced how goods and services were sold. Much of this owed to the rise of e-commerce. Often e-commerce benefited producers as well, giving them expanded options to sell. A book publisher, for instance, could use both Barnes & Noble and Amazon as retailers, and movie producers could distribute through both Blockbuster and Netflix. In 2001, Michael Porter, the well-known business strategist, characterized internet-driven business models as approaches that complemented traditional strategy.[11] They weren't seen as Earth-shaking disruptors.

The Entrenchment of the Digital Titans: The Central Role of Data

Today, two decades later, several businesses that emerged because of the widespread use of the internet have transformed themselves into the mighty digital titans. Broad technological trends—such as the ubiquity of smartphones, richer telecommunication bandwidths, and an overall rise in digital connectivity—helped amplify the power of the digital titans. Because such developments exponentially expanded opportunities for data-driven digital exchanges, these businesses became dominant conduits for the flow of data. Furthermore, while riding the wave of new technological opportunities, the digital titans also enhanced the role of data in their business models. Data are not just an ancillary to facilitate digital exchanges anymore; they are a central force driving the current dominance of digital exchanges. To understand this shift, it is useful to examine how the digital titans unlocked the potential of one particular facet of their data, namely, interactive data.

Interactive Data

Interactive data are intrinsic to digital platforms. To participate in a digital exchange, users interact with the platform. And because the platform's website or app captures the particulars of each interaction through software, user participation generates interactive data. Amazon obtains all the data generated when a customer browses for an item on its website. Similarly, Google obtains all the data generated when a searcher poses various questions before finding a satisfactory answer. The platform's website or app thus acts as a sensor, collecting these interactive data.

When interactions are tracked in real time, interactive data also become real-time data. Conducting an exchange on a digital platform requires real-time data. For instance, real-time data allow Uber to match a specific rider with a specific driver for a ride. Similarly, Google matches a search query to an answer by using real-time data.

Interactive data, however, have a greater value that goes beyond facilitating digital exchanges in real time. To unlock this value, the digital titans leverage three notable attributes of interactive data: the ability to develop deep insights, amenability to being shared with external entities, and the capacity for enriching digital experiences. Each of these attributes is explained below (see figure 1.2).

Deep Insights: Interactive data capture many aspects of a transaction in real time. The book or movie a user is searching for, the location at which a passenger is waiting for a ride, the query posed during an internet search, or how a friend is reacting to another friend's post are all examples of real-time data captures. These real-time data turn into after-the-fact data when each interaction ends. The digital titans

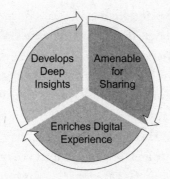

Figure 1.2
Attributes of interactive data.

accumulate after-the-fact data to create a profile for each user. Repeated interactions further fortify these data repositories, refining each profile by adding more data. Over time, such profiles offer deep insights into each user. Deep insights develop when large volumes of interactive data are generated that reflect nuanced and intricate facets of individual user personas.

Amazon, for example, generates interactive data every time a user browses for an item, even if those transactions do not result in a purchase. In contrast, without similar browsing data, a physical store's accumulated data are limited to what is purchased in the store. More important, the large scale of Amazon's operations generates massive amounts of interactive data. Amazon has now cornered almost 50 percent of all e-commerce.[12] It receives over four thousand unique visitors every minute of the day.[13]

More generally, the growing reliance on digital interfaces for day-to-day activities has significantly enhanced the flow of data into the digital titans' repositories. In 2012 there were 2.2 billion active internet users.[14] In 2019 this number grew to 4.4 billion.[15] The sheer scale of such traffic has enabled the digital titans to reel in unprecedented volumes of interactive data. Google processes 40,000 searches every second.[16] Facebook captures 2.7 billion "like" actions a day and scans more than 3 terabytes of data every minute.[17]

Interactive data also capture intricate and nuanced facets of user personas. Searches on Google or browses for items on Amazon can provide a lot of information about a person's genuine preferences. Similarly, the patterns of likes on Facebook or the moments shared on Instagram expose many inner thoughts of users. When large volumes of such intricate and nuanced real-time data feed into unique user profiles, deep insights can emerge. The digital titans further enrich those insights with the use of powerful algorithms and AI. They consequently know a lot about individual users. Facebook, for example, can predict when a couple is likely to get married even before the couple has decided.[18] Microsoft knows about your work skills and work relationships through Office 365 and LinkedIn (more on this in chapter 2). Facebook and Google together control around 60 percent of the $88 billion digital advertising market because their insights into each user's preferences and behavior helps them micro-target messages to users' precise needs.[19]

Amenability to Being Shared with External Entities: Suppose Uber's interactive data reveal that a woman is waiting for a ride at an unsafe location late at night. Real-time updates reflect when the passenger gets her ride, how she proceeds with her journey, and when she finally reaches her destination. Uber can share these data with app developers, who in turn can, say, facilitate the sending of text messages to the passenger's designated friends in real time to enable monitoring of her safety. This safety feature, however, is meaningful only if the data are shared in real time. It is of little value if the data are shared after the fact, such as a day after the ride.

The real-time element of interactive data thus unlocks a different kind of value, one obtainable only if the data are shared in real time. Put differently, some opportunities for value creation disappear if interactive data are not shared in real time. The value of such data also loses relevance for the data recipient after the fact. This transient value of real-time data thus makes the data amenable to being shared with external entities (such as app developers) without having to worry about losing proprietary advantages. The same is not true for accumulated data, whose value is not transient. In fact, the value of accumulated data strengthens over time. Moreover, it is risky to share accumulated data with external entities because data confidentiality is often necessary to maintain a competitive edge. Uber, for example, is unlikely to share its profiles on its riders and drivers with external entities.

Modern digital technologies also allow real-time data to be easily shared. Sharing is enabled through a technology protocol called an *application programming interface,* or API.[20] APIs enable two (or more) software programs to communicate with one another and share information across a broad set of entities (chapter 2 further elaborates on APIs). The amenability of real-time data to sharing drives the digital ecosystems of the digital titans' digital platforms. The more entities they share data with, the larger and the more vibrant are their digital ecosystems.

Digital Experience: By sharing data in real time with a rider's designated friends for the rider's safety, Uber offers a digital experience. A digital experience is a data-enabled experience. Uber offers other digital experiences as well. For a rider heading to the airport, Uber can help with online flight check-in services. For a rider heading to a restaurant, Uber offers restaurant ratings and helps choose an optimal restaurant. Uber may also assist in booking tables at the restaurant, providing an advance look at the menus, and recommending meals. All these digital experiences are made possible because interactive data generated during the ride are exchanged with external entities (airlines and restaurants) whose digital presence complements Uber's interactive data. A conventional taxicab, lacking interactive data, cannot provide equivalent digital experiences. It offers instead a physical experience, such as clean cars or polite drivers, which Uber can also offer.

Interactive data enrich digital experiences in many ways. First, interactivity facilitates the experience in real time—or at the exact moment a user is interacting with the data platform. Uber's digital experiences are real-time experiences that the user can enjoy during her ride. Similarly, a user browsing for a book on Amazon enjoys digital experiences such as being offered tips on more books written by the same author, on different authors writing on similar themes, or on user reviews, all while browsing in real time. Second, the amenability of interactive, real-time digital data to sharing incentivizes harnessing inputs from complementary entities that can add newer experiences. Uber can rely on a wide set of app developers, who may discover more creative services and experiences. Third, the deep insights into each user that interactive data build over time also shape and customize each digital experience. Uber's recommendations for restaurants or menus, for example, shape what Uber learns from the profile of each user.

The Power of Interactive Data

Interactive data make the digital titans even more powerful. They enable the digital titans to expand their influence beyond their core digital platform businesses. Consider how Alibaba and Tencent, dominant digital platforms from China, have made significant inroads into the Chinese banking business by leveraging the power of their interactive data. These digital titans have five core interrelated components in their platforms: search, e-commerce, payment services, chat with social networking, and entertainment services. In tandem, these services extract troves of interactive data on an array of attributes, including those concerning how money is spent.

When a user wants to buy a car, for example, Alibaba and Tencent know what car the user wants, when he wants it, the friends from whom he seeks advice, his credit history, and where he lives. These kinds of insights stemming from interactive data make Alibaba and Tencent far more competitive in offering a loan than a conventional bank. In addition, they offer popular digital experiences such as digital processing of the loan without the painful documentation required by conventional banks demand, finding a competitively priced car, and connecting the loan recipient to a conveniently located dealer. Not surprisingly, Alibaba and Tencent are among the leading lenders for consumer loans in China today. (We discuss Alibaba and Tencent more in chapter 8 when we introduce the concept of digital competitors.)

Interactive data allow the digital platforms to influence how goods and services are produced, in addition to how they are sold. Netflix is now producing movies and television series. Insights from the interactive data the company collects give it the strengths to mass customize its offerings in ways legacy producers of movies and music cannot. Here we recall from the preceding chapter the story of Ford offering an app platform for riders to automatically place a coffee order. Interactive data explain why Ford is pursuing such a service—and why Google and Uber are poised to be formidable competitors in the automobile business. The foundations the digital titans have established to generate rich user profiles through a variety of interactive data sources give them a strong competitive edge in a future world where users may prefer customized ride services to buying cars. Google can use what it knows of individual users (such as calendar itineraries, shopping preferences, family relationships) to offer far more seamless and personalized car-ride services.

The Data Advantage of the Digital Titans

In summary, the digital titans use data to propel a cycle of mutually reinforcing advantages (see figure 1.3).

Data facilitate digital exchanges that generate long tail and network effects advantages. These advantages strengthen firms' digital platforms.

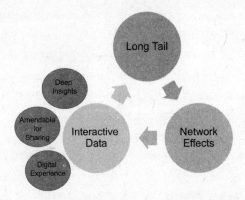

Figure 1.3
The data advantage of the digital titans.

And as these platforms become dominant, users continue to provide them with troves of interactive data, giving them deep insights and the benefits of data sharing that can be shaped into useful and alluring digital experiences.

Interactive data in turn also enhance long tail and network effects advantages. Netflix and Amazon, for instance, leverage the deep insights developed over multiple user interactions to benefit from their long tail of offerings. Netflix recommends movies that users may enjoy based on their prior history. Many of these are obscure movies from Netflix's long tail of titles that the user may not otherwise have picked. Over the years, because of its deep insights into each user's preferences, Netflix's recommendation engine has garnered tremendous power. More than 80 percent of its viewing hours are driven by Netflix's recommendations.[21]

Similarly, Amazon uses its deep insights to recommend items to users, many of which are part of its long tail of inventory items. Amazon generates user insights not just from interactive data from Amazon Prime but from other interfaces as well, such as Alexa. Consequently, Amazon too has built formidable strengths at recommending items to users. Over a third of product choices at Amazon are from the feature "People who bought this also bought this."[22]

By strengthening long tail advantages, interactive data also fortify network effects advantages. With the ability to showcase more movies, Netflix attracts not only more movie producers but also more subscribers. Amazon similarly attracts more sellers because of its strengths in matching long tail items with user preferences. As more movie producers and sellers join their platforms to offer more items, more renters and buyers also get attracted to their platforms. Both Netflix and Amazon thereby strengthen their network effects advantage.

The three core sources of data advantages—a long tail, network effects, and interactive data—thus reinforce one another.

Takeaways for Legacy Firms

What should legacy firms learn from the digital titans? How do they find relevance for these ideas insofar as most legacy firms are not platforms?

How do the insights highlighted above apply to legacy business models built around value chains? These are some of the questions the following chapters seek to answer. Before we dive into those details, however, a few takeaways, summarized below, may offer some food for thought.

First: Sensors and the IoT can provide interactive data. One important takeaway for legacy firms is the concept of interactive data and its role in building powerful data resources. Most legacy firms do not have interactive data. Most do not have the systems in place to track how their customers interact with their products in real time. However, modern sensors and IoT technologies allow them to build such systems. They too can generate interactive data from such sensors and infuse their legacy data resources with fresh vitality and new value-generating potential. They too can use interactive data to generate deep insights into their customers that allow them to offer exciting new digital experiences.

Second: It's essential to develop the means for sharing data. Another important takeaway relates to the sharing of data. Most legacy firms do not share data with external entities outside their value chains. This is understandable, as much of their data does not have a transient real-time component suitable for that kind of sharing. Interactive data from sensors can give legacy firms that option. Once legacy firms are able to find ways to share data, they are on the path to discovering their digital ecosystems, which will allow them to unlock far more value from their data.

Third: Using interactive data to build digital platforms creates new, profitable business models. Legacy firms have built their value chain–based models on supply economies of scale that favor standardization. Henry Ford's famous offer to sell cars painted "any color as long as it is black" epitomizes the foundations of an industrial world that has long relied on leveraging efficiencies through standardization. Business models emanating from such thinking fundamentally discourage variety—and consequently thwart the generation of long tail and network effects advantages. Interactive data generated by sensors can enable established firms to modify their business models. They can extend prevailing value chains into digital platforms, to benefit from the advantages long tail and network effects provide.

The ensuing chapters elaborate on these ideas. But before that we will first discuss another important facet of how the digital titans unlock the value of data. Chapter 2 discusses APIs and how they form the underpinnings of their digital ecosystems.

2 Leveraging Data Powerhouses: What Should You Know about APIs?

Chapter 1 highlighted the importance of interactive data and why they are an integral to digital platforms. It also described how the digital titans use data of this sort to develop deep insights into users and facilitate powerful digital experiences. This chapter delves deeper into how the digital titans make these outcomes happen. It describes the inner workings of how the digital titans unlock the power of interactive data and amplify their value through their digital ecosystems. Much of this is through application program interfaces, or APIs.

If legacy firms wish to emulate the digital titans' approaches to unlocking the value of data, they must grasp the significance of APIs. If they plan to use interactive data to dazzle their customers with new digital experiences, they must understand how APIs work. If they wish to extend their value chain business models into digital platforms, they must develop cutting-edge API management capabilities. If they aim to build new digital capabilities to compete in digital ecosystems, they must learn how to harness the power of API networks. Using the digital titans as examples, this chapter describes how APIs function and generate value. The chapter also highlights what legacy firms can take away from these examples and how APIs can help shape their modern-day digital strategy.

What Are APIs?

Application program interfaces are mechanisms that enable different software programs to communicate with one another. They also provide functions and rules to shape such communication. APIs can help weave together a diverse range of software programs and amalgamate data from a multitude of sources. They can initiate a vast set of instructions on how firms wish to transact with data. As a result, APIs have enabled unprecedented data sharing and collaboration among firms. It is through APIs, for example, that Expedia, a leading travel booking digital platform, integrates data across almost all competing airline companies; thousands of hotels, resorts, and rental car companies; and payment service providers.[1] In doing so, Expedia can offer a seamless travel experience: in one website visit, a customer can book air tickets, hotels, rental cars, and other such services for a vacation or a business trip.

The adoption of APIs started with the rise of software applications in business in the early eighties. In keeping with this trend, even legacy firms have long been using APIs to integrate functionalities of different software programs within their enterprises. Using APIs, for example, firms can connect their customer relationship management (CRM) software with their payroll software. One of the benefits of doing so is the automatic sharing of a salesperson's productivity data shared with payroll, enabling her salary check to reflect her earned bonus.

Until recently, however, many legacy firms saw APIs primarily as technology tools buried inside their enterprise resource planning (ERP) systems—a suite of software applications that an organization can use to collect, store, analyze, and manage data from several of its value chain activities. Often, APIs remain hidden within the purview of a firm's IT department. Today APIs have gained far greater visibility, going all the way up to C-suites. This is because legacy firms have begun to notice the larger strategic significance of APIs. They can see APIs as the key that opens a new world of digital ecosystems for them. They also realize that APIs can shape the underpinnings of their digital ecosystem strategy. In the modern digital world, developing a good understanding of APIs is a must for all executives. Observing how the digital titans use APIs helps in acquiring such an understanding.

The Functioning of APIs

APIs offer a structured approach for different digital services to communicate over the internet using a common language.[2] Consider, for example, two such digital services: Google Maps, a service that provides location data, and Yelp, a service that offers user ratings for service establishments (such as dental offices or coffee shops). Together, the two services can add value for an establishment that wants to offer location information and simultaneously showcase its reviews on its own website. APIs make that value addition happen. In this case, Google and Yelp are the "providers" and the establishments such as dental offices or coffee shops are the "consumers." Providers' software offers data and functionality; consumers' software uses that data and functionality. APIs help integrate such needs between multiple parties (see figure 2.1).

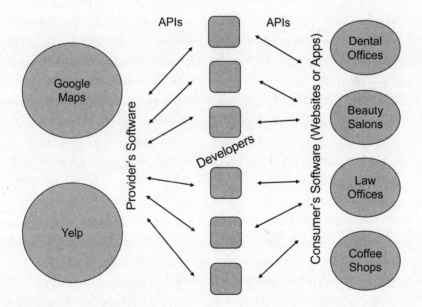

Figure 2.1
The functionality of APIs.

Such integration happens on a large scale because of a class of software programmers referred to as developers. There are millions of developers working on APIs.[3] These developers know how to discover APIs and weave them together with other APIs to create new functions for customers. A developer can, for instance, enable Fidelity Investments, an investment advising firm, to list its various office locations on its website using the functionality of Google Maps. Such web pages that integrate multiple digital service functionalities are also called *mashups* and are powered by APIs.

APIs provide the building blocks for developers to program new functions and provide flexibility to customize user experiences. These functions can be used on websites or apps, as in the Fidelity example. They can be also used to facilitate the business models of companies. Twilio is a communications platform that provides such APIs. Developers use them to customize the flow of such communications as voice calls, text, or video messages for different requirements. eBay, a leading digital platform, uses Twilio's APIs to facilitate communication between buyers and sellers on its marketplace. For example, the moment a buyer offers to buy a product, the seller is notified; once the seller confirms, a call automatically goes to a service that picks up and delivers the package. At any time during the process, buyers or sellers can call a help line to get questions answered. Twilio's APIs offer such flexibility to customize communication flows in ways that the services provided by telecommunications companies cannot. The core business models of most telecommunications providers involve selling standardized plans for communication connectivity, not customizing how various customers may want to shape its flows (the way eBay may want to). Twilio's APIs act as a convenient bridge between (inflexible) telecommunication providers and software developers who wish to create user-friendly communication-driven experiences for end users.

More fundamentally, APIs can serve as conduits for data and improve the functionality of digital services. Unpacking how the digital titans take advantage of this opportunity can help us understand how to replicate this work in legacy business settings.

How the Digital Titans Harness Value from APIs

The digital titans harness the attributes of APIs to generate value through two approaches. One approach takes an internal focus. Here APIs create stronger functionalities for the titans' digital services by shoring up internal efficiencies during software development. In this approach, the digital titans also use APIs as internal conduits for assimilating data. APIs help channel the data generated by the digital titans' services into their internal data archives, to refine user profiles and deepen user insights.

The second approach takes an external focus. Here APIs help improve the functionalities of the digital titans' digital services by drawing on external resources. APIs also serve as conduits to dispense data to external entities. In doing so, APIs help expand users' digital experiences, relying on the ingenuity of third-party entities. Yet this second approach also requires the digital titans to balance two countervailing outcomes of widespread data sharing through APIs: the greater convenience their digital experiences can offer and rising concerns over loss of user privacy (more on this topic later in this chapter and in chapter 9, which discusses the problem at length). The internal and external focus approaches are described below.

Harnessing the Value of APIs through an Internal Focus

With an internal focus, APIs bolster internal digital platform competencies. APIs focused internally are also described as *private* APIs.[4] For example, Google uses private APIs to harness the functionality of its search engine in multiple other products of its own, such as Google Maps, Google Photos, Google News, and Google Docs. This helps Google avoid duplicating its efforts and improves software development efficiencies. Parts of Google's already developed software can be reused in new software products. Similar to the mixing and matching of different Lego blocks, Google uses APIs to allow any piece of functionality (such as search) to be independently swapped, reused, and shared with multiple other functionalities (such as maps). Google consequently can provide the power of its search function across a wide array of its present and future products.

But Google products are also sources for interactive data. When interacting with Google Photos or Google Docs, a user tells Google whom they are sharing their pictures or documents with. Interactions with Google Maps informs Google about the locations a user is interested in or is associated with. Using Google News tells Google about a user's topic interests, political affiliations, and other preferences. APIs also integrate and stream such data into designated repositories. In addition to enhancing software design functionality, APIs act as internal conduits that help Google channel data from a multitude of its software products. This enriches the profile of each individual user and deepens insights into them.

Microsoft also uses APIs in similar ways with Office 365, a subscription-based version of the company's widely used Microsoft Office Suite. The Office Suite offers products that are familiar to millions of users around the world, such as Word, Excel, PowerPoint, Outlook, and OneNote. In addition, Office 365 offers other products, including Skype for business (for video conferencing), SharePoint (for smart and secure document sharing with co-workers), OneDrive (a cloud-based file hosting service), Microsoft Teams (for chat-based collaboration among co-workers), and Yammer (a social network for enterprises) for its enterprise customers.

As with Google, APIs help Microsoft swap and share many functionalities across these products. For example, the chat functionality in Skype is also used in Teams and Yammer, and the functionalities of Word, Excel, and PowerPoint are important components of SharePoint. Also as with Google, each of these products collects user interaction data. Microsoft consequently knows what a user does in its Office 365 environment. It knows a user's scheduled meetings (through Outlook), who her co-workers are (through Teams), and some of her skills (through SharePoint). It can track relationships based on who sends emails to whom. By identifying those who contemporaneously modify the same documents in SharePoint, Microsoft also knows who is collaborating with whom. APIs channel and help integrate the interactive data collected by these products. This helps Microsoft develop user profiles for people in the enterprise world, just as Facebook, Amazon, and Google do in the consumer world. Microsoft calls this the Office Graph.

By acquiring LinkedIn in 2016, Microsoft substantially enhanced its access to interactive data. LinkedIn has north of 500 million members globally and is the de facto social network for professionals. Using APIs, Microsoft merges LinkedIn's data with the data from other Office 365 products, thereby adding substantial power to its Office Graph. Microsoft also applies machine learning and business intelligence processes to these cumulative data. The result is an array of new personalized digital experiences. LinkedIn's Newsfeed, for example, serves up articles based on projects that an employee is currently working on. Office 365 suggests mentors or experts whom an employee can connect with for a current or future task. Microsoft is also providing targeted advertising based on user profiles, just as Google and Facebook do: between 2016 and 2019 Microsoft earned over $7 billion in revenue from advertising.[5]

Beyond channeling data collected by the titans' own products, APIs also help collect data from external entities. Facebook's APIs, for example, make it possible to offer a Facebook "like" button on the websites of third-party entities. Every time a user clicks on the Facebook like button—say, on a beauty salon's website—the beauty salon gets visibility with all of the user's friends on Facebook's platform. Facebook in return captures more data through these "likes," which supplement the likes collected by its own platform. The positioning of Facebook's like button on third-party websites thus is akin to Facebook placing sensors on those websites. APIs channel such sensor data internally into their repositories. Widespread adoption of the like button (achieved through APIs) helps Facebook capture and channel (through APIs) troves of additional interactive data in its reserves that deepen its insights into individual users.

Harnessing the Value of APIs through an External Focus

With an external focus, the digital titans use APIs to marshal the resources
of external entities to enhance what their digital platform can do. Such
APIs are also known as public APIs. In this approach, the digital titans
expose their data to the external world through their APIs. By exposing their data, the digital titans motivate developers and other external entities to find ways to further enrich the functionalities of their
digital platforms. The premise is that innovative ideas are more likely to
emerge when thousands of independent entities are working on generating them, as opposed to just one organization. It is the "let a thousand
flowers bloom" approach. Let's consider the example of Twitter.

APIs Let a Thousand Flowers Bloom

In its early days, Twitter's user interface was not good enough for regular users, and the platform floundered for a while after its initial launch.
To its benefit, however, Twitter at that time was using an open API policy, freely giving developers access to its data feed. TweetDeck, a third-
party developer, used these APIs to build a better user interface on top
of the Twitter engine. TweetDeck's dashboard allowed users to send and
receive tweets, along with observing user profiles in more innovative
ways. Its features became so became popular that it led to an explosion
in Twitter usage. Twitter ultimately bought TweetDeck in 2011.

Google's Nest, an electronic, programmable, self-learning smart thermostat (acquired from the Palo Alto–based Nest Labs for $3.2 billion in
2014), similarly has APIs open to the outside world through its "works
for Nest" initiative.[6] Through this initiative, Google looks for partners
who can find innovative ways of linking their products to Nest. Open
APIs, however, also allow the partners to find Nest, rather than Nest
alone making all the effort to find them. With open APIs, many companies have found ways to connect their products with Nest. Mercedes-
Benz cars connect with Nest, alerting it when drivers are about to arrive
home to enable timely adjustments of home temperatures. Nest also
knows when a driver leaves home and can change home temperature

settings accordingly. Similarly, Samsung's robotic vacuum cleaner starts cleaning when informed that a user has left home. JennAir ovens, when in use, help Nest lower home temperature settings to adjust to the extra heat generated. Jawbone wrist bands that track a person's movement tell Nest when a user wakes up or falls asleep, to modify temperature settings accordingly. Whirlpool and home energy providers connect with Nest to run appliances, such as washing machines and dishwashers, during off-peak energy consumption times. APIs channel data from a variety of sources, including GPS data from cars and Internet of Things (IoT) data from various appliances, that Nest can analyze with modern analytical tools so as to offer new services.

All these collaborations began as experiments. Some were expected to work while others were expected to fail. But just a few blockbuster applications make all the effort worth it. APIs help set up such experimentation. This is what Eric Schmidt, the former CEO and executive chairman of Google, called a URL strategy—ubiquity first, revenue later. He explained it by saying, "If you can build a sustainable eyeball business, you can always find clever ways of monetizing them."[7] Investing in the ubiquity or large-scale exposure of APIs invites more interest in a firm's data offerings from third parties. This in turn increases the odds of successful partnerships. Increased revenues, consequently, are a likely outcome.

APIs Expand the Usage of Digital Services

Exposing APIs to developers also helps expand the usage of digital services. For example, Netflix exposed its APIs in 2008, giving the outside world unprecedented access to its internal data assets. Developers could browse and search its extensive content catalog, retrieve user ratings, manage a user's video queues, and insert video play buttons into their applications. Consequently, Netflix saw a surge in its usage. By 2014, their APIs were supporting around 58 million subscribers, up from around 9 million subscribers in 2008.[8] These new subscribers could watch their content on a myriad of digital devices, from the Nintendo Wii console to smartphones.

Similarly, the popularity of Slack, a business communication platform, skyrocketed in a few short years because of its API strategy. Founded in 2009, it attracted 12 million daily active users and had a valuation of over $20 billion by 2019.[9] It is known for its creative functionalities and seamless integration with several digital services, including Gmail, Google Docs, and Google Calendar, and project management apps such as Trello. Among its functionalities, it creates customized workplaces within a company within which users can have real-time conversations; it creates "channels" to extend collaboration even with people outside the company; and its "bots," web robots that are programmed to run specialized tasks, can crawl into different calendars to find optimal meeting times among co-workers automatically. Slack's users enjoy an array of clever functionalities because of the company's open API policy.[10]

But APIs need not be kept exposed forever. An API can be shut off or its access modified whenever strategically desired. Netflix currently does not provide the same open access to external entities that it offered in 2008. It has kept its APIs open for a select few partners but closed it for the rest. After achieving its early objective of getting widespread adoption into multiple devices in ways that established a uniform experience, the company changed its API policies. Twitter has made a similar move after achieving a desired user base. Wanting more control over the way users interact with its service, Twitter has cut off many developers who had once relied on Twitter's APIs to build their own offerings. APIs thus can be used as strategic levers by providers and harnessed for their advantage. Consumers or partners of API providers should keep that in mind when determining how much to rely on any particular provider's APIs for their own business models.

APIs and Privacy Concerns

Keeping APIs open to developers can vastly enhance a digital platform's functional attributes. The functionality of modern smartphones, for instance, has exploded because of millions of apps created by developers who use the APIs associated with Apple's iOS and Google's Android, the two dominant operating system platforms in most smartphones. The functionalities these platforms have provided for smartphones have transformed our lives. At the same time, these capabilities raise understandable privacy concerns.

The efforts of Apple and Google during the COVID-19 pandemic serve as an example. The companies partnered to set up a contact tracing service to tackle the challenges of reining in the spread of infection.[11] They have offered interoperable APIs that allow developers to build services usable for all the devices using the iOS and Android platforms. The functionality is planned to work as follows: smartphones sense and track people who come within a certain proximity of each other. If someone in this set of people finds she is COVID-19-positive, she enters that information into her smartphone through a public health authority app. People who were tracked as being within her vicinity receive messages from the public health authority for appropriate action (such as to quarantine themselves for fourteen days).

For this functionality to work, however, participants must provide consent. And understandably, users may have significant privacy concerns about allowing public agencies to monitor their whereabouts and whom they meet. Indeed, as of this writing, privacy concerns have prevented this initiative from being implemented in the US. (Other countries, such as Austria, Belgium, and Canada, have, however, implemented this initiative.[12])

Privacy concerns weigh heavily for all firms collecting interactive data from individuals and using them to develop user profiles. Interactive data streams and the profiles they create can certainly be used to enhance digital experiences. Such digital experiences can provide useful conveniences for everyday life. But knowing who you are by tracking many things you do on a daily basis can also lead to abuse of individual privacy.

Alexa can eavesdrop on users.[13] Such eavesdropping, however, can provide consumers with convenient services. For example, Alexa hears that a dishwasher just broke, and immediately initiates calls from three competing dishwasher service companies. However, eavesdropping can be a huge problem, too: no one wants calls from competing divorce lawyers when one is overheard arguing with one's spouse, for instance. Similarly, Ford may learn of a driver's preferences for coffee and recommend new coffee shops during a ride. Some may see it as an invasion of privacy; others may see it as a convenience.

Threading the needle between offering cutting-edge conveniences and protecting consumers' privacy is a growing challenge for firms in the modern digital world. It is a thorny problem, with governments around the world considering regulations and enterprises searching for solutions. And APIs can be in the middle of this imbroglio. It is important to note that APIs are just a tool. It is up to every firm to discover how to use this tool in ways that offer conveniences without exploiting privacy. How should companies deal with these issues? Improved screening of who uses the company's open APIs and careful monitoring of API consumption are a start.

Apple has introduced a tool that lets individuals know what Apple knows about them.[14] The question is whether other firms will follow Apple's example and offer transparency on what they know about you. Also, will all digital businesses use the API diligently? And how do we know that they are taking adequate precautions to protect users' privacy? These are issues that concern regulators.[15] One consumer acting on her own can do little to influence how these issues are resolved. Staying away from the internet or not using smartphone apps are not realistic options. However, when mobilized in large groups, individuals can sway governments to legislate meaningfully. The road to achieving such goals may be full of meanders and byways as companies, individuals, and governments experiment with various approaches. Chapter 9 in this book provides more details as to how legacy firms can manage issues around data privacy, data security, and the changing regulatory environment around data sharing.

Takeaways for Legacy Firms

How should legacy firms harness APIs for value creation? This is another important question to which the digital titans can offer useful answers.

Although many legacy firms may be familiar with APIs, emulating the titans can help expand their prevailing usage of APIs within their traditional enterprise resource planning (ERP) systems (such as connecting customer relationship management [CRM] to payroll) in several ways.

APIs make digital connectivity happen because they are intrinsically meant to connect various software units. With the proliferation of sensors and expansion of the IoT, there are far more software units that APIs can connect to (all sensors and IoT items have software components). APIs make it possible to take advantage of this proliferation of software. That is, by expanding APIs, firms make more connections among these emerging software units. This in turn helps legacy firms activate new digital ecosystems that provide more avenues to unlock the power of their data. APIs thereby provide legacy firms the key to compete in a new world of digital ecosystems.

The internal and external approaches the digital titans employ to use APIs can further help legacy firms develop a structured pathway to expand their API applications and shape their digital ecosystem strategy, whether in a production or a consumption ecosystem. As discussed in the introduction to this book, production ecosystems use linkages between the groups and activities within a company that are involved in producing and selling products, including R&D, manufacturing, assembly, and distribution channels. Consumption ecosystems focus on external connections and stem from a network of external entities that complement a company's own source of data, such as the sensors on a product the company makes.

This distinction can help legacy firms take stock of their current use of APIs while also detecting where they can expand that use. APIs thus can provide legacy firms with the underpinnings of their digital ecosystem strategy (see figure 2.2).

Within production ecosystems, the "interface" part of the API initialism has two layers. The first layer, the *intrafirm interface*, is activated when APIs connect internal software programs or software units within the enterprise. Connecting a company's CRM software with its payroll software through APIs is an example of an intrafirm interface. The second layer, the *supply chain interface*, expands API connectivity to

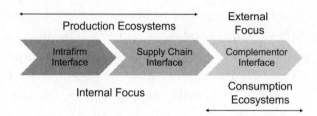

Figure 2.2
The layers of APIs.

units outside the enterprise but within its supply chain. Connecting inventory-level tracking software at a supplier (or a retailer) with production scheduling software at a manufacturing plant is an example. A firm can ask, Where in these two layers is our current usage of APIs? What purposes are those APIs serving? How can we expand on what we have?

Within consumption ecosystems, the third interface, the *complementor interface,* is activated when APIs are opened to the outside world. The introduction described Ford's onboard computer system connecting the vehicle to a nearby coffee shop to order a perfectly timed beverage for the driver. This illustration is an example of a complementor interface at work. This particular approach of Ford is similar to that of Nest, described in this chapter.

The APIs in the complementor interface are crucially important to legacy companies if they intend to expand their prevailing products into digital platforms. Here a legacy firm can ask, Do we have APIs in the complementor interface? If not, how can we initiate them? What additional digital services and associated experiences can we generate from them?

The upcoming chapters explain how legacy firms can expand their use of APIs across these three interfaces. Here are two essential concepts that we will explore in depth:

First: Legacy firms can do more to leverage APIs in their production ecosystems. Many legacy firms use APIs to coordinate the communication between software applications underlying various business functions, such as managing inventory levels, machine outputs, or production schedules. In this role, APIs can also rewire how these software applications interact, to help enterprises reconfigure their business processes for greater agility in their value chains.

These prevailing functionalities of APIs expand in a world of digital ecosystems, where enterprises benefit from newer technologies such as sensors, the IoT, and AI. In this new world, value chains are elevated into digital production ecosystems. APIs here play a far more significant role as they provide the underpinnings for smart business processes, such as self-optimizing inventory levels, machine outputs, or production schedules. They also provide the foundations for new data-driven services.

Second: Legacy firms can develop new APIs for their consumption ecosystems.   Digital ecosystems bring fresh opportunities for firms to offer new user experiences through smart products. Many new user experiences devolving from smart products stem from engaging with consumption ecosystems where product-user interaction data are shared with external third-party entities. For many legacy firms, consumption ecosystems may be new. They may not have APIs designed to share their data with the outside world. They may also not have much experience in dealing with third-party entities such as developers necessary to activate the complementor interface of APIs. This is an area where legacy firms have much to learn from the digital titans. This learning is especially necessary when a legacy firm plans to extend its value chain–based business into a digital platform.

Whether in production or in consumption ecosystems, APIs are powerful mechanisms to channel data for new digital experiences. APIs thus establish the foundational data conduits for a firm's digital ecosystems. Chapters 3, 4, and 5 elaborate on how legacy firms can unlock the value of their data from their digital ecosystems.

3 The Structure of Digital Ecosystems for Legacy Firms

A core objective of this book is to illuminate how legacy firms can unlock new value from the data they acquire and harness the data for competitive advantage. An associated aim is to provide insights into how a legacy firm can shape its competitive strategy with data as a key input. The introduction framed these goals, describing this book as a "data to digital strategy journey" for legacy firms. Chapters 1 and 2 started this journey by highlighting what legacy firms can learn from the digital titans about the new and explosive power of the data they harness. They provide valuable lessons. One important takeaway is that digital titans use their digital ecosystems to draw formidable market power from data. It is through their digital ecosystems that the digital titans amplify the worth of their data and harness the data to provide rich digital experiences to their customers. Their digital ecosystems thus shape much of their influence in the modern economy.

Legacy firms too can construct digital ecosystems to amplify the value of their data. They too can offer new value-creating services and experiences to their customers through their digital ecosystems. To do so, however, they need new strategic thinking. Legacy firms have long anchored their business models on products and industries. Shifting from products and industries to data and digital ecosystems requires new approaches to managing their businesses. Moreover, legacy firms must make this shift while continuing to build on their prevailing strengths, which is derived from products and industries. Put simply, legacy firms have to construct digital ecosystems that are tailored to their needs.

This chapter highlights the unique attributes of a legacy firm's digital ecosystems and how legacy firms should construct their digital ecosystems to balance their old product-centric strengths with new data-centric ones. The chapter lays out the core concept of this book, a new digital ecosystems framework tailored to the needs of legacy firms. According to this framework, legacy firms' digital ecosystems have two interrelated components, production ecosystems and consumption ecosystems. A production ecosystem is an internal data-generating and data-sharing network built on the foundations of a legacy firm's own value chains. A consumption ecosystem is an external data-generating and data-sharing network, built on the foundations of third-party entities, that complements product-generated sensor data. Taken together, production ecosystems and consumption ecosystems give legacy firms a variety of different options to choose from to unlock fresh value from their data while maintaining their legacy strengths. Production and consumption ecosystems thereby provide legacy firms with the foundations to craft a digital competitive strategy (see figure 3.1).

This chapter develops this digital ecosystems framework. It underscores the significant role digital ecosystems play in shaping a legacy

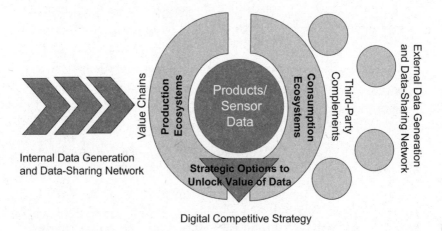

Figure 3.1
The digital ecosystems framework for traditional firms.

firm's digital competitive strategy. It also takes an important step forward in a legacy firm's data to digital strategy journey.

What Are Digital Ecosystems and Why Are They Significant?

Digital ecosystems are networks comprised of data originators and data recipients. A special attribute of these ecosystems is that they amplify the value of data when the data are shared within the ecosystem's network. The digital titans provide more than ample evidence of this attribute. The millions of riders, drivers, app developers, and third-party entities that are originators and recipients of Uber's digital platform data, for example, make up Uber's digital ecosystem. We also know from chapters 1 and 2 how digital titans unlock unprecedented value from data by harnessing it in their digital ecosystems. They do so primarily through their digital platforms. Their business models, predicated on the existence of digital platforms, necessitate generating and sharing data. The richer their digital ecosystems, the more abundantly they generate and share data—and the more they prosper and thrive. Through their digital platforms, the digital titans have made digital ecosystems their natural habitat. And, as their digital ecosystems magnify the power of the firms' data and build their competitive strengths, they also form the digital titans' primary competitive environment.

Legacy firms, however, do not follow the same approach. For many, digital ecosystems may not even appear to be relevant as they primarily compete with their products, not with data. While legacy firms may have troves of data on markets, customer segments, sales, inventory, and other operational aspects of their business, this voluminous data collection is largely used to support and enhance their products and their competitive position. Data are also collected for internal use within legacy firms' value chains. And as most legacy firms do not operate as digital platforms, their data are not widely shared with and amplified through external entities, nor are the data easily amenable to such uses.

Because products drive their key value propositions, legacy firms draw their strengths from the industries they compete in. Indeed, the characteristics of their industries amplify the value and competitiveness of their products[1]—a point explained in more detail shortly. Not surprisingly, legacy firms have long considered industries, not digital ecosystems, their principal competitive canvas.[2] Also, with industries shaping their strategic thinking, leaders at many legacy firms have yet to notice any particular value that digital ecosystems could offer for their prevailing business models.

This dynamic changes when a legacy firm considers adding data to its competitive arsenal. Its industry then ceases to be the firm's sole domain for value creation; neither does its industry remain its predominant anchor for competitive strategy. To amplify the value of data, a legacy firm needs digital ecosystems. And when firms move from industries to digital ecosystems, the data firms acquire become a value generator in themselves, right along with a firm's products. As a consequence, the role of data within digital ecosystems expands from merely supporting products to being an equal partner to products in driving revenues.

It is important to note that a firm seeking to expand its competitive domain into digital ecosystems does not mean that industries will lose their significance for the firm. Legacy firms must not overlook how industry parameters such as scale empower their products. Products, after all, are the means by which new user interaction data are generated. The stronger their products, the better conduits for data they can become. Instead, legacy firms need to erect fresh digital ecosystems on the scaffolding of their prevailing industry structures. And they must find ways to draw strengths from both their prevailing industries and their new digital ecosystems.

Digital ecosystems constructed specifically for legacy firms thus are not the same as the ecosystems that the digital titans compete in. They may have some common characteristics because in both cases, the digital ecosystems generate and share data. But a legacy firm's digital ecosystem has some unique features tailored to the firm's needs because it is built on the foundations of the firm's prevailing industry structures. These features help legacy firms unlock new value from data shared in digital ecosystems even as the firms retain their old strengths, drawn from their prevailing products, business models, and industries. To appreciate the unique features of the digital ecosystems in which legacy firms operate, it is useful first to recognize what strengths legacy firms draw from their industries. These strengths must endure in their new digital ecosystems.

Why Are Industries Important?

There are many good reasons why firms consider industries their primary competitive environment. First and foremost, industry boundaries offer a straightforward way for firms to find and maintain their bearings when competing with their products in their markets. They help firms recognize who their rivals are—or identify who offers similar products to their target customers. This helps focus their attention on relevant competitors and allows them to track their competitors' moves more easily. Industries also help firms identify suppliers, as they are generally from a common pool shared by all rivals. Industries further help firms recognize common trends, opportunities, and threats. They help firms take cues from their industry rivals to adapt to collective developments. For many such reasons, industries have evolved over the years as institutions that provide firms with a powerful identity. An automobile manufacturer, for example, sees itself as "belonging" to the auto industry; a bank identifies itself as a member of the banking industry.

Beyond such pragmatic appeal, the value of framing business environments as industries is supported by a well-established body of research that has deep theoretical and empirical foundations in the fields of economics and business. Scores of studies tell us why and how industry attributes shape competition and firm performance.[3] Their cumulative evidence reinforces the "structure-conduct-performance" paradigm.[4] *Structure* stands for key and relatively stable attributes of an industry. One such attribute, for example, relates to the number of competitors and their relative market share. An industry is said to have a "concentrated" structure when a few firms dominate the market and a "fragmented" structure when a large number of firms compete without any one or two having a sizable market share. Such structural attributes of an industry influence firm conduct, or the strategy with which the firm competes. For example, a firm is more likely to price its products with high margins in a concentrated industry and with low margins in a fragmented industry. Furthermore, both industry structure and firm conduct influence firm performance. A firm is likely to perform better in concentrated industries with few competitors. Coca-Cola and PepsiCo, for instance, have enjoyed handsome profits for decades, deriving benefit from a concentrated industry (together the two enjoy around a 70 percent share of the global soft drink market). Yet a firm can also overcome negative odds in a fragmented industry through innovative strategies or conduct. Budweiser, Heineken, and Miller, for example, transformed what was once a largely fragmented beer industry with thousands of microbreweries into a concentrated industry through scale-intensive plants, massive efforts at branding, and large distribution networks.

Michael Porter's work exemplifies this line of thinking.[5] His well-known five-force framework captures an array of structural intricacies of an industry as influenced by five forces, namely, the relative power of buyers, of suppliers, and of substitutes; the threat of new entrants; and the intensity of rivalry. Together these forces determine the attractiveness of an industry and influence the odds of a firm performing well in it. When these five forces are stacked in a firm's favor, the firm is more likely to do well; conversely, when these five forces are not stacked in its favor, it is likely to do poorly. In other words, industry structure, captured through the nature of the five forces of a firm's industry, influences firm performance.

The Significance of Value Chains within Industries

The five-force framework also highlights how firm conduct, or firm strategy, influences firm performance. A firm can bend the five forces in its favor by strategically positioning itself in its industry. Positioning reflects unique attributes of how a product is offered to its market vis-à-vis rival products. Such positioning is enacted through a firm's value chain, an array of activities, such as procuring from suppliers, manufacturing, assembling, R&D, marketing, and selling, that are involved in producing and selling products.[6]

Nike's unique and differentiated position in the athletic footwear industry, for example, stems from the various approaches by which the company administers its global supply chain, invests in R&D, shores up its brand, and manages its vast retail network. Through its R&D, it develops high-quality shoes that improve the performance of athletes. Through its branding, Nike connects sports performance to its products. In doing so, Nike not only generates significant power over its buyers, it also makes it hard for rivals to imitate the company's products. Through scale in procurement, Nike generates power over its suppliers. And through scale in its advertising, R&D, and sales, Nike reduces the potential threat of new entrants desiring to compete with their products.

Products thus draw their competitive strengths both from their industry structure and from their value chains. Industry structure can provide favorable conditions for products to thrive. Value chains can help firms position themselves to make those conditions even more favorable for their products to build competitive advantage. This, in a nutshell, is the premise of traditional competitive strategy. It also is the underlying rationale for why industries play such a significant role in shaping a legacy firm's business environment.

Can Industries Turn into Digital Ecosystems?

So, what attributes do industries share with digital ecosystems? They are both networks. Digital ecosystems are networks of data generators and data recipients. The primary focus of digital ecosystems is to amplify the worth of data through sharing. Industries too are networks of various interdependent entities, activities, and assets.[7] But the primary aim of an industry network is not to amplify the worth of data but to amplify the worth of products. The two networks, the industry network and

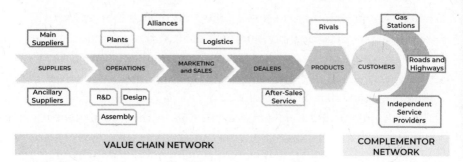

Figure 3.2
Industry networks: Ford Motor Company.

the network represented by digital ecosystems, can be blended together to great benefit for a legacy business. Through such blending, legacy firms can construct digital ecosystems that are designed to retain their prevailing strengths while adding new strengths. To learn how, it is important to understand the nature of industry networks.

Industry as a Network

Consider the industry network that Ford engages with, when competing with its products, as depicted in figure 3.2. One part of this network, shown on the left side of the figure, emanates from Ford's value chain, helping it produce and sell its products. The other part of the network, shown on the right side of the figure, is formed by complementary entities, including gas stations, highways, and repair shops, that support the use of Ford's products after they are produced and sold. Each part is described below.

The Value Chain Network
Ford's value chain network stems from an intricate set of relationships among interdependent entities, assets, and activities that enables Ford to produce and sell its cars. This network includes Ford's suppliers, manufacturing and assembly units, R&D, marketing, distribution, and after-sales service dealers. Ford has around one hundred main suppliers

and several more ancillary suppliers. It operates sixty-five manufacturing plants across the world. It has over 7,500 dealerships worldwide that support Ford in its sales and after-sales service efforts. Each of these suppliers, plants, and dealerships has a myriad of assets and activities whose roles and inputs need to be synchronized to achieve one overarching goal: delivering products to customers in ways that maximize revenue and profit generation.

Ford further expands its value chain network when it attracts alliance partners to shore up select facets of its value chain activities such as R&D, manufacturing, or marketing. Its recent alliance with Volkswagen to develop electric cars, self-driving technology, and transport services is an example.[8]

Ford's network also includes its rivals. These rivals are connected to Ford's value chain activities because each of Ford's competitive actions invariably attracts competitive responses.[9] A price cut by Ford is usually countered by a commensurate price cut by Ford's rivals. Similarly, if Ford decides to launch a new product or enter a new country market, rivals can be expected to make equivalent retaliatory moves. In other words, competitive actions are not isolated events but are interdependent moves and countermoves. The unwritten rules behind these moves and countermoves are implicitly understood and followed by key rivals to maintain competitive equilibrium in the industry.[10]

For instance, Ford and its rivals match their presence in product offerings and global market presence to situate themselves for quick and effective retaliation in response to competitive moves, a concept known as multimarket contact.[11] With multimarket contact, if Toyota cuts prices in the US market, for instance, Ford has the option of retaliating by cutting prices in Toyota's home Japanese market, where it may hurt Toyota the most. Such an option is possible because Ford matches Toyota's presence in its home market with Ford's own presence in Japan. The idea is to provide a credible threat of retaliation and thereby discourage initiation of competitive attacks in the first place. Multimarket contact, consequently, as many empirical studies show, increases the likelihood of maintaining profitability in an industry.[12]

The scope of Ford's value chain shapes its multimarket contact because Ford's choices for where and how it locates its value chain activities determine how evenly Ford matches its key rivals with its global presence in manufacturing, sales, and after-sales service. This in turn helps Ford manage its network of rivals in ways that strengthen its products' competitiveness.

The Complementor Network

Ford's industry network also extends beyond its value chain, into a network of complements. The roles various complements play emerge after Ford produces and sells its cars, or after the scope of Ford's value chain ends. Such a complementor network can include, for example, gas stations and a road and highway infrastructure that are necessary for car usage. Other examples include independent service providers such as the Midas and Meineke franchises that help Ford's customers maintain their cars and extend their use. Ford does not play any role in setting up gas stations or in building roads and highways, nor does it intervene in the operations of Midas or Meineke. It does, however, rely on its complementor network to boost demand for its cars.

Industry Networks Are Well Established

In sum, Ford's industry can be seen as a network of value chain and complementor entities, assets, and activities. Almost all firms that produce and sell products have value chains. Large legacy firms such as Ford, Boeing, Bank of America, and Progressive Insurance have massive value chains with thousands of intricate interdependencies among various entities, assets, and activities. Even the smallest of legacy firms, such as restaurants, operate with a functioning value chain. Almost all products also have complements. Light bulbs need electrical sockets, wiring, and electricity. Commercial aircrafts need airports. Toothpastes need toothbrushes. Soft drinks need refrigerators or ice. Banks that sell loans need objects—homes or cars—that people want to borrow money for. And so on.

The value chain networks of most legacy firms are usually larger and more complex than complementor networks. Also, legacy firms pay far more attention to their value chain networks than to their complementor networks. In most cases, legacy firms rely on their customers to arrange for the complements necessary to use their products. Ford's customers can find gas stations on their own. Similarly, customers of copiers make their own arrangements for acquiring paper; customers of light bulbs arrange for sockets, wiring, and electricity on their own. In a few cases, a firm may sell both products and complements, such as Gillette does with its razors and blades. In select cases, a firm may sell complements separately but cobrand them, such as Colgate does for its toothbrushes and toothpaste. These are, however, exceptions rather than the rule. By and large, complements play a much smaller role for legacy firms than does their value chain. While most legacy firms recognize the significance of complements, they usually adopt a hands-off approach in managing them.

Injecting New Vitality through Data in Established Networks

These dynamics change in important ways when legacy firms turn their industry networks into digital ecosystems. The role of complementor networks in particular expands significantly because of modern digital connectivity. The core focus and thrust of value chain networks also undergo major change when these networks are converted into digital ecosystems. The existence of value chains and complementors as established concepts for legacy firms, however, indicates that networks per se are not new to them. What is new is using their prevailing networks as digital ecosystems.

Here is the big difference: industry networks focus on supporting products and creating value from product positioning. Digital ecosystems focus primarily on generating and sharing data to create data-driven services, experiences, and value. While there may be considerable data generation and sharing within value chain networks (less so in complementor networks), value chain networks channel data primarily to improve the operational efficiencies of producing and selling products. Such operational efficiencies are certainly important. However, by turning industry networks into digital ecosystems, legacy firms can further expand these benefits through offering new data-driven services and digital experiences.

The task ahead for legacy firms is to reinforce prevailing strengths embedded within their industry networks while generating new strengths by turning those industry networks into digital ecosystems. To do so, legacy firms must make it possible for the various entities, assets, and activities within their prevailing value chain and complementor networks to become different kinds of data generators and recipients. They must turn their prevailing networks' data-generating and data-sharing potential into wellsprings of new data-driven services, experiences, and value. Modern digital technologies can help them do that. And because value chains and complements are widely established concepts among legacy firms, they provide excellent foundations on which legacy firms can build digital ecosystems. The stronger these foundations, the greater are the opportunities for legacy firms to adapt the conventional product-centric roles of their industries to the new data-centric roles of digital ecosystems.

Building Digital Ecosystems on the Foundations of Industry Networks

To effectively utilize the foundations provided by a legacy firm's industry network, it is important to appreciate that value chains and complementors play different roles in amplifying the worth of products. Value chains shore up the supply-side strengths of firms and their products. They help maximize how effectively a company produces and sells its products to customers. Nike's network of R&D, supply chain, marketing, and sales organizations, for example, amplifies the effectiveness with which Nike produces and offers its products to customers. In contrast, complementors shore up the demand-side strengths of those products. They increase the worth of products by making them easier to use or consume. The widespread availability of electricity and standard electrical sockets, for example, improves the demand for light bulbs, making them a mass consumer product that is widely and easily consumed.

Because of these differences in their roles, value chain networks and complementor networks provide different kinds of foundations on which legacy firms can build digital ecosystems. Value chain networks lead to *production ecosystems*. Complementor networks lead to *consumption ecosystems*.

From Value Chain Networks to Production Ecosystems

Let us first consider how Ford's value chain network turns into a production ecosystem. It is important to remember here that the origins of value chain networks lie in task interdependencies entailed in the production and selling of goods, not in data generation and data sharing. Unlike the digital platforms of the digital titans, this network can function even if there is no data generation or data sharing within it. Indeed, Ford's value chain network emerged in the early 1900s, long before the advent of modern computers and their associated abilities to help generate and share data. Back then, coordination between different value chain activities was done manually.

Yet value chains greatly benefit when their activities are coordinated through data. These benefits also improve progressively as the role played by data intensifies. The transition from a raw value chain network, one in which data play no part, to a rich network, where the role of data is maximized, is what characterizes the conversion of a legacy firm's value chain network to a digital production ecosystem. Figures 3.3a, 3.3b, and 3.3c depict such a transition for Ford. Figure 3.3a shows the raw value chain network with no digital connectivity.

Figure 3.3b shows the introduction of IT systems and software-driven services, initiating some element of data generation and sharing within the value chain network and thereby starting its conversion to a production ecosystem. This step improves operational efficiencies within the value chain network.

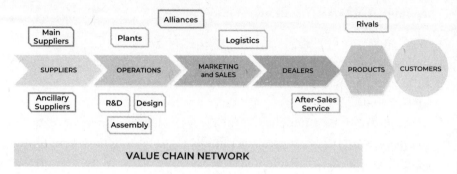

Figure 3.3a

Raw value chain network: Ford Motor Company.

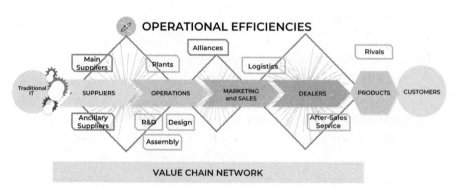

Figure 3.3b

From value chain to production ecosystem with IT: Ford Motor Company.

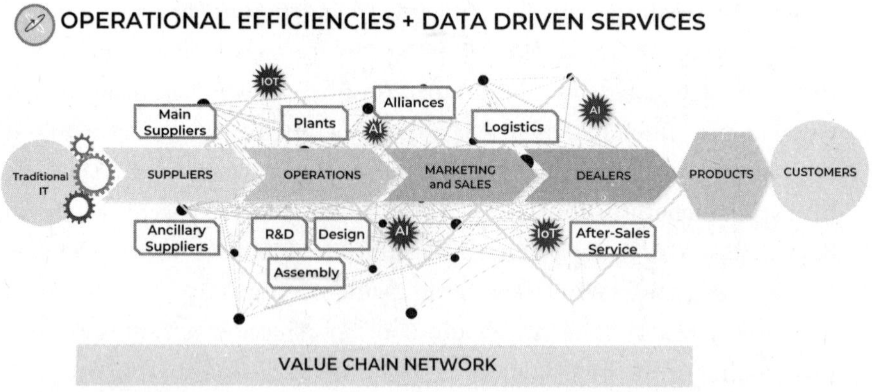

OPERATIONAL EFFICIENCIES + DATA DRIVEN SERVICES

Figure 3.3c

From value chain to rich production ecosystem with modern technologies: Ford Motor Company.

Figure 3.3c depicts continuing progress toward an ever-richer production ecosystem because of advances in modern digital technologies such as sensors, the IoT, and AI. This step allows Ford not only to further improve its operational efficiencies but also to offer new data-driven services that can expand its value scope and revenue generation.

The journey is ongoing. The more ways Ford finds to augment the role of data in its value chain network, the richer it makes its production ecosystems. Because IT services initiated the progression of value chain networks into production ecosystems, their role is discussed first.

The Role of Traditional IT Services: Initiating Production Ecosystems

Ever since the 1970s, enabled by computers, software, and the rise of various IT services, legacy firms have automated many of their workflows to make their value chains more efficient. Such efforts understandably started small and had a narrowly circumscribed scope. In its early days, Ford's procurement division, say, would have one particular kind of IT system that helped keep track of inventory, such as what inventory was ordered, received, and in stock. Similarly, Ford's production scheduling unit would have a different IT system that helped keep track of the sequence in which components were manufactured and assembled. As these systems were different and used different kinds of software, integration was difficult. Even when the data generated in each unit were shared across units, such sharing was done in clumsy and time-consuming ways, often by sharing data files at the end of each day. For example, a procurement unit might share files at the end of each day with a production scheduling department to reconcile inventory ordered during the day with the inventory that was consumed that day.

Over time, advances in IT services improved integration across such self-contained software systems and their idiosyncratic workflow automation efforts. Among the notable advances was the introduction of enterprise resource planning (ERP) systems by business software companies such as SAP and Oracle. Gaining considerable traction by the 2000s, ERP systems helped firms connect the software used by different units. This empowered companies such as Ford to have a more inte-grated view of the performance of different business processes. Ford could, for instance, track the status of diverse aspects of its business related to its overall performance, such as cash, inventory, production capacity, purchase orders from its dealers, and payroll, across its global units. ERP systems also continuously updated the status of these met-rics using common databases. All this was also possible because of APIs that allowed different software programs to talk to one another. Chap-ter 2 described this kind of API usage as an intrafirm interface appli-cation. Such applications enable data and systems integration within Ford's internal units.

ERP systems also made possible data generation and sharing across wider parts of firms' value chain networks, to include their suppliers—and even, in some circumstances, their rivals. For instance, Ford, along with its key domestic rivals, GM and Chrysler, adopted the Automo-tive Network Exchange, or ANX. This exchange enabled the Big Three's common pool of suppliers to use a standard IT system to interact with each of the three automakers. This reduced administrative costs not only for the automakers but also for their suppliers. Here again, APIs allowed software programs across Ford, GM, Chrysler, and their com-mon suppliers to talk to one another. Chapter 2 described this kind of API usage as a supply chain interface application.

Over the years, IT services have steadily improved workflow integra-tion within value chain networks using data. These efforts continue. More recent advances include cloud technologies that allow legacy firms to outsource the infrastructure behind the software and IT services they need to software companies. Salesforce.com for instance, offers software as a service (commonly referred to as SaaS), whereby client firms can coordinate their sales and marketing activities through their software without owning and managing the underlying infrastructure needed to generate those services. Similarly, Amazon, Microsoft, and Google offer infrastructure as a service (IaaS), providing options for leg-acy firms to outsource a host of other services. For instance, an athletic shoe manufacturer such as New Balance wanting to complement its existing distribution outlets (such as Amazon or Footlocker) with its own e-commerce channel can opt to use third-party remote infrastructures that create and run its e-commerce business for the manufacturer on a subscription basis. Cloud services simplify the management of infrastructure for legacy firms and provide better flexibility and alignment of IT with their business goals. In addition, cloud services can also help remove barriers to sharing data across the organization.

These advances in IT services have certainly improved data integration within the value chain network through software. Such integration leads to better operational efficiencies in producing and selling products. Despite these advances, however, many legacy firms still remain mired in old systems that run on idiosyncratic software languages and shoehorn data into siloed data storage formats. These conditions continue to pose barriers to effective data sharing. Moreover, the data generation and sharing powered by such IT services do little to help value chain networks go beyond improving their operational efficiencies. Recent advances in digital technologies, however, allow legacy firms to break through such barriers. They further transform value chain networks into richer production ecosystems. Let's discuss them.

The Role of Modern Digital Technologies: Enriching Production Ecosystems

There is a slew of digital technologies that are described as "modern." These technologies have gained momentum in the last few years and show tremendous promise to transform the way we live our lives. For example, blockchain has the potential to verify the authenticity of financial transactions and traded goods by providing an electronic ledger for auditing. Augmented reality can improve the efficiency of warehouse and factory workers by showing data on the next actions they should take to pick up a package of repair equipment on an assembly line. 3D printing makes it possible to deliver spare parts electronically rather than physically, among other uses. Also included in this mix are advances in telecommunication such as 5G that allow larger amounts of data sharing at greater speeds between connected devices.

Yet when we narrow our focus to those technologies that have the greatest impact in turning industry networks into digital ecosystems, a few stand out. These are technologies that empower legacy firms to generate and share interactive data the way the digital titans do (as highlighted in chapters 1 and 2). These technologies expand frontiers for legacy firms with respect to what they can do with their data. Three such modern technologies are sensors, the IoT, and AI.

Sensors allow firms to collect real-time interactive data from assets, products, and customers. The IoT allows various physical assets to be connected to the internet through protocols such as Wi-Fi, Bluetooth, or Zigbee. Its connectivity increases with more assets having sensors and software interfaces and with greater telecommunication power— such as afforded by the greater wireless bandwidths available with 5G technology. AI is a term that encompasses many different technologies, such as statistical machine learning, neural networks, natural language processing, or robotic process automation.[13] For the purposes of this book, when we say "AI," we mean a technology that recognizes patterns in large amounts of data that humans may miss. It also enables making probabilistic predictions based on these patterns, which can help decision-making.

Sensors, the IoT, and AI exponentially improve on the operational efficiencies delivered by traditional IT. In so doing, they also further help with the original objectives of value chain networks—to support products and product positioning. More important, however, these technologies also make it possible for value chain networks to go beyond their legacy product-centric scope. These technologies empower legacy firms to use their industry networks to generate new data-driven services and digital experiences.

Improving Operational Efficiencies   Let us first consider how sensors, the IoT, and AI improve the operational efficiencies offered by traditional IT services in Ford's value chain network. Sensors can capture a wide range of interactive data. They are versatile. They are ubiquitous. They can be retrofitted to existing assets. And they can be connected to form vast networks permitting data generation and sharing through the

IoT on top of the IT system's infrastructure. Sensors and the IoT thus allow broader data generation and sharing beyond what IT systems can provide.

It is important to note that sensors, the IoT, and AI do not replace the functions of various IT systems. These IT systems have evolved over the years to provide sophisticated and intricate ways of automating various complex workflows. Sensors, the IoT, and AI complement those systems by creating a broader data generation and sharing network on top of those systems. This added network can generate far more data because of the ubiquity of sensors. Retrofitted sensors allow assets to generate data not earlier envisaged by the creators of their underlying software or IT systems. The network can customize the kinds of data generated by an array of different entities, assets, and activities because of the versatility of sensors in generating different kinds of data. Also, data can be shared within the network for use by AI systems to generate additional insights. Indeed, AI adds considerable power to this network by injecting fresh intelligence as to how data should be used for problem solving within the value chain. All these affordances improve operational efficiencies.

Let's consider a scenario in which an IT system in one of Ford's assembly units detects a spike in defects in the door assemblies received from a manufacturing unit. That IT system then alerts a different IT system in the manufacturing unit that produces the door assemblies. The alert requests more shipments of door assemblies. This is done in order to have enough non defective door assemblies so that the assembly operation flow is not disrupted. Clearly, such data generation and sharing solve an immediate problem of maintaining assembly workflow. However, the solution does not address the root cause or sources of those defects.

Sensors and the IoT cast a much wider net for data collection and sharing beyond the assembly and manufacturing units' siloed IT systems. Armed with more voluminous data from a broader set of sources, AI gets a better shot at detecting the underlying source of the problem. Its solution goes beyond avoiding workflow interruptions in one particular assembly unit. The solution tries to reduce the overall time needed to produce a car. Chapter 4 provides more examples to further explain how firms can develop a production ecosystems strategy to improve operational efficiencies with the help of sensors, the IoT, and AI.

New Data-Driven Services   A far more significant difference that sensors, the IoT, and AI provide over what traditional IT systems offer lies in their abilities to generate new data-driven product features and services. These new features and services are possible when firms install sensors on their products and track product-user interactions. Unlike the benefits from operational efficiencies, which help to reduce costs, data-driven services can generate fresh revenue streams for firms. Enabled by data, they can expand their competitive scope beyond what is possible with their products to new pastures. Data-driven services can transform a firm's interactions with its customers. They can even help a firm reinvent itself.

Data-driven services arise from new data-enabled product features that provide added benefits and new experiences for a firm's customers. Ford's cars, for example, self-park. They help drivers stay in their lane. They brake before collisions happen. Ford monetizes such features, offering them as added options for enhanced prices and margins.

Data-driven services stemming from such smart product features can be extended in two special ways, depending on the kind of data generated, the product generating the data, and the needs of the customers. One is through predictive services. Ford can, based on sensor data and AI, detect the likelihood of failure of a car's components, such as an engine, axle, or brakes, and alert a driver ahead of time. Such predictive services, made available as options, can generate new revenue streams. Ford is using these services for its fleet customers (such as car rental companies and police) to reduce the downtimes of their fleets of cars. Predictive services for maintenance are particularly valuable for situations in which product downtime is costly. Predictive services can be used wherever sensor data can provide alerts before bad outcomes happen. In assisted living facilities, for example, predictive services help avoid client hospitalizations by providing alerts before clients' likely falls or illnesses. In agriculture, they can predict crop disease or pest activities and initiate corrective actions before costly damage occurs.

The second way in which data-driven services stemming from smart product features can be extended is through mass customization. Here mattresses provide an example. Using real-time data on users' heart rate, breathing, tossing, and turning, mattresses can be mass-customized to provide users with better sleep experiences. Put differently, mattresses can change their features (contours) to accommodate every individual's sleep patterns each night. Chapter 4 provides more examples and details on how firms use their production ecosystems to offer such new data-driven services to expand revenue generation.

From Complementor Networks to Consumption Ecosystems

The complementor network is the other foundation on which legacy firms can build new digital ecosystems. Compared to value chain networks, the complementor network has been smaller and less significant for legacy firms. Furthermore, unlike with value chain networks, traditional IT has not played any notable role in managing data generation and sharing within complementor networks. The links between different entities, assets, and activities in complementor networks have traditionally remained nondigital. Some of these links are created through cobranding efforts, as illustrated by the example of Colgate's toothbrushes and toothpaste. Most of the links, however, are established through commonly adopted industry standards. Standards in socket designs, voltage levels, and electrical wiring make it possible for consumers to buy any light bulb and use it in their homes. Similarly, standards applicable to gas and fuel dispenser nozzles in gas stations make it easy to complement any car with gas.

Today, sensors and the IoT are dramatically transforming nondigital complementor networks into vibrant digital consumption ecosystems. Figures 3.4a, 3.4b, and 3.4c depict such a transition for Ford from its traditional complementor network to a new consumption ecosystem.

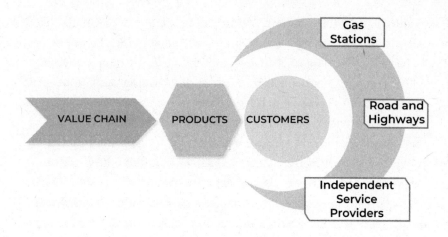

COMPLEMENTOR
NETWORK

Figure 3.4a

From complementor networks to consumption ecosystems: Ford Motor Company
with traditional nondigital complements.

Before the establishment of modern digital technologies, Ford's complementor network included a handful of entities and objects that were
not digitally connected. We noted gas stations, independent service
providers (such as Midas), and roads and highways as examples. This is
depicted in figure 3.4a.

With sensors and the IoT, these complements can now be digitally
connected to Ford's sensor-equipped cars and made accessible to Ford's
digital customers for new digital platform services. As examples, a car
running low on gas can locate the nearest gas station. A car with a
potential brake problem can be connected to a conveniently located
Midas or equivalent independent service provider to schedule an
appointment. A car receives a traffic jam alert and is provided with an
alternative route (see figure 3.4b).

These scenarios all revolve around connecting preexisting nondigital
complements through modern digital technologies. In addition, a car

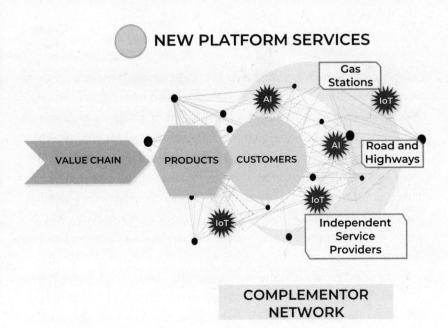

Figure 3.4b

From complementor networks to consumption ecosystems: Ford Motor Company with traditional complements digitally connected.

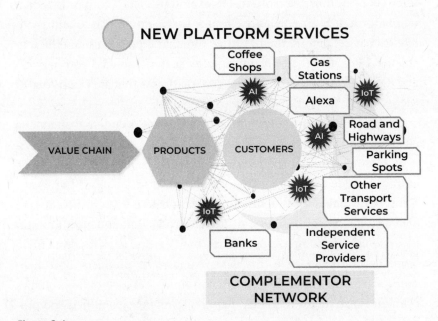

Figure 3.4c

From complementor networks to consumption ecosystems: Ford Motor Company with expanded digital complements.

today has many new complements that have emerged solely because of digital connectivity. The introduction described how drivers can order coffee from their cars. This is possible through new digital complements such as Amazon's Alexa and connected entities such as Starbucks and banks. Just like Starbucks, there could be thousands of other retailers that can be similarly connected. Ford can find many other such connected entities and assets as complements to its sensor-equipped cars. They include connected parking spots and software interfaces with an array of transportation services such as buses, subways, and trains (see figure 3.4c).

By connecting with these new complementors, Ford can offer an even wider array of new data-driven services and digital experiences. Herein lies the new power of consumption ecosystems. Coffee-ordering services, timely after-sales service by independent service providers, finding empty parking spots, and traffic jam avoidance are some examples of such data-driven services and digital experiences. To offer these services, however, Ford has to extend its value chain onto a digital platform. It has to digitally connect various third parties and facilitate exchanges among them, just as the digital platforms described in chapter 1 do. How legacy firms can offer such new data-driven services and digital experiences through digital platforms that are extensions of their value chains is the main focus of chapter 5.

Unlike production ecosystems, which provide an internal and value chain–based avenue to unlock the value of data, consumption ecosystems offer an external avenue through a proliferation of "connected" entities outside prevailing value chains. For a vast majority of legacy firms, these digital ecosystems did not exist before modern advances in data and digital connectivity. Although production and consumption ecosystems offer different approaches, both expand a firm's competitive scope beyond products to the data generated by products. Both help transform a firm's interactions with customers. Yet each of them shapes competitive strategy differently, requires different capabilities, and provides different strategic options for firms. They have to be understood as different but related facets of digital ecosystems.

Differences between Production and Consumption Ecosystems

Table 3.1 summarizes the key differences between production and consumption ecosystems.

Foundations: Production ecosystems and consumption ecosystems stem from different foundational networks. Production ecosystems stem from value chain networks, while consumption ecosystems stem from complementor networks. These different foundations shape production and consumption ecosystems differently. Production and consumption ecosystems thus generate distinct opportunities for new value creation. They project different trajectories for digital competitive strategy.

Network participants: Value chain networks offer an array of well-established entities, assets, and activities as network participants. The

Table 3.1
Differences between production and consumption ecosystems

Criterion	Production Ecosystems	Consumption Ecosystems
Foundation	Builds on value chain networks	Builds on complementor networks
Network participants	Data generation and sharing among prevailing assets, entities, and activities	Data generation and sharing among new and expanded set of assets, entities, and activities
Competencies used or extended	Reinforces and reinvigorates prevailing value chain competencies	Builds on new digital platform competencies
Input sources for new data-driven services	Internal value chain competencies	External complementor ideas and competencies
API focus	Internal API focus	External API focus
Scope of new value	Purposeful and bounded by value chain boundaries	Serendipitous and unbounded, as in an app economy
Governance mechanisms	Utilizes prevailing value chain governance mechanisms	Requires new governance mechanisms anchored on external APIs

process of data generation and sharing within this network started years ago with IT services, long before the arrival of modern digital technologies. Production ecosystems use this already established network of participants for further and more enriched data generation and sharing.

Complementor networks, on the other hand, start with few network participants and depend on the range of physical connections to a product. For a light bulb, for example, the physical complements are limited to sockets, electricity, and wiring. With new digital complements instilled by modern digital technologies, however, the scope of this network expands. Smart bulbs, for instance, have far more digital complements than traditional light bulbs. As highlighted in the introduction, smart bulbs generating data on motion in homes that are supposed to be empty find security services, alarms, and mobile apps as complements. When generating data on the movement of inventory in warehouses, smart bulbs find various entities, objects, and activities connected to logistical services as complements. When detecting data on gunshots, smart bulbs find camera feeds, 911 operators, and ambulances as complements. Consumption ecosystems thus generate and share data within new and expanded sets of network participants.

Competencies used or extended: Because production ecosystems stem from value chain networks, they reinforce and reinvigorate prevailing value chain competencies. One way they do so is by improving operational efficiencies within value chains through expanded data generation and sharing. Even beyond operational efficiencies, new data-driven services derived from predictive maintenance capabilities and mass customization enabled by production ecosystems enhance the strengths of a legacy firm's value chain. Predictive maintenance improves on a legacy firm's prevailing after-sales service capabilities. Caterpillar arranging for a critical spare part for an excavator *before* a breakdown through predictive maintenance services improves on its older practice of ensuring spare part availability *after* a breakdown through efficient spare part inventory planning. Mass-customized products similarly improve prevailing product functionality. A GE jet engine that guides pilots to fly in ways that reduce fuel consumption according to the unique flying conditions of each flight is a better product than jet engines that do not adapt their fuel efficiencies to flying conditions, which allows GE to strengthen its prevailing product functionalities of high averages in fuel efficiency.

Consumption ecosystems, on the other hand, can generate new data-driven services that are different from the prevailing functionalities of the product. Depending on the nature of the digital complements a smart bulb relies on, it can generate new data-driven services in home security, logistics, and street safety, among others. All these services are far removed from the light bulb's primary function of providing illumination. Such data-driven services achieved through consumption ecosystems also need new digital platform capabilities. In fact, the competitiveness with which a legacy firm can offer such new data-driven services from its consumption ecosystems hinges on such new digital platform capabilities (a subject elaborated on in chapters 5 and 8).

Input sources for new data-driven services: Production ecosystems leverage internal value chain capabilities when generating new data-driven services. Predictive maintenance services, for instance, are built on the foundations of prevailing after-sales service capabilities. Similarly, mass-customized products rely on many prevailing value chain strengths such as R&D, product design, and manufacturing. Even new organizational units—created specifically to handle fresh responsibilities of managing sensor data and AI—have to fit in with prevailing value chain activities and merge with their processes and capabilities.

Consumption ecosystems, by contrast, rely on the innovations of third-party entities. The primary inputs for new data-driven services stem from how creatively external entities find ways to complement their data. Chapter 2 described this approach as "letting a thousand flowers bloom." Nest thermostats offer data-driven services to enable Google customers to automatically adjust home heating from their cars or to run their washing machines at off-peak hours because scores of external third-party entities such as auto companies, appliance

manufacturers. and energy companies found creative ways to complement Nest's data.

API focus: Production ecosystems adopt an internal API focus whereby
interactive data generated by products and digital customers are chan-
neled internally within the ecosystem's value chains. Such internal
channeling of data generates insights that improve operational efficiencies and support stronger data-driven services such as predictive maintenance and mass-customization services. Chapter 2 described these
internally focused APIs as applications of intrafirm and supply chain
interfaces.

Consumption ecosystems, on the other hand, require an external
API focus. Consumption ecosystems expand and become increasingly
vibrant as more third parties find ways to complement product data.
Data-driven services emerging from consumption ecosystems are likely
to be stronger as the number of network participants increases and the
associated network effects multiple. This likelihood increases with an
open and externally focused API policy that improves the odds of external entities finding ways to complement the traditional firm's data.
Chapter 2 described such externally focused APIs as applications of a
complementor interface.

Scope of new value: In so far as production ecosystems rely on internal
value chain strengths and have internally focused APIs for data sharing,
the scope of new value they create is also bounded by those choices.
The new value they generate is a function of how they improve operational efficiencies or how they provide new data-driven services. All
this is done through the data they internally share and by using their
internal strengths. Such efforts are usually purposeful, with planned
targets to be reached and specified goals for outcomes.

Because consumption ecosystems rely on external inputs and externally focused APIs, the new value they generate is not bounded by their
internal strengths. Instead it is open to a wide array of digital complements that find ways to co-create new services from the data. Such new

value generation is also serendipitous. As in an app economy, it is hard to predict which platform service will gain traction or which creative idea will go viral in its application.

Governance mechanisms: Finally, production ecosystems and consumption ecosystems need different governance mechanisms to manage their network relationships. The network participants within production ecosystems are already part of their prevailing value chains. The governance mechanisms for production ecosystems thus do not change much from what legacy firms employed to manage their value chains. For internally owned units, such governance mechanisms are driven by established organizational processes, hierarchies, reporting relationships, and specific job expectations. For value chain partners such as suppliers and dealers, there are norms for and expectations regarding the quality of components they produce or the customer relationships they manage. Companies enter into contracts to govern each of these relationships. Production ecosystems continue to rely on these prevailing governance mechanisms.

Consumption ecosystems, by contrast, need new governance mechanisms. Because legacy firms have historically taken a hands-off approach with their complementor network participants, there is no established practice to rely on akin to those in production ecosystems. As all consumption ecosystems participants are entities external to their value chains, there is no hierarchical governance possible similar to what legacy firms employ to manage internal units. The governance approach with external entities in consumption ecosystems is also different from what firms have traditionally used for their value chain partners such as suppliers and dealers.

Ford, for instance, expects its dealers to provide genuine Ford components during car repairs and to meet minimum thresholds of service quality. On the other hand, if Ford connects a driver to a convenient Midas location in its consumption ecosystem, the relationship is just that—a simple connection. It is no different from Ford connecting a driver to Starbucks. It neither expects Midas to use Ford components nor sets up any expectations with the driver that she is receiving Ford's service, just as a driver does not associate the quality of Starbuck's coffee with Ford. Such network relationships are governed through API policies, much as the digital titans manage their relationships with the users of their digital platforms through API policies. API policies are software-driven. Software automates the underlying rules for sharing of data and functionalities among different entities, along with their associated commercial terms. Through software, Ford's APIs, for instance, can set the rules as to which independent service provider a driver can connect to in case of a component malfunction and what each service provider must pay for that connection. Through software updates, Ford can modify the terms it offers providers or set the terms to vary based on the volume of transactions. Fundamentally, API-driven governance mechanisms are far more flexible than traditional value chain governance mechanisms.

Digital Ecosystems and Industry 4.0

Before we conclude this chapter, it is useful to understand how digital ecosystems, presented here as a combination of production and consumption ecosystems, relate to the concept of Industry 4.0, also known as the fourth industrial revolution. The progression of industry networks into data-enriched digital ecosystems, highlighted in this chapter, has parallels with the evolution of Industry 4.0. It is also useful to appreciate the context Industry 4.0 provides for traditional firms to construct, shape, and engage with their new digital ecosystems.

Briefly, Industry 4.0 refers to the ongoing modernization of traditional industries through the application of smart technologies. The origin of the term and concept is commonly associated with Germany's new industrial policy, which emerged around 2010. At the World Economic Forum in Davos in 2015, German chancellor Angela Merkel highlighted its importance to established industries:

We must—and I say this as the German chancellor in the face of a strong Germany economy—deal quickly with the fusion of the online world and the world of industrial production. In Germany, we call it Industrie 4.0 . . . because otherwise, those who are the leaders in the digital domain will take the lead in industrial production. We enter this race with great confidence. But it's a race we have not yet won.[14]

The term Industry 4.0 thus acknowledges that modern digital technologies have ushered in a new era in industry. It signals to legacy firms the necessity of changing and adapting to this new era, and further suggests a path and direction for legacy firms to take. To sense its gravity, one must consider the other momentous changes in our industrial history that preceded it and are now equated with Industry 4.0. These are Industry 1.0, 2.0, and 3.0.

Industry 1.0 marked an era when technologies changed hand production methods to machine-based production with the help of steam and waterpower. Industry 2.0 refers to the establishment of extensive railroad networks, the telegraph, and electricity. Industry 3.0 picked up momentum with rapid progress and the widespread adoption of IT systems, which allowed industrial firms to automate workflows and begin leveraging the power of data. Such major shifts are rare, transpiring approximately once per century. The Industry 4.0 revolution happening now is driven by modern digital technologies, including sensors, the IoT, and AI, as discussed in this chapter.

Each one of the epic landmarks from Industry 1.0 to 3.0 pertains to radical changes in how firms produce and sell their products. Technological developments such as machines, electricity, and computers brought about such changes during each of those industry transformations. From this history, it may appear that Industry 4.0 is a continuation of that trend, that Industry 4.0, like its predecessors, is yet another milestone in how traditional firms transform their value chains by taking advantage of quantum jumps in technology trajectories. Indeed, Industry 4.0 is often closely associated with such terms as "smart factories" and "lights-out factories"—facilities where human intervention in decision-making is progressively minimized. FANUC, a Japanese company that makes robots, for example, has a factory that can operate for up to six hundred hours with just a skeleton staff to perform routine maintenance and be ready for unanticipated trouble shooting. Such associations might give the impression that Industry 4.0 is essentially about legacy firms benefiting from their production ecosystems.

The scope of Industry 4.0, however, goes beyond production ecosystems. Industry 4.0 also accounts for the possibilities of firms offering new user experiences through smart products. And many new user experiences associated with smart products stem from engaging with consumption ecosystems. The key point here is that to seize the full scope of value that Industry 4.0 offers, a legacy firm must strive to engage with both its production and its consumption ecosystems. Also, unlike the three previous epochs in industrial development, Industry 4.0 offers new possibilities that go beyond pathbreaking improvements in operational efficiencies. The next two chapters, which go into more detail on production and consumption ecosystems, respectively, further establish this point. They elaborate on how digital ecosystems help legacy firms unlock the value of their data, in ways that not only enhance operational efficiencies but also generate fresh revenue streams through new data-driven services.

Summary Takeaways

This chapter laid out the core framework of this book, presenting digital ecosystems as a combination of production and consumption ecosystems. In doing so, we took one step further on our data to digital strategy journey. The digital ecosystems framework allows legacy firms to choose different options to engage with their production and consumption ecosystems to unlock more value from their data. The framework thus establishes an important foundation for legacy firms to craft their digital competitive strategy. The concept that digital ecosystems help unlock more value from data is one that we borrowed from the digital titans and their digital platforms. However, we adapted the idea to suit the prevailing business models of most legacy firms.

Legacy firms compete with products and draw their strengths from their industry structures and value chains. Seeing their industries as networks helps them expand their business environments into digital ecosystems. Industry networks, as combinations of value chain and complementor networks, provide the foundations to build new digital production ecosystems and consumption ecosystems. Digital ecosystems, specially adapted for legacy firms, allow those firms not only to reinforce their prevailing product-centric strengths but also to build new data-centric strengths. How legacy firms choose to engage with their production and consumption ecosystems determines the shape and scope of their digital competitive strategy. Chapters 4 and 5 focus on this next step.

The introduction to this book referred to digital myopia stemming from a firm's continued insistence on relying on products and industries for competitive advantage. The framework of digital ecosystems presented in this chapter can help legacy firms see new prospects for value beyond what their products and industries can offer. Yet digital myopia may persist if firms see the value of data and digital ecosystems only in improving their operational efficiencies. Many CEOs of legacy firms still expect the primary benefits of modern digital technologies to address old priorities: How do we introduce new products faster? How can our product innovations drive greater profits? How do we reduce downtime? How can we better manage our global supply chain? These are important priorities, but addressing them unlocks only a part of the full potential of data. Much more can be unlocked if firms and their CEOs shift to a different set of priorities: What new data-driven services can we offer? How can we shift more of our revenue from products to data-driven services? What new data-driven services can we offer through our production ecosystems? What new data-driven services can we offer through our consumption ecosystems? The following chapters continue this discussion.

4 Unlocking Data's Value from Production Ecosystems

This chapter elaborates on how production ecosystems can unlock the newfound opportunities from data that modern technologies offer. It also discusses how legacy firms can use their production ecosystems to shape select facets of their digital strategy. Figure 4.1 depicts two broad approaches by which production ecosystems help legacy firms unlock more value from their data. One approach is through achieving greater operational efficiencies, the other approach is through offering new data-driven services. Greater operational efficiencies stem from generating and sharing data within value chains to improve productivity and reduce costs. Data-driven services, on the other hand, empower legacy firms to generate new revenue streams.

It is useful at this point to recall the four tiers of digital transformation discussed in the introduction of this book.[1] Production ecosystems help firms traverse through the first three tiers of digital transformation. Firms engage in the first tier of digital transformation when they use data from their value chain *assets* to drive their operational efficiency gains. Firms progress to the second tier when they use data from their *products and users* to advance their operational efficiency gains. Firms move into the third tier of digital transformation when they harness data from products and customers to offer new data-driven services using their production ecosystems. The fourth tier entails a firm engaging its consumption ecosystems, elaborated in the next chapter.

This chapter describes how legacy firms can use their production ecosystems to progress through the first three tiers of digital

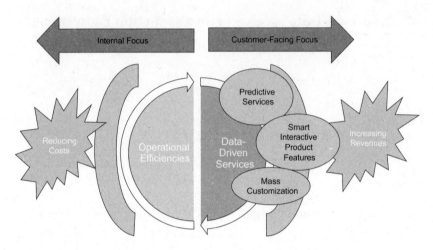

Figure 4.1
Unlocking the value of data from production ecosystems.

transformation. Let's start with the first two tiers that entail enhancing operational efficiencies.

Operational Efficiencies from Production Ecosystems

Production ecosystems are value chain networks injected with greater data-generating and data-sharing capabilities through the use of modern digital technologies. These modern technologies improve on the capabilities of older IT systems, which began the process of automating and integrating workflows within companies. Not surprisingly, production ecosystems enriched by these modern technologies also enhance prevailing operational efficiencies.

This section highlights various examples, representing different ways in which firms can use their production ecosystems to generate greater operational efficiencies: the first two examples highlight how firms can use data from value chain assets, while the third discusses how firms can generate more advanced operational efficiencies using data from their products and customers. These examples are meant to suggest some of the many choices legacy firms have at their disposal in seeking to use their production ecosystems for operational efficiency gains. They are also offered to spark ideas on how the principles highlighted in these examples can be applied to other contexts in which operational efficiency gains might be possible.

Matching Supply and Demand in the Fast-Moving Consumer Goods Business

The fast-moving consumer goods (FMCG) business sells nondurable household goods such as beverages, toiletries, packaged foods, cosmetics, and over-the-counter drugs. FMCG companies concentrate on low-priced items that are meant to move fast from retail store shelves. Globally, FMCG products generated over $10 trillion in revenues in 2018. Among the dominant companies in this business are Nestlé, Procter & Gamble, Unilever, PepsiCo, and Coca-Cola. Each of these companies has multiple brands. Nestlé, the largest, has more than 8,000 brands. Unilever has 400. Each of these brands in turn has thousands of items with unique identifiers known as stock keeping units (SKUs) that help retailers keep track of the inventory they receive and sell. P&G's umbrella brand Tide, for instance, has several products, including liquid detergents, detergent pods, sanitizing fabric sprays, and other cleaners. Each of these products is differentiated by package size, color, and packaging material, among other attributes. Each package type is also a unique SKU. One can see why the number of SKUs proliferates quickly for FMCG companies.

Thousands of such SKUs are also sold through an intricate network of millions of large and small retailers worldwide. One of the most significant challenges for FMCG companies is to match the demand for these SKUs arising from these diverse set of retailers with supply from their distribution centers.

A well-known problem with matching demand and supply in the FMCG sector is referred to as the "bullwhip" effect.[2] The bullwhip effect refers to small changes in demand at individual retail stores leading to large misperceptions in supply requirements to meet aggregate demand. A small shake of the handle at the top can lead to large-amplitude waves at the other end of the whip. Likewise, small changes in demand in individual retail outlets can lead to large swings in inventory response from further up the supply chain. There are several reasons why FMCG companies might experience a bullwhip effect. Sales staff may give bulk discounts, incentivizing retailers to buy more than their typical orders. Similarly, transportation companies may give discounts, skewing the number of SKUs retailers ask for. Retailers may also respond idiosyncratically to short-term promotions. Poor communication across the supply chain further exacerbates the impact of all such events on the bullwhip effect.

FMCG companies with thousands of SKUs also face complexity and unpredictable variability in their supply. In part this is because of the inability of traditional enterprise software to help supply chain planners properly manage inventory over the eight- to twelve-week execution planning horizon. Because of unanticipated swings in demand, it is common for some of these companies to miss fulfilling between 8 and 10 percent of their orders, despite having the necessary inventory somewhere in their supply chain. They are just not able to get the right inventory to the right location in time. "It is as if this is the cost of doing business," says Raj Joshi, the cofounder and president of Noodle. ai, a company that offers AI solutions to enterprises. "Modern digital technologies offer a huge opportunity for supply chain executives to solve such problems," he adds.

Traditional enterprise resource planning (ERP) systems can churn out massive amounts of data on demand and supply patterns. However, the traditional approaches to utilizing such data rely on retrospective analysis. They deliver insights into what went right or wrong in the last week, month, or quarter. The difference with enterprise AI, says Joshi, is that it can help predict or peek into the future in a probabilistic sense. Through algorithms that interpret and analyze various patterns in the data, AI engines can tell you, for instance, that there is an 80 percent chance that a large order for specific SKUs in a specific geography for a valued customer is likely to go unfilled. AI engines, based on data from a firm's ERP systems, can then recommend actions that supply chain planners could take to ensure increasing inventories so that the order gets filled. Conversely, AI can predict inventory overages, thereby helping supply chain planners appropriately reduce production levels and reduce inventory costs. AI can thus avert putting substantial value at risk. According to Joshi, a conservative improvement in unfilled orders of one percentage point—say, from 10 percent to 9 percent—for the FMCG companies has the potential to increase contribution margins and profits by multiple millions of dollars.

Improving Productivity in Pharmaceutical Research Labs

Drug discovery is the lifeline of the pharmaceutical business. Firms in this businesses live or die based on their pipelines of new drugs. Not surprisingly, the pharmaceutical sector invests substantially in R&D—around 17 percent of their annual revenues.[3] In comparison, aerospace companies spend around 5 percent on R&D and the chemicals sector spends around 3 percent. Microsoft and Google spend around 12 percent. While 17 percent is the average R&D spend in the pharmaceutical sector, leading firms spend even more. AstraZeneca's R&D spend was around 25 percent of its annual revenue in 2019, Eli Lily's was around 22 percent, and Roche's was 21 percent. The total amount spent on R&D in the pharmaceutical industry totaled $179 billion globally in 2018. This amount reflects money that goes into all phases of pharmaceutical R&D, from the initial research on drugs and disease to testing compounds in preclinical and clinical trial stages. Around $56 billion of this amount goes into early drug research that is done in research labs.[4]

Figure 4.2 shows a simplified version of the value chain network for pharma research labs. It starts with various supplies, such as kits, assays, and reagents for cell-based analysis, genome analysis, and protein purification; live animals; and general lab items such as chemicals, glassware, and disposables. The next step in the value chain entails scientists using these supplies and lab equipment for experiments. Thousands of such experiments over several years lead to lab outputs, which may include discoveries of new compounds that may work in combating

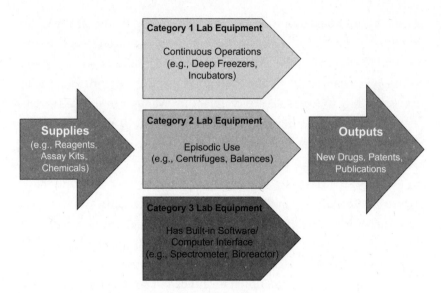

Figure 4.2
Value chain networks in research labs.

various diseases, along with patents and publications related to such breakthroughs.

Traditional Use of Lab Equipment: Largely Analog, with Little Data Integration Lab equipment can be characterized as falling in three categories. The first category entails equipment operated around the clock, such as deep freezers and incubators. Deep freezers are necessary to store certain reagents, antibodies, and assay kits at temperatures such as minus 20 or minus 80 degrees centigrade for preservation. Incubators, another example, are needed to maintain cell cultures at predetermined temperature and humidity levels, apart from providing requisite oxygen and carbon dioxide for the cell culture. Such equipment usually runs round the clock in research labs. Any interruption can alter the composition of cell cultures in ways that may ruin ongoing experiments using them.

The second category equipment is used as and when needed. Centrifuges are used whenever an experiment needs to separate liquids and substances of different densities. For example, centrifuges are used to separate different components in blood such as red blood cells, white blood cells, platelets, and plasma. Some specialized lab balances similarly are used whenever an experiment requires measuring small masses in the submilligram range with great precision. The first two categories of equipment are usually analog. Records of their use are usually kept manually. A scientist may, for example, measure the mass of a compound and note the reading in a paper lab notebook.

A third category of equipment comes with built-in software that can be connected to external computers. Such equipment generally outputs data files rather than just numbers. A mass spectrometer, for example, used to determine the molecular composition of a sample based on observing the spectrum of ions within it, needs software. It detects, among other things, small amounts of proteins, biomarkers, or drug molecules, even when they occur in low concentrations. Interpreting such mass spectra data entails analyzing large amounts of data and performing tedious calculations, both of which are difficult to do without software-driven algorithms. Although such equipment can generate and record data digitally, these data are siloed within each piece of equipment and its connected computer. The data are not designed to be easily shared and integrated with data from other lab equipment.

The three categories of equipment depict the "raw" value chain network of a typical research lab. Because of the massive investments involved in research labs, any increase in operational efficiencies can have a big impact on a lab's bottom line. So how can firms transform this value chain network into a digital production ecosystem? What kind of benefits can they expect?

New Operational Efficiencies through Data and Data Integration   Meet Sridhar Iyengar, the CEO and founder of Elemental Machines, a company that turns an array of discrete lab equipment into a connected network through sensors and the IoT. Sensors help track various contextual variables such as temperature, humidity, air pressure, and light as scientists conduct their experiments using various pieces of lab equipment. Why are such data important? Sridhar explains through a personal anecdote that he heard from two colleagues in two different institutions.

During their days as lab bench researchers in biology, Sridhar's friends noticed something unusual during their experiments. As all researchers know, experiments are deemed successful only when they are replicable. In other words, results must not change when the same experiment protocol is repeated. With these particular experiments, the results were inconsistent. As the researchers kept repeating them, however, they noticed a pattern. The results were off only on certain days of the week, while consistent on others. The reason? The experiment involved mice. On certain nights of the week a construction site next door had night shifts, and the associated noise and vibration affected the nocturnal patterns of the mice in the lab.

When Sridhar heard the same story from two different people in two different research labs, he had an epiphany: context matters in lab experiments. The context for most experiments in pharmaceutical labs, of course, is highly complex. Yet even measuring some basic variables such as temperature, humidity, air pressure, and light (or in the case of mice, sound and vibration levels) as an experiment progresses helps. Using such data, researchers can determine, to some extent, the reasons behind the variability in their results. In other words, they need not throw away all experiments that show variable results by assuming faulty scientific hypotheses as the sole cause. This can lead to substantial productivity improvements. Sridhar's company, Elemental Machines, has recently joined forces with PerkinElmer, a global life sciences company, with the aim of improving productivity in research labs through data and data connectivity.

Figure 4.3 shows how the value chain network of a pharma lab turns into a production ecosystem for operational efficiency gains. This happens when an array of different lab equipment gets connected through sensors and the IoT. And in some special cases, AI also helps.

Sensors in the first category of equipment, such as cell culture incubators, keep track of conditions under which cell growth occurs for synthetic biology applications. Smart labels on the fermentation flasks that hold the cells can record the ambient conditions relevant to their growth (temperature, humidity, CO_2, and so on) and alert a

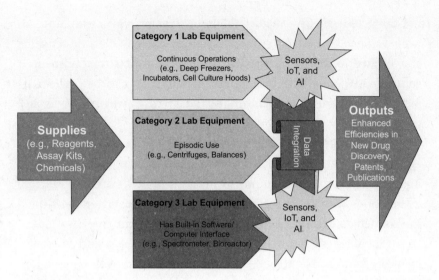

Figure 4.3
Production ecosystems in research labs.

scientist when any unexpected variation occurs. Such variations can creep in when, for example, multiple scientists share an incubator in a lab. The number of times an incubator door opens during the time cells are growing in the incubator can affect the outcome of an experiment. Further complicating this situation is that cell growth can take several days, and it may take weeks before the data become available to determine whether those cells grew successfully. Timely alerts thus help avoid such losses of scientists' valuable time. This idea applies to some of the second category of equipment, too. For example, readings of specialized balances measured in micrograms can be affected by the opening or closing of the equipment's breeze break door. (A breeze break is designed to prevent minute changes in temperature or air flow from altering the extremely sensitive weight-measuring device.)

The first category of equipment also needs to operate without interruptions to ensure that the materials stored in it are preserved. Sensors alert concerned scientists directly in case of unexpected interruptions so they can make alternate plans for their experiments.

Connected second category equipment helps in coordinating lab work among scientists. The use of a centrifuge may be time-sensitive and needed exactly after a particular protocol of an experiment is completed. Having data on equipment schedules can help scientists plan their experiments accordingly and avoid wasted protocols and wasted time.

The third category of equipment already produces data in digital form, but the data are restricted to the core functions of the equipment. Adding sensors to such equipment makes it more flexible to integrate its functions with other equipment. For instance, data generated by a spectrometer are usually restricted to the spectrometric analysis of specimens. Such data do not help coordinate or schedule a scientist's experiment program, nor do they take into account the ambient temperature of the room when the reading was taken (which can affect the calibration of the instrument). Third-category equipment retrofitted with sensors and connected to other assets through the IoT can help do that.

The above efforts reduce experiment variability and improve the utilization of assets in a lab. They thereby improve the operational efficiencies of a lab. The savings for a typical big pharmaceutical company, according to Sridhar, are in the millions. "Considering the billions spent on research labs by pharmaceutical firms, research labs have historically been remarkably analog," he says. All that can change with modern digital technologies converting analog value chains into rich production ecosystems.

Using Data from Products and Users for Advanced Operational Efficiencies

Data driving operational efficiency gains need not just come from a firm's assets such as enterprise resource planning (ERP) systems or lab equipment. They can also come from products and users through embedded sensors. The book's introduction highlighted how Caterpillar's motor graders (machines used in construction sites), embedded with sensors, generate interactive data providing new and unique insights.

Caterpillar had designed its motor grader imagining that its customers would use it to flatten dirt. Sensor data on actual usage told a different story. Customers mostly used the motor graders to flatten gravel, a lighter material. This discovery helped Caterpillar develop new blades for the motor grader that flattened gravel better. It also helped Caterpillar design a machine that was less expensive to produce for this task, pricing the product more competitively and yet improving margins. Sensor data from customers in other words, helped Caterpillar make their R&D and product development processes more productive. Arriving at such an efficient design would have taken much longer and expended far more resources if Caterpillar relied on traditional approaches to collect product usage data such as surveys or focus groups.

Receiving interactive data from customers is possible even if it is difficult to envision embedding sensors into products. Consumer packaged-goods companies such as P&G and Red Bull are using web-based sensors with the aid of creative customer-relationship management (CRM) programs to generate interactive data from their customers. CRM programs help attract current and potential customers to their websites, eventually providing them with interactive data that they ordinarily do not get when their products are sold through third-party retailers.

P&G's baby diaper brand, Pampers, has CRM programs that offer advice to young or expectant mothers on caring for their babies and toddlers. Similarly, Red Bull's CRM programs offer videos of wild stunts—attracting their customer base in keeping with its "Red Bull gives you wings" brand image. These customers offer interactive data by liking various content, participating in loyalty programs, or in the case of Pampers, asking questions related to motherhood. Such interactive data helps them mass-customize and micro-target their advertising and promotion campaigns. Advertisements based on messaging that are most likely to appeal to individual customers are placed on digital channels, such as Facebook or Google, in ways that will probably get attention. In doing so, P&G improves its efficiencies in ad spend.

Operational efficiencies gained from product and user data are more advanced as they go beyond improving asset utilization and apply to broader processes such as R&D, product development, marketing, and advertising. Harnessing such advanced operational efficiencies also pose additional challenges for legacy firms (and hence at a higher tier of digital transformation), as it is much harder to get sensor data from products and users as compared to value chain assets. This point will be further explored in chapter 6 in a discussion of the challenges in acquiring digital customers, or customers who provide interactive data.

Many Ways to Improve Operational Efficiencies

As the above examples depict, there are a host of different ways legacy firms can enhance their operational efficiencies using production ecosystems. No matter what the industry, the ideas behind these examples have relevance; they can be applied to different contexts, and every firm can enhance their operational efficiencies using their production ecosystems. All such approaches are impossible to cover in this book. Suffice it to say that if a firm identifies an area where it believes operational efficiency improvements are warranted, modern technologies can offer a solution. There are several third-party entities (like noodle. ai and Elemental Machines referred to earlier in this chapter) that offer IoT-based solutions to connect a variety of different value chain assets and entities to generate operational efficiency gains. Legacy firms can use such resources.

Operational efficiency improvements, though significant, are not the only benefits offered by production ecosystems. Legacy firms can use their production ecosystems to generate new data-driven services as well. In this way, production ecosystems can help legacy firms generate new revenues in addition to reducing costs, as the examples in the next section highlight.

New Data-Driven Services from Production Ecosystems

Caterpillar Inc., referred to in earlier examples, is one of America's iconic manufacturing companies. A merger between Holt Manufacturing company and L. Best Tractor company in 1925 marks its origin. Today it is the world's largest construction equipment manufacturer.

Several of its products, such as loaders, excavators, and bulldozers, with their instantly recognizable yellow livery and familiar CAT logo, are prominent features on the landscape of most construction sites. Caterpillar understandably is deeply entrenched in a culture of manufacturing rugged mechanical engineering products meant to operate in tough weather conditions and on difficult terrains. It is often referred to as "big iron." Yet in recent years, Caterpillar has also made its mark in the digital world, offering an array of new, sophisticated data-driven services.

Caterpillar sells and services a diverse range of products, such as construction and mining equipment, diesel and natural gas engines, industrial gas turbines, and diesel-electric locomotives. These products are used by a wide range of industries, including construction, mining, oil and gas exploration and extraction, power generation, marine transport, rail transport, and a host of others. Caterpillar has traditionally structured itself to ensure that each of its products effectively caters to the unique needs of the user's industry. Accordingly, in the early 1990s, Caterpillar organized the company into autonomous business units. Each business unit, such as the Global Excavator Division, became responsible for its own profit and loss. Each unit decided how much to produce, what product designs to introduce, where to produce, and which suppliers to source, among other decisions.

This kind of structure was quite common among conglomerates during the 1990s. Business strategies then were primarily shaped by industry characteristics, as discussed in chapter 3. A core maxim was that profitability stemmed from products and how products effectively marshaled competitive forces within their own relevant industries.

By the middle of the following decade, however, digital technologies started changing Caterpillar's business landscape. New and different types of companies from outside Caterpillar's industry started entering the company's various markets. These new entrants were not competing with products similar to Caterpillar's; instead, they were offering new services to customers through data. Using data, they could offer innovative digital services that helped construction equipment users more effectively manage their assets, whether they were sold by Caterpillar or by Caterpillar's prevailing rivals, such as Komatsu, Hitachi, or Volvo.

Two examples of the new entrants are Trimble and Teletrac Navman. Both companies came with a background in GPS and cellular technologies, along with the capabilities to provide a host of new data-driven services to construction equipment users regardless of the brand of equipment they used. Through their services, construction equipment owners could monitor, for example, the real-time locations of their entire fleet of front loaders, backhoes, bulldozers, and skid steers at a construction site. Through the installation of retrofitted sensors these companies also offered real-time data on ignition status, engine diagnostics, vehicle activity, and fuel consumption of each asset, enabling productivity assessments of fleets.

Such digital capabilities were not new to Caterpillar. In fact, many of the company's mining products were already equipped with sophisticated sensor and IoT technologies and were designed to operate as autonomous vehicles to do jobs. Acquiring modern digital technology, in other words, was not Caterpillar's primary challenge. Rather, expanding technology adoption from a few select products to all its products was the challenge. Caterpillar had a business unit–driven organizational structure in which not all of the (independent) business unit heads saw the same urgency to equip their products with sophisticated digital technologies. A business unit responsible for small skid steers, for example, could find adding sensors difficult from a product design perspective. Unless the business unit could convince customers there was value in the added cost, these products' prices could become uncompetitive.

By 2010, however, the company's leadership, spearheaded by CEO Doug Oberhelman, was convinced that to meet growing customer needs in the new digital world, Caterpillar needed major internal cultural changes. Their "big iron" culture was not sustainable in its prevailing form. Yet Caterpillar also recognized the significance of getting buy-in from the company's key business leaders when making major changes. The business unit heads, after all, were important stakeholders. They would have to be convinced before any meaningful adoption of connected products could go forward as a strategic plan.

New Data-Driven Services through Interactive Product Features Caterpillar developed a matrix that helped the company's business unit leaders prioritize when, where, and how to justify making their products connected. This matrix allowed them to visualize an array of new data-driven services for their customers through technology-enabled interactive product features. Such visualization also helped in finding ways to accelerate the adoption of connected products. Four broad categories shape the scope of Caterpillar's interactive product features and related data-driven services. These categories are equipment management, productivity, safety, and emissions. Furthermore, each of the features within these categories could be applied to single assets, fleets of assets, or an enterprise that has multiple projects going on in different locations globally (see table 4.1).

Each box in this matrix represents an illustration of an interactive product feature. For example, information on whether an asset is in use or idle at any given point of time is an interactive product feature. It allows both customers and business unit managers to visualize and

Table 4.1
Interactive product features and data-driven services

	Equipment Management	Productivity	Safety	Emissions
Assets	Total engine idle time?	Tons of material lifted?	Is the asset operating safely?	Asset emissions?
Fleets	What part of the fleet will need maintenance, and when?	How many assets are needed for a job?	Gamification to incentivize operators for safety	How to reduce fleet emissions?
Enterprise	Which project is on or behind schedule?	How to allocate resources across projects?	How to maintain safety standards across geographies?	Which projects have high/low emissions, and why?

choose the features they think would be appropriate to adopt. Each of the features can be presented as a value proposition to Caterpillar's clients. If attractive enough, each can also be offered as a data-driven service that provides, say, a more detailed and pertinent analysis of the factors causing the asset to be idle or working. Likewise, each of the boxes represents such an opportunity. To take one more example, consider data-driven gamification to incentivize operator safety as a feature (in the matrix with fleets as the row and safety as the column). The feature, based on operator tracking, generates a safety score for each operator; the score is used to incentivize operators to win gift cards, if their scores are better than other operators. Caterpillar can facilitate such a data-driven service for interested fleet owners.

This matrix helped business unit managers determine how best to adopt connected products for their businesses and what kind of digital services to offer. A manager may decide that for his business unit's smaller products, such as skid steers or backhoes, new data-driven services may make economic sense only for enterprise customers. Also, the matrix helped a business unit manager focus on the appropriate level at which data services made sense. A skid steer, for example, does not need continuous real-time streaming of data. Instead, what is useful is basic information on location and service meter hours provided once or twice a day. Offering a service that did just that would make its cost/value trade-off more attractive to customers.

Caterpillar started implementing these initiatives in 2012. At that time, approximately two-thirds of the company's products left the factory as connected products. By 2015 *all* Caterpillar products had interactive product features as standard offerings. Several factors helped: sensors became smaller and cheaper; Caterpillar created teams of digital specialists, including a centralized "digital factory" to help business units, distributors, and customers see the value in integrated machine sensors and the IoT (with business unit approval); and—quite important—Caterpillar went about this initiative ensuring that it secured buy-in from key stakeholders such as various divisional managers, finance managers, dealers, and customers.

In 2008, Caterpillar also formed a joint venture with Trimble (mentioned earlier as one of the new digital entrants in the construction space). Trimble offered Caterpillar proven expertise in GPS and building information management (BIM) technologies.[5] BIM technologies are used to help manage digital representations of physical and functional characteristics of places, such as topographies of construction sites. In addition, Trimble entered the joint venture with experience in building IoT connectivity within assets and in data analytics. "Trimble's skills and experience were ideal complements to Caterpillar's strengths in construction equipment," said Prakash Iyer, senior vice president of software architecture and strategy at Trimble, who played a leadership role in the joint venture. Trimble provided machine control hardware that was installed in Caterpillar's machines. It also provided sensors and software that generated and collected data. This collaboration with Trimble helped Caterpillar accelerate the implementation of many of its strategic digital initiatives.

Predictive Services for Product Maintenance Caterpillar soon realized that its products, equipped with sensors and connectivity, could also offer a more specialized and lucrative service, namely, data-driven product maintenance, commonly referred to as predictive maintenance. Such services are based on analyzing sensor data, predicting component failures, and providing alerts when equipment needs attention before it breaks down. Through such predictive services, Caterpillar's customers could benefit from reduced machine downtimes. Machine downtimes represent significant costs for construction projects. All construction projects have different machines working in tandem to complete a job. A hauler, for example, has to move dirt, after which a compactor comes in to level the dirt. If any one of these machines breaks down, the sequence is interrupted, leading to lost time and money.

Prevailing approaches to reducing such occurrences involve scheduling regular maintenance of machines. Such schedules usually are preset based on the number of hours of operation. Historical information on average machine usage and related wear and tear determines the optimum number of hours of operation after which a machine is recommended to be taken off-line for maintenance. New data-driven product maintenance, on the other hand, uses real-time operating data from each individual machine or machine component to predict when to take a machine off-line for maintenance. This is possible because of a network of sensors in the machine that captures all kinds of data related to the machine's wear and tear. Some of the data concern the conditions in which the machine is working, such as the nature of the terrain, its elevation, soil composition and hardness, and weather conditions. In addition, sensors also capture data on the real-time status of different components of the machine, such as turbocharger speed and temperature or engine oil pressure. AI helps make sense of all these data to produce reliable predictions.

With such data, a user gets a far more refined estimate of when to take a machine off-line for maintenance. The user also finds a better balance between maintaining a machine before it fails and not taking the machine off-line when doing so is not really warranted. All this can save substantial costs. For large projects, these savings could run into the millions of dollars. In 2015, Caterpillar partnered with Uptake, an industrial AI and software company, to begin offering predictive maintenance services to its customers.[6]

AI engines such as Uptake's need substantial amounts of data to be effective. Caterpillar's earlier joint venture with Trimble further aided its predictive maintenance initiative by enlarging the pool of data available for Uptake's AI algorithms. Separate from its role with Caterpillar, Trimble is an independent vendor that sells its hardware and software not just to Caterpillar but to all construction equipment manufacturers, including Caterpillar's competitors, such as Komatsu and Volvo. Because its products are installed across brands, Trimble could facilitate the sourcing of a larger pool of machine data, beyond just Caterpillar's, and strengthen Uptake's AI engine and algorithms. Trimble not only had the necessary hardware and sensors installed in a large pool of assets operating across different construction sites, it also had the requisite APIs to facilitate data transfer from these machines to Uptake. Caterpillar and Trimble would, of course, need the permission of the asset owners at various construction sites to access that data. The incentive for these owners to share the data? Bigger pools of data lead to better predictions to avoid machine downtimes.

Caterpillar's example relates to using predictive services to reduce product downtimes. Insurance companies can similarly use predictive services to reduce risk and bad outcomes. Through sensors in homes, for example, it is possible to predict water leaks and take corrective action by shutting off water lines to avoid costly damage and reduce risks for home insurance underwriters.

Revenue Generation   As new data-driven services provide benefits for customers, it also stands to reason that companies such as Caterpillar would want to monetize such value propositions. Caterpillar monetizes its value offerings in several ways. The most direct way is through subscriptions for different services. Caterpillar began offering several interfaces, such as CAT Connect, Minestar, and Insight, to do so. Through these interfaces, Caterpillar's customers could select the subscription services they preferred from a menu of different options.

In certain sectors, such as mining and power plants, 80 to 90 percent of users subscribe to a large array of data-driven services. In these sectors, the value offered by remote data-driven monitoring is more evident. Not all sectors, though, have such high adoption rates, nor do they extensively use many of the offered data-driven services. Overall, around 70 percent of Caterpillar's customers use some form of remote monitoring. Monitoring may be as simple as letting a fleet owner know whether all the machines are accounted for at the end of each day. Thirty percent of Caterpillar's customers do not use any form of data-related features, even those offered free of charge. Some may not find the time to analyze all the options data present on a day-to-day basis. Others may have more jobs than they can handle and think their current practices are working well without the addition of modern technologies. These are some of the challenges Caterpillar faces as it aims to increase its revenues from data-driven services through subscriptions.

Subscriptions, however, are not the only way to generate new revenues. As Caterpillar discovered, there are indirect sources, too. For instance, Caterpillar found that customers that opted for predictive maintenance services were also more likely to buy a larger number of spare parts. The reason? Customers using predictive maintenance services are more likely to use other data-driven services, such as remote monitoring of their machines with real-time data. These services offer alerts, such as when a machine is idle. Reacting to such alerts, and motivated to reduce idle times, customers are able to use assets for longer stretches of time. Doing so causes faster wear and tear, hence raising the demand for more spare parts. In sum total, however, predictive maintenance brings down costs for Caterpillar's customers. It does so largely by reducing machine downtimes and by avoiding catastrophic failures. The money saved here is far greater than the money customers might spend on additional spare parts purchases.

In addition, Caterpillar found that customers employing more remote monitoring of their assets on their job sites also purchased more assets. If a customer finds data indicating that adding a new wheel loader at a job site could further improve productivity, that customer is more likely to buy that additional wheel loader. Data, in other words, can be a very effective sales tool and a driver of increased revenues.

That was Caterpillar's transition into the digital world. Let us turn to another example for a different facet of data-driven services: mass customization.

Mass Customization   Some interactive product features make products work or act differently for each individual customer or for each use. Our example here is Sleep Number, a company that designs and manufactures smart beds. As a company, Sleep Number has long recognized that no two individuals sleep the same way. Starting in the 1980s, Sleep Number introduced innovations to improve sleep quality for individuals and, especially, couples with its DualAir Technology. Every individual has a unique Sleep Number setting, which adjusts the level of firmness of each side of the bed. Sleep Number's beds use a combination of proprietary foam and adjustable air technology to conform to each user's body pressure points on the mattress. Each sleeper finds a "Sleep Number setting" appropriate for them based on how soft or firm they like the mattress and how well the bed conforms to their body, allowing couples to sleep on different levels of firmness. Users typically try different setting options until they find the most optimal setting that provides the highest level of comfort. Settings may be adjusted at any time; the company encourages adjustments to ensure optimal comfort.

In previous Sleep Number bed models, simply because of the nature of air, a mattress setting could change throughout the night based on how much someone moved, body temperature, room temperature, and other factors. Today, Sleep Number's newest models intelligently adjust using sensor data to ensure that a Sleep Number setting remains stable throughout the night and maintains optimal comfort. Biometric sensors integrated into the mattress track a user's breathing, heart rate, and tossing and turning; the sensors send this biometric data to a cloud-based infrastructure that is fed into an app. An algorithm determines a personal sleep score—called a SleepIQ score—for each individual user that reflects the quality and restfulness of his or her sleep, which the user can see in the SleepIQ smartphone application.

The SleepIQ algorithm dynamically refines sleep scores based on incoming streams of sensor data. Over time, with access to more and more data, the algorithm learns about every individual's sleep patterns. On the basis of over 13 billion biometric data points worth of sleep data gathered through the SleepIQ technology,[7] these smart mattresses can make individualized recommendations to improve sleep experience. The smart mattresses offer users personalized insights into their sleep patterns and circadian rhythms, and suggest lifestyle changes that can improve their sleep.

Looking ahead, Sleep Number expects to be able to identify chronic sleep issues such as sleep apnea and restless leg syndrome, and eventually predict other health conditions such as heart disease and strokes. In 2020, the company entered into a partnership with Mayo Clinic to further sleep science research with an emphasis on cardiovascular medicine and a dedicated R&D fund to improve health quality. It expects to expand its business scope from being a mattress producer to being a company offering wellness services.

Data not only allow Sleep Number to mass customize its mattresses, they generate new data-driven features and also become a significant resource for brand differentiation and competitive advantage.

Traversing the First Three Tiers of Digital Transformation Using Production Ecosystems

Modern technologies can enrich a legacy firm's value chain network in several ways. The greater the enrichment, the more vibrant are the firm's production ecosystems. And, with a vibrant production ecosystem, a legacy firm can unlock the value from data in a multitude of different ways. This chapter categorized two broad approaches to unlocking the value of data: one by improving operational efficiencies, and the other by generating new data-driven services. Improved operational efficiencies can reduce costs, while new data-driven services can generate new revenue. Through these approaches production ecosystems help legacy firms ascend the first three tiers of digital transformation highlighted in the introduction.

Tier 1 is a must for firms, as most can benefit from operational efficiencies. Not surprisingly, a vast majority of digital transformation initiatives are in this tier. This tier is particularly relevant for firms where operational efficiencies are a big part of their strategic thrust. Oil and gas companies, for instance, run wells, pipelines, and refineries that require investments running into several billions of dollars. Wrong estimates of where to drill or how much to drill, for example, can cost millions of dollars. Firms can save up to 50 to 60 percent of their operational costs using IoT devices, AI, and other modeling techniques to better improve likelihoods of finding reserves.

Some businesses may find it hard to go beyond tier 1, if acquiring product-user interactive data is cumbersome. Steel, aluminium, and soda ash are examples. Key challenges in tier 1 include establishing a widespread use of interactive data in asset utilization and breaking silos around how data across assets is generated and shared. Legacy firms may benefit from the following strategic questions:

- Have we exhausted the possibilities of capturing interactive data from our assets?
- Have we instituted processes to share this data optimally?
- Are there creative ways by which we collect and use product-user interactive data to ascend onto higher tiers?

Tier 2 presence is imperative for firms where products have the potential to access interactive data from users. This potential, if exploited, provides firms with added strategic advantage beyond tier 1. Tier 2 becomes the final stop in a firm's digital transformation journey if available product-user interactive data is not amenable for revenue generating services. Many consumer-packaged goods fall in this category. The primary use of interactive data in such businesses is to improve advertising or product development efficiencies.

Establishing digital customers, or customers who provide interactive data, is a key challenge in tier 2. P&G's challenge in its diaper business referred to earlier, is to generate content on their websites that excite current and prospective customers and motivate them to actively engage. A related challenge is to set up data mining processes to interpret large volumes of interactive data and use them for improving advertising efficiencies. Firms may find the following strategic questions useful:

- How do we find digital customers?
- How can we equip our products with sensors? If sensor-equipped products are not feasible, in what other ways can we capture interactive data from customers?
- How do we enhance our data mining capabilities?
- How can we creatively think of extending the use of interactive data for revenue generating services to ascend onto the next tier?

Tier 3 presence is necessary for businesses where generating data-driven services from products and value chains is feasible. Such firms must enrich their production ecosystems to broaden their strategic advantage from delivering operational efficiencies to generating new data-driven services. In reaching tier 3, firms cross an important barrier between using data for operational efficiencies and using it for revenue generation. Many firms however find themselves unable to cross the next barrier—that between generating data-driven services from their value chains and doing so through digital platforms. One reason may be an inadequate development of consumption ecosystems, a point that will be elaborated more in chapter 5. Home appliance companies are examples. Sensor equipped dishwashers for instance, can offer data-driven services from their value chains. They can predict component failures before they happen to offer subscription services for predictive maintenance. But dishwashers are hard to digitally connect to other objects that complement them. They cannot easily operate as digital platforms.

That said, many firms also miss opportunities to extend their products into platforms, thus curtailing their digital initiatives to tier 3. They overlook their product's consumption ecosystems or perceive risks to outweigh rewards in extending their products into digital platforms. Peloton and NordicTrack have extended their products into digital platforms. Many of their rivals in the exercise equipment business have not.

Generating competitive data-driven services requires substantial amounts of data. Algorithms that drive many of these services get smarter with more data. Smart toothbrushes, for example, improve their accuracy in reporting brushing quality with increasing data. Caterpillar better predicts downtime of equipment when armed with more data. Firms that attract more digital customers can thus provide better data-driven services because of network effects. Yet, to attract digital customers, establishing the superiority of services is important—which in turn builds momentum only after a critical mass of digital customers are engaged. Creating a network effect advantage through data-driven services is therefore a key challenge in tier 3. Also challenging is to establish new data-driven services, as it entails a significant change in business models long anchored on producing and selling products. Legacy firms may benefit from the following strategic questions:

- How do we build network effects for our data-driven services?
- How should we price our sensor-equipped products to attract more digital customers?

- How can we ascend to the next tier by expanding our data-driven services from value chains to digital platforms?

Production Ecosystems and Operational Efficiencies: New Solutions to Solve Old Problems

Using production ecosystems for operational efficiency gains is akin to employing new solutions to old problems. Improving procurement efficiencies, reducing unfilled orders, improving R&D productivity—examples highlighted in this chapter—are long-standing objectives for executives. Modern digital technologies provide new solutions to these old problems. Stanley Black & Decker, for example, a manufacturer of industrial tools and household hardware, reduced product-labeling errors by 16 percent using modern digital technologies.[8] Sub-Zero, an appliance manufacturer, attributes a 20 percent reduction in its new product introduction times to its connected factories.[9] Ford's automated vision-based inspection system of paint jobs on its cars has improved defect detection by 90 percent over manual means.[10]

Because age-old issues such as improving product introduction times, reducing errors, or saving energy are well-understood problems for legacy firms, they are easier targets to tackle. The cost-benefit trade-offs involved in tackling such challenges are also well understood. For many legacy firms, these operational efficiency improvements may be low-hanging fruit in return for investing in digital technologies. They represent the first and most accessible payoff from legacy firms' investments in production ecosystems. A key point to remember, however, is that improving operational efficiencies is only a first step—and that production ecosystems can deliver much more.

Initiating Data-Driven Services from Production Ecosystems: New Risk-Reward Trade-offs

Initiating data-driven services is a new endeavor for most legacy firms focused on products and product market strategies. It may require them to acquire new digital capabilities, hire new talent, and develop new mindsets (discussed in chapter 8). The risk-reward trade-offs are also new. The benefits of data-driven services may not be apparent to customers until producers have access to massive amounts of data—for which widespread adoption often becomes a precondition (this point is further elaborated on in chapter 6). Going after such widespread adoption may involve substantial investments, can be risky, and can even break a legacy firm's back if not thoughtfully executed.

In this context it is interesting to compare and contrast GE and Caterpillar, two iconic industrial giants that made significant digital transformation forays in their own ways. Both were on a journey of transforming their "big iron" into "smart iron." Caterpillar's approach, as noted in this chapter, involved convincing a fairly decentralized organization about the benefits of introducing new data-driven services. The company instituted processes (such as the matrix highlighted in table 4.1) to provide key stakeholders a say in how to go about their digital transformation efforts for their respective businesses and products.

GE's approach in retrospect appears to have been far more top-down. GE spent over $1 billion on new software capabilities and the development of a technology called Predix that offered a common interface to generate new data-driven services for the company's assets across multiple divisions (jet engines, locomotives, medical equipment, turbines). GE relocated its software talent from different business units and geographies to a centralized location in San Ramon, California. The idea was that all the company's products would take a similar approach to data-driven services, all anchored on Predix. Just as GE's jet engines advised pilots on optimally flying planes to save on fuel, the company's locomotives advised drivers on navigation, for similar benefits. Just as GE's turbine could offer predictive maintenance, so could its MRI machines. In the process, GE also established new common guidelines for its sales and marketing staff.

These were, however, early experiments. Both GE and its customers were uncertain about the returns on their investments. These initiatives also introduced uncertainty among GE's sales staff. These sales professionals were trained in selling complex engineering products, and now had to shift to selling data-driven services. Maybe GE was ahead of its time. Maybe the transformation efforts were too much and rolled out too fast. In the end, GE's digital transformation vision did not unfold as planned.

At the same time, GE gave the rest of the industrial world valuable new concepts, ideas, and ways to frame digital transformation. It was at the 2012 "Minds and Machines" conference that then CEO Jeff Immelt proclaimed GE's commitment to the "industrial internet," making that term famous. The world was well aware of the consumer internet's having ushered in the e-commerce and smartphone revolution. Immelt's proclamation crystallized the idea that the industrial internet could make machines and assets do the same and spark a parallel revolution. Similarly, the idea of a "digital twin," or a digital representation of an asset enabled though streaming interactive data from products, is another important GE contribution.

The key takeaway here is that legacy firms may find introducing data-driven services far more challenging than improving operational efficiencies. Yet the rewards have the potential to be greater. Chapter 8 discusses how legacy firms can build the necessary digital capabilities to earn those rewards. Before we get there, chapter 5 elaborates on the other facet of digital ecosystems, consumption ecosystems.

5   Unlocking Data's Value from Consumption Ecosystems

Fundamentally, production ecosystems are constructed from a legacy firm's value chain networks. They emerge when value chain entities, assets, and activities generate and share data within their internal network. Most legacy firms have fairly well-established value chains. Most legacy firms also have experience with generating and sharing data within their value chain network through IT systems. Further enriching their production ecosystems using modern digital technologies may therefore appear to them to be a natural extension of their digital initiatives.

Consumption ecosystems, on the other hand, are constructed from complementor networks. They emerge because digital connectivity enables a network of third-party entities, assets, and activities to complement product-generated data. Nearly all products have complements. Yet these complements rarely played any significant role in traditional business models. Until recently, most of these complements were not even digitally connected. Furthermore, legacy firms do not control the processes by which these complements get connected to grow into consumption ecosystems. Rather than through internal digital initiatives, consumption ecosystems are driven by external forces of digitization. The billions of connected entities and assets emerging around *all* firms because of modern trends in digital technologies are what generate complements for any particular legacy firm's product-generated data.

These trends are new. Legacy firms may not even detect many of the opportunities presented by these emerging consumption ecosystems. In fact, their familiarity and comfort with their value chains are likely to bias them to heed new data-driven opportunities within their production ecosystems. Thus they may overlook opportunities waiting within consumption ecosystems. When it comes to consumption ecosystems, then, firms are more likely to fall into digital myopia traps, referred to in the introduction to this book.

Last, to engage with consumption ecosystems, legacy firms need to extend their value chains onto digital platforms. Digital platforms can facilitate data exchanges among various entities, assets, and activities that complement a firm's product-generated data, thereby providing an effective approach to steering a firm's consumption ecosystems toward generating data-driven services. A light bulb company that wants to offer a home security service using its motion-sensing bulbs needs a digital platform. It is only through such a platform that the company can effectively facilitate data exchanges among security alarms and smartphones, among other such complements. The need for such digital platforms that facilitate data exchanges among various complements is a significant factor differentiating consumption ecosystems from production ecosystems.

How Legacy Firms Can Build Platforms

Most legacy firms do not operate on digital platforms. This approach is new to them. Hence, even when legacy firms recognize fresh opportunities from the new consumption ecosystems emerging around them—and even if they intend to profit from them through new digital platforms—their path to do so is not straightforward. They may have several questions as they contemplate enacting such a significant change to their prevailing business models. At the outset, they may want to know what they are getting into, and ask, how would *their* digital platforms compare with those of the digital titans discussed in chapter 1? In what ways are they similar? In what ways are they different?

Similarities are to be expected: in both cases the underlying business models of the digital platforms rely on data exchanges among platform participants. However, there also are important differences. The digital platforms of legacy firms emerge out of product-generated data. These digital platforms are therefore tethered to products and product-generated data.[1] Such tethering makes these platforms different from the digital platforms of many of the digital titans discussed in chapter 1.

The digital titans' digital platforms, discussed earlier, usually start with an innovative idea that identifies a market need to create value by utilizing data through the internet. This leads to a business model in which a digital platform attracts relevant users and creates value through data generation and sharing. In many of the examples referred to in chapter 1, such as Facebook or Netflix, the underlying idea entailed eliminating a physical presence during transactions and using data to create value; the consequent business plans were facilitated through digital platforms. Similarly, other famous digital platforms, such as those of Uber or Airbnb, started with asset sharing using data and the internet as a core idea. Here again their digital platforms enacted their business plans. These digital platforms thus started with a clean slate and plans to serve unmet needs and use creative ideas.

Tethered digital platforms do not start with such a clean slate. Their initial business idea itself is tethered to the product and the data that a company's products generate. Their platform users similarly are tethered to these data. Such tethered data open up new market opportunities but also restrict the range of these opportunities. Put differently, product-user interaction data circumscribe the scope and feasibility of tethered digital platforms.

Because products and product-user transaction data form the genesis of tethered digital platforms, this connection raise several additional questions for legacy firms interested in moving onto digital platforms. Are the products and product-generated data suitable for creating a digital platform? How can firms gauge the potential of their product-user transaction data to drive a commercially viable digital platform? How do product-generated data shape the tethered digital platform? Do digital platforms vary with the kind of products legacy firms have? How does a legacy firm decide on the kind of platform it should build? How should it compete using such a platform?

Finding answers to such questions will yield some understanding of how a legacy firm can engage with and create value within its consumption ecosystems. This chapter addresses such questions by constructing a framework useful for analyzing tethered digital platforms.[2] Before that, let us examine the key components of a tethered digital platform.

The Tethered Digital Platform

Figure 5.1 shows the principal components of a tethered digital platform.

A tethered digital platform has four essential components. First, it has a sensor-equipped product; second, it has product-user interaction data emerging from the sensor-equipped product; third, it has platform users, who include direct users of the sensor-equipped product (such as users of smart toothbrushes) and users whose data complement the interactive data generated by the direct users (such as dentists); and fourth, it has platform services generated through sharing and exchanging these data among all platform users. Because sensors and sensor-equipped products are foundational to tethered digital platforms, they are discussed first.

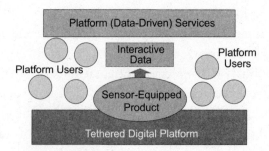

Figure 5.1
Components of a tethered digital platform.

The Rise of Sensors and Sensor-Equipped Products

Rafael Nadal, one of tennis's all-time greats, has played with a Babolat tennis racket since 2004. Babolat is among the leading tennis racket brands. In 2012, Nadal was introduced to Babolat's "connected" racket with built-in sensors.[3] Using this racket in his practice sessions, he could monitor how he hit his shots to prepare for his matches. According to his coach (and uncle) Toni, Nadal more likely wins a match when 70 percent of his shots are forehands and 30 percent are backhands.[4] With the smart racket, Nadal and his coach can track how many forehands and backhands he hits during practice sessions. In addition, they can assess many other attributes of his shots, such as how much topspin (or forward rotation) the ball has, how much slice (or backspin), how hard the serve was, where in the racket the ball hits the strings, and the number of shots in every rally. The sensor sends the data to a smartphone, where they can be reviewed and analyzed. In 2013 the International Tennis Federation approved the use of connected rackets during matches. It amended its rules to allow professional players to collect interactive data—between them, their rackets, and the ball—while playing tournaments.

Today, connected tennis rackets are available not just to professional tennis players and champions like Nadal but to any tennis enthusiast. With a Babolat connected racket it is even possible to check how one's best tennis shots compare with those of Nadal (Nadal is a spokesperson for the brand).[5] This is because Babolat makes selected aspects of the interactive data generated during Nadal's practice sessions available to other Babolat users. Connected rackets are now being offered by several top companies, such as Head, Yonex, Wilson, and Prince. In addition, Sony and Zepp Labs offer stand-alone sensors that can be attached to any tennis racket. These sensors are miniaturized electronic chips. They can be attached at the bottom of the racket handle or on the shock or vibration dampener, usually found on the racket's strings. Sensors are also available as wrist bands, allowing users to enjoy the benefits of a connected racket.

Sensors do more than play tennis. For instance, different kinds of sensors can be embedded in an ingestible drug. In November 2017 the

US Food and Drug Administration (FDA) approved the first drug with an ingestion sensor.[6] Abilify Mycite, the approved digital drug, is used to treat mental disorders such as schizophrenia, bipolar disease, and depression. The sensor, one millimeter in diameter, embedded in the tablet is referred to as an ingestible event marker. Once swallowed, the sensor in the pill comes in contact with gastric fluid. This triggers the chemicals in the sensor to react and activate a signal that is sent to a wearable Bluetooth patch, which in turn allows data to be viewed on a smartphone. The data help track whether a patient has taken his medicine. For patients with mental disorders, taking medications regularly can be challenging; the smart pill feature helps family members and doctors assist in managing the patient's well-being by monitoring medicine intake and watching behavioral symptoms.

In addition to being made from electronic chips or ingestible ingredients, many sensors today are constructed primarily through software. One such example is that of Samba TV, a TV content recommendation engine and a viewer tracking app maker. Samba TV provides sensors to TV manufacturers such as Sony, TCL, and Sharp that enable capturing what a viewer is watching on a smart TV. Use of the automated content recognition (ACR) technology requires installing a software-based algorithm on the TV. This software processes and computes a video "fingerprint" for every video frame broadcast on the TV. This fingerprint is sent to a server, which compares it with a database of source videos for content recognition, enabling Samba TV and the TV manufacturer to capture data on what a viewer is watching. Samba TV and TV manufacturers use the data to provide TV entertainment content providers (such as NBC or ABC) feedback on the popularity of their shows. The data also help advertisers (such as Toyota or Coca-Cola) better align their advertisements on TV, with the knowledge of who is watching which show and in what geography or household.

The Samba TV sensors illustrate how a legacy manufacturer can add a software sensor to its products. A vast majority of software-based sensors today function as smartphone apps. For instance, almost all banks offer software apps for features such as online banking or check deposits. In the process, these apps also act as sensors, capturing data such as when and where a user spends her money, the user's preferences for products or vendors, and the user's credit history. Gaming companies similarly use software-based sensors to collect interactive data from their users. The data tell them, among other things, whether a gamer is left-handed or right-handed and what her preferred strategies are when playing games, and can help predict her next moves.

From Sensor Data to Platform Users and Platform Services

Each of these sensor-equipped products can generate unique product-user interaction data. And in each case, the data can be used to generate exchanges among various third-party entities, assets, and activities that are part of the product's consumption ecosystems. To facilitate such exchanges, these third-party entities, assets, and activities have to be onboarded as tethered digital platform users. By connecting various users and orchestrating data exchanges among them, the tethered digital platform offers new data-driven services.

Using sensor-equipped tennis racket data, a smart tennis racket producer can identify groups of smart racket users who could be matched for pickup games; the producer can also identify appropriate coaches who could be matched suitably with players according to their skill level. Groups of players and coaches are part of the tennis racket's consumption ecosystem because they complement the racket's sensor data; they also complement the tennis-related needs of any individual racket user generating those data. When they join a tethered digital platform, they become platform users. And by orchestrating exchanges among such users, a tennis racket producer can offer new data-driven platform services that include coordinating pickup games or coaching.

Similarly, a video game producer that has interactive data on its various game users can develop such matching services to make its competitive games even more interesting. It can, for example, match different video game players with similar skills or complementary game strategies. Abilify, the creator of smart drugs for bipolar disorders, can similarly orchestrate data-driven interactions among patients, relatives, and doctors. Banks that garner sensor data from their apps, providing insights into spending patterns, creditworthiness, lifestyle, and desired purchases of their customers, can do the same. Using such data, they can orchestrate exchanges between their customers (with the customers' consent) and relevant merchants that can compete with attractive discounts to fulfill the customers' purchase desires.[7] In doing so, banks can extend their legacy banking services into purchase experiences for their customers.

The underlying pattern in each of these cases is similar. The process starts with a sensor-equipped product that generates product-user interactive data. The sensor data attract complements from the product's consumption ecosystems. When added to the platform, these complements become platform users. By facilitating exchanges among these users, the tethered digital platform offers data-driven services. The larger the vistas of a product's consumption ecosystems, the greater the number of complements and the larger the number of platform users. All of the above broaden the scope of a firm's tethered digital platform and its platform services.

The widespread availability and versatility of sensors make it possible for all kinds of firms to adopt sensor-equipped products, identify complements to their data, visualize the possibility of constructing a tethered digital platform, and offer new data-driven platform services. Does this imply that all products can become platforms? The answer to this question depends on whether a product's tethered digital platform can offer commercially viable services. Much of such viability depends on the kind of sensor data the product generates. As discussed next, certain key attributes of these data critically influence the underlying business model of any tethered digital platform.

Sensor Data Attributes

That product-user interactive data are closely related to the product's use is to be expected. These data closely follow a product's key features and its primary intended use; they flow from the interface the product offers for its use. Toothbrushes interface with a user's teeth; the sensor data harvested from a toothbrush accordingly are primarily connected to dental care. As a consequence, the data also attract complementary entities connected to dental care, such as dentists or dental insurance companies. Mattresses similarly interface with their users when they sleep. Sensor data acquired from a mattress pick up and convey attributes of a user's sleep, such as data on heart rates, breathing patterns, or tossing and turning during sleep. The most obvious objects that complement this data are those that can help improve sleep, such as adjustable lighting or soothing music. Sleep specialists too can complement the data by helping prevent the medical consequences of sleep apnea, a breathing disorder during sleep. Likewise, sensor data acquired from excavators concern what these products do on a construction site. Excavator sensor data are most relevant to other assets on a construction site that work in conjunction with the excavator.

Product-user interactions thus not only shape the kind of sensor data a product generates, they determine the kinds of complements the data may attract and thereby the nature of platform services. Sensor data thus can significantly influence the commercial viability of these platform services. Primarily, for a tethered digital platform to be commercially viable and successful, its platform services should have a strong market potential, should have few rivals, and should provide seamless data exchanges for powerful digital experiences. Three specific attributes of sensor data that vary across products and product-user interfaces are notable in assessing these considerations. *Sensor data scope* influences the market potential of a firm's platform services; *sensor data uniqueness* limits the influence of rivals; and *sensor data control* determines how seamlessly data on a tethered digital platform can be exchanged among platform users for powerful digital experiences. Each of these attributes is explained below.

Sensor Data Scope

Sensor data scope provides an initial estimate of the value of the services expected from a tethered digital platform. For a smart tennis

racket producer, for instance, this may take the form of an initial estimate of the revenues that a partner matching service or a coach matching service can generate. For a mattress company it may take the form
of an estimate of subscription revenues for a platform service that connects sleep data to external objects in the room (lights, music, etc.)
to improve sleep experiences. A company like Caterpillar can estimate
the scope of its sensor data in other ways. Apparently, billions of dollars annually are wasted through rework on construction sites.[8] Even a
small fraction of savings enabled through a data-driven coordination
of construction activities can run into multiples of millions; Caterpillar
can estimate potential revenues from platform services that make those
savings possible for the company's customers.

In some ways, sensor data scope is similar to the market scope of a
new product about to be launched. Most legacy firms understand how
to estimate a new product's market scope. They know how to assess the
market need addressed by the new product's features, the profiles of
potential customers, and the overall market size in which the product
is expected to compete for a share. In that respect, sensor data scope is
similar to a new product's scope. Instead of new products, the estimates
in this case are for the expected value from new platform services.

In addition, sensor data scope varies with the network effects the
sensor data generate for a tethered digital platform. Because sensor data
determine the kind and number of platform users that are likely to join
a tethered digital platform, they determine the network effects that a
tethered digital platform can generate. Depending on the kind of platform users the sensor data attract, the platform services may benefit
from either direct or indirect network effects—or both. As discussed in
chapter 2, direct network effects stem from the value a user gets from
other similar users, such as the value friends on Facebook get when
they find more friends on the platform. Such similar users form one
side of a platform. Indirect network effects stem from other kinds of
users or other sides of a platform, such as a professional on LinkedIn
benefiting from more recruiters on the platform.

A tethered digital platform anchored on sensor data from a smart
toothbrush, for instance, may attract other smart toothbrush users and

complementary third parties such as dentists. Its platform service may enable timely attention to dental problems from dentists and hence better dental health for each platform user. This kind of tethered digital platform benefits from indirect network effects because the more dentists that are available on a producer's platform, the more potential benefits exist for each smart toothbrush user, and vice versa. It may also enjoy direct network effects if, with a greater number of smart toothbrush users and larger volumes of user data, the platform's algorithms become smarter.

In the case of a tennis racket's sensor data that attract other smart racket users to a tethered digital platform offering a player matching service, the platform service benefits from direct network effects. The more players on the platform, the more choices there are for an optimal match, and hence the more value exists for each player. This tethered platform also generates indirect network effects when it attracts other third-party complementors such as coaches to its platform. The more complementary entities a product's sensor data attract, the greater are its tethered digital platform's direct or indirect network effects. Because these network effects enhance the potential value of a tethered digital platform's services, they are an important facet of sensor data scope.

Sensor Data Uniqueness

Sensor data are unique when the same sensor data are not readily available to other types of products. Conversely, sensor data are not unique when several types of products have access to the same data. For a toothbrush producer, for example, sensor data stem from toothbrush-to-user tooth interactions. Data of this sort are likely available only to other competing sensor-equipped toothbrush producers—in other words, familiar product rivals. Oral-B may find itself competing with Philips or other similar electric toothbrush producers that adopt sensors in their products. On the other hand, a smart light bulb producer relying on motion data for its tethered platform services will find that its product's motion-related sensor data are not restricted to other smart bulb producers. The data are accessible to an array of other smart products in the same room, such as thermostats, fire alarms, or security cameras. The producers of any such products are likely contestants for the same platform service customers. In other words, sensor data can attract rivals from outside a product's prevailing industry boundaries.

Furthermore, sensors can be retrofitted to products, attracting even more nontraditional competitors. Chapter 4 referred to such nontraditional rivals for Caterpillar. New competition came from companies in the software, telecom, and GPS space, such as Trimble and Teletrac Navman. These rivals could retrofit construction-related equipment and objects with sensors to offer the same kind of construction management services highlighted earlier as potential value offerings for Caterpillar. Chapter 8 describes such rivals that have access to similar data as digital competitors and elaborates on their influence on a legacy firm's digital competitive strategy.

When they have access to similar sensor data, the digital titans are among the most formidable digital competitors. The digital titans often have powerful vantage points, giving them access to a broad range of data that legacy products may be seeking through their sensors. Through their omnibus platforms and apps, Alibaba and Tencent, for example, collect far richer data on the spending habits, credit histories, and loan requirements of the average Chinese consumer than what Chinese banks could ever expect to capture from their own app-based sensors.[9] Alibaba and Tencent therefore have a stronger competitive edge over the legacy Chinese banks when offering loans to customers.

The key point here is that sensor data uniqueness can influence the competitiveness of a tethered digital platform's services. The more unique the data, the more likely it is that a tethered digital platform will be commercially viable.

Sensor Data Control

Finally, sensor data control refers to the degree to which a producer can freely use a product's sensor data to facilitate exchanges among users and complementary entities without restriction. Restrictions are likely in cases in which product-user interactions entail intermediaries. These intermediaries may not allow a producer to freely share sensor data with external entities.

GE's sensor data from its smart locomotives, such as expected time of arrival at specific destinations, serve as an example. These data can potentially be shared among cargo shippers and receivers and used to generate exchanges to offer an array of different platform services. GE's potential platform could provide transparency to both cargo shippers and receivers as to the precise locations and expected deliveries of their merchandise at any given time. The platform could offer invoicing and payment collection services tied to precisely when goods are shipped and received. The platform could also offer cargo shippers and receivers options to select routes for their cargo shipment that best match their needs (such as shortest shipping times or best shipping rates). Such services could also allow cargo shippers and receivers to modify their choices, even when goods are en route, if their circumstances change (such as needing merchandise delivery earlier, later, or at different destinations). The platform can add last-mile delivery agencies such as truckers to broaden its contributions to shaping the overall logistical plans of customers.

The cargo shippers and receivers, however, are not GE's direct customers. Instead they are customers of GE's customers, namely, the railway companies. Railway companies are thus intermediaries between GE and the intended platform users—cargo shippers and receivers. These railway companies may restrict GE from sharing what they consider to be *their* sensor data (because they own the locomotives) with *their* customers to facilitate exchanges for intended platform services. The presence of intermediaries can thus introduce impediments to a product company freely sharing its sensor data with its intended platform users.

Data privacy is another important factor that can restrict the free sharing of data with external entities. Products in the health care space, for example, may find even their own customers resisting the sharing of sensor data they may deem sensitive and private. Customers of Abbot's sensor-equipped product 14-day Libre, for example, may restrict the sharing of their real-time blood glucose levels among possible complementary entities, being wary of how the data may be leaked or used against them by insurance companies.

In addition, various regulatory regimes may restrict different kinds of sensor data sharing. Several regulations prevent the free sharing of health care–related data across hospitals. Similarly, there are regulations that restrict banks from sharing their customers' finance-related data freely. Such regulations may restrict the scope of many platform services. Chapter 9 further elaborates on issues around data privacy and regulatory regimes with respect to the unfettered sharing of sensor data.

In sum, three attributes of sensor data—namely, their scope, uniqueness, and control—can influence the commercial viability of a tethered digital platform and its services. These three attributes can help legacy firms assess whether or not they should extend their products onto platforms, and may also help legacy firms determine the optimal way to construct their tethered digital platforms. In other words, depending on a product's sensor data scope, uniqueness, and control, a firm can find optimal ways to maximize the potential of the data it acquires to extend products onto platforms. The tethered digital platform framework outlined below describes how to do so.

Tethered Digital Platform Framework

Consider the tethered digital platform framework depicted in figure 5.2.

The horizontal axis of this framework represents sensor data scope and uniqueness. Its vertical axis represents sensor data control. The minimum threshold to vie for a tethered digital platform is a sensor-equipped product. Yet, as the lower left quadrant of the framework suggests, not all product firms crossing that minimum threshold can compete as a platform. They could, however, compete as suppliers to other platforms. The three other quadrants represent different approaches by which product firms can compete as tethered digital platforms: as full, collaborative, or enabled tethered digital platforms. The center circle represents a hybrid approach in which firms may

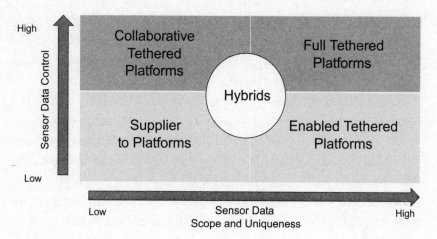

Figure 5.2
Tethered digital platform framework.

opt to implement select attributes from each quadrant. Each of these approaches is discussed below.

Full Tethered Digital Platform

This option is for products whose sensor data are strong on all three attributes of scope, uniqueness, and control. With such sensor data, a firm can run its own platform, directly invite platform users and orchestrate exchanges among users with full autonomy.

Consider Becton, Dickinson and Company (BD), a medical technology company whose business repertoire includes manufacturing and selling medical devices to hospitals. Some of its well-known products include needles, syringes, intravenous catheters, insulin syringes, local anesthesia syringes, and anesthesia trays. More recently, BD has been expanding its business scope to data-driven services through connected devices, in addition to the company's legacy stand-alone products. To do so, BD made a few significant acquisitions. One of them is Care Fusion, acquired for around $12 billion in 2014. In acquiring Care Fusion, BD acquired several smart products and software technologies. Among them are Alaris smart pumps, Pyxis automated medication dispensing systems for nursing stations, and Rowa technologies, which automate medication storage and dispensing in hospital pharmacies. To understand how these three products and technologies come together to form a tethered digital platform, let us first consider the basic functionalities of bedside pumps, nursing stations, and hospital pharmacies.

Bedside pumps dispense medications or fluids from intravenous bags or syringes at predetermined rates and frequencies. Doctors prescribe the fluids and medications. A nursing staff member administers them from a nursing station, generally centrally located on medical floors or patient recovery units. Nursing stations also maintain required medications and fluids for the patients in their treatment areas. They are supplied with requisite fluids and medications from hospital pharmacies. These hospital pharmacies are dedicated for specific hospitals and are also located on the hospital's premises.

Hospital pharmacists prepare customized doses based on doctors' prescriptions. For example, a doctor may prescribe 500 milligrams of amoxicillin to be given intravenously every eight hours to a patient. To prepare this prescription, the hospital pharmacy mixes 500 mg of amoxicillin in 10 milliliters of water for injections and then adds this mix to a bag of intravenous fluids. The nursing staff receive such bags and store them at the nursing station to administer the medication when needed by the patient by attaching the bags to the bedside pump. For different prescriptions the hospital pharmacy prepares bags differently, mixing different components.

For the bedside pump, patients, the medications delivered through the intravenous bags, the nursing station, and the hospital pharmacy are complements. They are important pieces that must be connected to administer treatment to a patient. When digitally connected, they emerge as a bedside pump's consumption ecosystem. And by facilitating relevant data exchanges among them, the bedside pump functions as a tethered digital platform. Let's look at how BD's Alaris smart pumps can function as a full tethered digital platform when patients, along with select functionalities of Pyxis and Rowa technologies, are onboarded as the pump's digitally connected complements and platform users.

What does Alaris do? As a smart pump, Alaris adds new features to the regular bedside pump. One of these new features is patient-controlled analgesia (PCA). Analgesia refers to insensibility to pain and can be achieved with a range of drugs, usually prescribed after an operation when a patient is recovering in the hospital. Common analgesics include morphine and other narcotics. PCA allows patients to self-administer predetermined amounts of pain medication based on when they need pain mitigation, with the pump monitoring and controlling prescribed minimum gaps between dosages. At the same time, the Alaris pump also monitors a patient's respiratory and CO_2 levels. This is because the narcotics often used for pain management can depress a patient's respiratory system and cause respiratory failure if the patient is not monitored closely. In other words, Alaris collects real-time sensor data on a patient's respiratory and CO_2 level status when its PCA feature is used.

A patient's real-time respiratory status and CO_2 level are the kind of data acquired by sensors that make Alaris suitable to function as a full tethered digital platform. First, the data have a strong scope because of the value BD's platform services can offer. As an example of a platform service, the pump can anticipate respiratory failure and alert the nursing staff for immediate medical attention. The event is automatically registered by the Pyxis system at the nursing station. The Pyxis system then generates an alert if the same dosage dispensation is planned again for the same patient by oversight. The event is also registered by Rowa's system in the hospital pharmacy, which generates similar alerts when the same prescriptions are requested for the same patient by oversight. The value of the service? Timely alerts for medical attention and prevention of medication errors.

Apart from its strong scope, the ability to measure a patient's respiratory status and CO_2 level in real time and make the connection to medication administration is also unique to Alaris (and other competing smart pumps). While there may be other monitors around a patient's bed that record respiratory status and CO_2 levels, none is specifically tied to analgesic administration. Only the smart pumps can connect the respiratory or CO_2 symptoms to the pain medication being administered. This functionality allows the nurses and physicians to intervene with more precision and speed.

And finally, because Pyxis and Rowa are also owned by BD, Alaris faces few restrictions or barriers in sharing data across BD's systems. With strong scope, uniqueness, and control over data sharing—here, the data are the patient's respiratory status and CO_2 level—Alaris can operate as a full tethered platform.

BD's legacy products, such as syringes and catheters, can also be sensor-equipped. However, it is hard to imagine how sensor data from such products could propel them into becoming platforms and into offering data-driven services the way smart bedside pumps can. Note that a patient's respiratory status and CO_2 level are just one kind of sensor data that Alaris collects with its PCA feature. Alaris has access to many other kinds of sensor data. Pyxis and Rowa have many other functionalities that can complement these kinds of data in other ways. For instance, based on how medications are consumed by a patient through Alaris pumps, Pyxis can anticipate how to replenish medication stocks and Rowa can anticipate how to supply them. Through such data sharing, the hospital is able to manage medication administration for each patient seamlessly.

Even a patient's respiratory status and CO_2 level may have other complements beyond what was described in this example. Put differently, smart pumps have far more vibrant consumption ecosystems than BD's legacy products. Acquiring Care Fusion and expanding its product portfolio from syringes and catheters into bedside pumps has helped BD make an emphatic entry into the digital realm with new data-driven services.

Supplier to Digital Platforms

This option is diametrically opposite to that of the full tethered digital platform, per the framework shown in figure 5.2. Whereas the full tethered digital platform option is for the strongest attributes of product-generated sensor data, the supplier to digital platforms option is for the weakest. Products in this option are sensor-equipped, but their sensor data are unlikely to generate viable platform services on their own. These smart products may have few identifiable complementary entities and as a result have weak consumption ecosystems. Such products may face substantial barriers to generating any platform services on their own and thus may not be able to operate as platforms. They can, however, serve as suppliers to other digital platforms. That is, they can connect to other digital platforms and rely on them to find ways to use their data connectivity.

Many home appliances today, such as microwaves, washers, and dryers, are sensor-equipped and connected to digital platforms such as Amazon's Alexa[10] or Google Home. Users can activate any of these appliances through voice commands. For instance, a user can activate microwave ovens to cook particular foods (such as popcorn), dishwashers to start a wash cycle, washers and dryers to run specific cycles, or faucets to fill bowls, merely by using voice commands. Each of these home appliances and fixtures is sensor-equipped, yet they do not facilitate any data exchanges among themselves to be able to develop into a digital platform on their own. They rely on other digital platforms such as Alexa or Google Home to coordinate their functionalities with those of other home utilities.

Collaborative Tethered Digital Platforms

This option is for products whose sensor data are strong on control but may lack scope or uniqueness. This option allows smart products to facilitate some exchanges on their own while also taking assistance from other platforms to deliver the full span of the planned platform services. Put differently, this option elevates a smart product from being a pure supplier to a third-party platform to an operating a platform of its own. Its platform, however, requires collaborating with other platforms to offer the intended platform services.

Whirlpool's new offerings of smart refrigerators, smart cooking ovens, and smart microwave ovens afford an example of a collaborative tethered digital platform. These products generate data exchanges among one another through an integrated cooking app, Yummly,[11] to offer a smart cooking service. The service is offered through Alexa's platform and as one of Alexa's smart home features. This is how it works.[12] Whirlpool's refrigerator and cooking oven can talk to one another through the integrated Yummly app. The service begins with the Whirlpool refrigerator letting the Yummly app know what ingredients are stocked in it that could be used for a recipe. If some ingredients are missing, Alexa arranges for them to be delivered through Amazon. The app helps a user walk through the various steps needed to prepare a dish. All through these steps, the oven anticipates how to operate for the particular recipe—preheating, baking, or broiling, as needed—by automatically adjusting its settings. Alexa is available at all times to add instructions at any point for the appliances, such as "stop broiling" or "increase oven temperature," when activated to do so through a user's voice commands.

By connecting its refrigerators and ovens and offering a cooking service through the Yummly app, Whirlpool goes beyond being just a supplier to Alexa. It facilitates a part of the exchanges required for the desired platform service, namely, cooking assistance. Here it should be noted that ovens are natural complements of refrigerators. What refrigerators stock, ovens use for cooking. Traditionally these utilities were not digitally connected. Through the Yummly app, Whirlpools connects them.

Moreover, Whirlpool collaborates with Alexa to deliver the full scope of the cooking assistance platform service. For instance, Whirlpool relies on Alexa and Amazon to arrange for deliveries to stock its refrigerators. Whirlpool could do it on its own—but then it would compete with Amazon. Amazon has access to the same data Whirlpool has through Dash, or through the refrigerator user, who can ask Alexa to replenish the low-stock items. By choosing to limit its platform scope to a subset of the exchanges required, Whirlpool avoids direct competition with Amazon. Whirlpool also realizes that its sensor data scope driving a cooking assistance service is limited when compared to Alexa's broader set of smart home services, of which cooking is just a part. Whirlpool's best option thus is to develop a collaborative tethered digital platform for its smart refrigerators and ovens.

This option is similar to those adopted by Spotify, a music streaming platform, and Zynga, a gaming platform, which collaborate with Facebook's social network platform. Spotify expands its scope by using the wider network of Facebook friends who could share the music they stream. Zynga similarly expands its scope by relying on Facebook friends to find players of its games. Both also avoid direct competition with Facebook. Facebook in turn benefits from greater indirect network effects by having Spotify and Zynga as part of its platform. So does Alexa, with Whirlpool joining its broader home services platform with niche cooking assistance services.

Enabled Tethered Digital Platforms

This option is for products with sensor data attributes of strong scope and uniqueness; however, sensor data of this kind may face many restrictions to being shared across complementary entities and among potential platform users.

Intuit, one of the leading providers of business and financial management software for consumers, small and medium-sized enterprises (SMEs), and tax professionals, provides the example here.[13] Intuit started off as a products company, first offering products as packaged software and subsequently as software as a service (or SaaS). One of Intuit's offerings is QuickBooks, which helps SMEs manage their accounting needs such as payroll, invoicing, or paying bills. The software also acts as a sensor, collecting interactive data such as data on receivables, invoices, inventory, and working capital levels. These data attract several complements, such as vendors to pay, customers to collect money from, suppliers who can replenish inventory, or lenders who can arrange for short-term loans. By connecting them, QuickBooks acts as platform that generates services for Intuit's clients, such as easing payments to vendors, making timely collections, inventory replenishments, and maintaining steady working capital levels.

The platform is a tethered digital platform because it is tied to the underlying QuickBooks product. The platform is also an enabled tethered digital platform. Intuit enables each client to manage its own platform by allowing clients to select their platform users—specific vendors, customers, and lenders—and giving them the freedom to shape the scope of their platform services according to their needs. Most important, it is Intuit's clients, not Intuit, who decide whom to invite as platform users to share their data with. This is because Intuit's clients own the data; and they may not want Intuit to share their data with other third-party entities without their approval. An enabled tethered platform allows Intuit to extend QuickBooks into a digital platform that allows the company's clients to maintain their rights as to whom to share data with. Intuit provides the software, cloud, and AI infrastructure that helps several clients manage their platforms independently.

The enabled tethered digital platform is suitable for many business-to-business firms where the product generates data that have to be shared with a customer's customer. The GE locomotive example mentioned earlier falls into this category. GE's locomotive generates sensor data (ETA) with strong scope (good value from matching cargo shippers with receivers) and uniqueness (precise ETA data). Yet the data belong to GE's customers (the railway companies) and are intended to be shared with GE's customers' customers (cargo shippers and receivers). This arrangement limits GE's control over that data, making an enabled tethered digital platform the most suitable option for GE in case it wants to extend its locomotives into a digital platform.

Hybrid Approach

Each of the four quadrants covered so far represents a strategic option in its pure form. Yet some products may adopt a mix of these options to balance different strengths and weaknesses, and adapt their tethered digital platform accordingly. GE locomotives could run GE's own full digital platform through agreements with some of GE's clients while running enabled platforms for others. Whirlpool is a supplier to Alexa for some of its appliances (washers and dryers), yet it is a collaborative platform with Alexa for its refrigerators and ovens. The hybrid approach helps firms experiment with different options and strategically move

Table 5.1
Summary of tethered digital platform options

Type	Supplier to Platforms	Collaborative Tethered Platform	Enabled Tethered Platform	Full Tethered Platform	Hybrid Tethered Platform
Underlying Principle	Participates in third-party platforms as a supplier	Runs a subplatform on a larger or more powerful third-party platform	Runs platform on behalf of customers	Runs platform directly	Blends two or more platform types.
Examples	Delta Faucet connects to Alexa or Google Home.	Whirlpool offers cooking assistance services through its refrigerators and ovens with Alexa.	Intuit enables customers to exchange data with banks and suppliers via its accounting platform.	Becton, Dickinson runs a full tethered platform for Alaris pumps, delivering safe and fast medical services.	Whirlpool is a supplier for Alexa and runs a subplatform on Alexa.
Platform Ownership	Not yet a platform	Owned by a product firm but shared with a stronger platform	Owned by a product firm's customer	Fully owned by a product firm	Owned and shared
Ownership of Sensor Data	Handed over to mother platform	Owned by a product firm	Owned by a product firm's customer	Owned by a product firm	Owned and shared

from one option to another depending on a firm's circumstances and business goals. Table 5.1 summarizes the different options for tethered digital platforms.

Strategic Takeaways

Consumption ecosystems provide opportunities for legacy firms to expand their strategic vistas with new data-driven platform services.

In consumption ecosystems, product-generated data can evolve into becoming a product's strategic partner, allowing joint discovery of new value propositions and new ways of generating revenue streams. This chapter has highlighted specific ways in which a legacy firm can do so. Firms' efforts, however, need the anchor of tethered digital platforms; it is through such platforms that legacy firms can expand their strategic scope from products to data-driven services to avail themselves of new opportunities in their consumption ecosystems.

As a firm contemplates its tethered digital platform approach, the following three questions can shape its strategic thinking.

1. *What is our sensor strategy?* Sensor data underpin a tethered digital platform's commercial viability and its competitive scope. The three attributes of sensor data—its scope, uniqueness, and control—are important determinants of what a product can do with these data. The three attributes also depend largely on the nature of the product, its core functionality, and its product-user interface. Yet firms can find ways for their products to generate sensor data through innovative product-user interfaces that strengthen the data's attributes. Such product-user interfaces need not be tied to the core functionality of their products.

   An example is Roomba, iRobot's robotic vacuum cleaner, whose core functionality is vacuuming floors. It is equipped with sensors to help Roomba anticipate obstacles, navigate its way around them, and more effectively clean floor areas. Imagine if, with modifications, Roomba sensors could also detect mouse droppings, termites, or mold as the device scanned floors. Such sensors would expand the scope of Roomba's product-user interface beyond vacuum cleaning. With the sensor data, iRobot could develop a tethered digital platform that connected its users to pest control vendors and home contractors to solve users' pest or mold problems. iRobot could accordingly expand its strategic scope from selling vacuum cleaning robots to new data-driven platform services helping homeowners anticipate and protect their properties from pests and mold.

iRobot currently is a supplier to Alexa's platform (a user can activate Roomba through voice commands) and intends to broaden its role as a platform.[14] By adding new kinds of sensors, iRobot can elevate itself into a collaborative tethered platform, offering its home protection services from pests or molds on Alexa's broader home services platform.

2. *What is our strategy to attract platform users?* The three core attributes of sensor data—scope, uniqueness, and control—reflect the potential of sensor data to serve as the basis for developing a commercially viable tethered digital platform. To make it work, however, the platform needs to attract platform users. The effort begins with attracting customers, who begin using their sensor-equipped products and generate data that can be exchanged with other complements and other platform users. Chapter 6 defines such customers as digital customers and elaborates on how legacy firms can attract them. Once digital customers begin generating product-interaction data, the next step is to attract those entities that complement those data, namely, other platform users.

Mattress maker Tempur Sealy, for instance, has introduced a line of mattresses with sensors to detect heart rate, breathing patterns, and snoring during sleep. The company may first want to use its established marketing and distribution channels to attract customers and sell its sensor-equipped products.[15] The company may also decide to retrofit sensors on mattresses already sold. The next step is to identify other platform users, especially users that can complement user data to help improve sleep experiences. These additional platform users may include providers of smart adjustable lighting or smart music players to aid in the sleep experience. They may include sleep apnea specialists to monitor the user's sleep disorders.

Digital titans have long mastered strategies to attract platform users,[16] notably through open APIs (see chapter 3).[17] Open APIs can attract application developers and put the onus on them to find third-party entities that can complement one another and serve platform customers.[18] The digital titans have also pioneered pricing strategies tailored to both attract and benefit from platform users. As we saw in chapter 2, Facebook subsidizes its primary users with free access, and it profits from advertisers and app developers. Legacy firms can seek similar ways to subsidize some users and generate revenues from others. These choices, however, entail substantial upfront costs and require persistence to succeed. Chapter 6 provides some examples of how legacy companies could follow these best practices.

3. *What is our optimal tethered platform strategy?* Finally, a firm must determine how best to leverage its sensor data and platform users to offer new data-driven platform services that generate competitive advantages for the firm. Apart from evaluating the strength of their sensor data, the platform users, and the platform services, legacy firms must consider how their prevailing product strengths can help bolster their proposed platform strengths.

For a maker of athletic shoes, for example, arriving at an optimal approach to compete as a tethered digital platform involves two steps. The first step is to assess the product's sensor attributes and envision its intended platform service and its commercial viability. Let us assess the three attributes of an athletic shoe's sensor data first. Sensor data on running have strong scope—keeping in mind the commercial value in connecting runners to other runners or athletic trainers. Sensor data uniqueness may be moderate, owing to the existence of other potential competitors such as Apple, Garmin, or Fitbit, which have access to similar data. Sensor data control may be high if one assumes that most athletic shoe users would be willing to share their data for value-added services. With these attributes, the shoemaker may find the value proposition of a platform service connecting runners to other runners and athletic trainers worth further consideration. It may now want to choose an optimal tethered digital platform option.

Here it needs to go through a second step. This step entails considering its prevailing strengths and the competitive positioning of its core product. A market leader like Nike can bring to the fore its formidable branding and operational scale in a business centered on fitness services. For Nike, a full tethered platform may appear to be an optimal option. For second-tier firms the threat of potential rivals in their envisaged platform service space may appear more ominous. For them a collaborative platform may be a better option. Alternatively, they may experiment with a hybrid approach. For smaller firms it may make more sense to be a supplier to a dominant athletic services platform.

Closing Thoughts

Unlocking value from consumption ecosystems entails substantial changes from prevailing business models. The digital transformation efforts involved in engaging with consumption ecosystems are also correspondingly more arduous. Hence, it represents the fourth and highest tier of digital transformation. Unlike with production ecosystems, wherein a legacy firm may opt to focus mainly on operational efficiency improvements (or stay in tiers 1 or 2), value propositions from consumption ecosystems come primarily from new data-driven platform services. It necessitates reaching tier 4 of digital transformation.

Establishing *tier 4* presence is also strategically important for any firm whose products are witnessing emerging consumption ecosystems. Firms that stay within their production ecosystems in such scenarios risk being commoditized. In a world where light bulbs generate an array of new platform services alluded to earlier, stand-alone light bulbs lose significance. A key challenge in tier 4 is to learn how to run digital platforms. It requires attracting third-party entities to complement their product's sensor data and interfacing their input through APIs (application program interfaces). Legacy firms may benefit from the following strategic questions:

- What does our consumption ecosystem look like?
- What are the key digital complements to our product's sensor data?

- How do we make our APIs accessible to them and leverage their input for new customer experiences?

Engaging in consumption ecosystems also puts a special onus on a firm to acquire digital customers (to generate sensor data), jostle with new digital competitors (to maintain sensor data uniqueness), and build new digital capabilities (to run tethered digital platforms). The following chapters discuss these issues.

6 Digital Customers

Data and digital ecosystems are the new drivers of value in the modern digital economy. We saw in the preceding chapters how legacy firms can build and engage with their digital ecosystems to participate in this new economy. Digital ecosystems allow legacy firms to harness data not only for new operational efficiency gains but for value scope–expanding services. They are thus the foremost and most critical enablers of a legacy firm's data to digital strategy journey. After three chapters on digital ecosystems (chapters 3, 4 and 5), we turn our attention to other important enablers of this journey. These other enablers are digital customers, digital competitors, and digital capabilities. Each of them plays an important role in shaping a legacy firm's digital competitive strategy. This chapter focuses on the role of digital customers.

Digital customers are customers that use sensor-equipped products and thereby provide firms with interactive product-user data. Interactive data provide deep insights into customers and serve as the foundation for a firm to offer unique digital experiences. For production ecosystems, digital customers can help improve operational efficiencies; they are also key enablers of smart interactive product features and drivers of predictive and mass customization services. For consumption ecosystems, digital customers are primary tethered digital platform users. They provide the foundations to attract other platform users.

For the digital titans, such as Amazon, Facebook, or Google, *all* customers are digital customers. All their customers provide interactive data whenever they use these companies' digital platforms. In contrast, for legacy firms that do not yet offer sensor-equipped products, *all* customers are nondigital customers. None of these customers provides interactive data. This chapter discusses the unique strategic challenges legacy firms face when converting their prevailing legacy customers into digital customers who use their sensor-equipped products and provide interactive data. The chapter also suggests approaches by which legacy firms can overcome these challenges.

More broadly, through the concept of digital customers, this chapter offers legacy firms a framework to collect data on product-user interactions. Acquiring data of this sort is new for most legacy firms. Yet such data also help expand their offerings from prevailing product feature–based experiences to new data-driven digital experiences. Indeed, interactive data collected from digital customers are a powerful lever for legacy firms to expand the scope of their value propositions through the provision of new data-driven services, as highlighted in chapters 3, 4, and 5. Making all this possible today is an exponential growth in the availability of sensors that are suitable for all kinds of products, from jet engines to medical devices to sporting goods to banks. While chapter 5 elaborated on sensors, it may be useful here to discuss how legacy firms can expand the adoption of sensors in their products, as sensors are indeed the foundations on which a firm attracts digital customers.

Expanding the Adoption of Sensors in Products

Sensors are ubiquitous today. They are also poised to open opportunities for all kinds of products to be sensor-equipped. Yet these opportunities may not be equally apparent to all legacy firms. Some products are more amenable to being sensor-equipped than others. For instance, it may be easier to equip tennis rackets with sensors than soft drinks. This differential requires legacy firms to be creative when adopting sensors and to take advantage of the widespread availability and different forms of sensors.

It's also important that legacy firms take an expansive view of what sensors can do in any business. It is sometimes assumed that sensor-equipped products generate interactive data that are associated only with the primary purpose of the product. Sensors in tennis rackets, for example, would be expected to offer data related to tennis and sensors in toothbrushes would be expected to offer data on dental health. However, sensors are versatile and can capture all kinds of data. If producers take advantage of this versatility, their products' sensors can generate interactive data that may even be far removed from the primary purpose of the product. Chapter 5 discussed possibilities for iRobot's robotic vacuum cleaners to have sensors that would detect mold, termites, or mouse droppings. Such innovative ways of looking at sensors help expand the scope of a legacy firm's prevailing business models.

Ongoing innovations in sensors are also poised to further expand the realm of options. For example, advances in nanotechnology-based sensors[1] are pushing out the frontiers of what sensors can do, such as enabling the monitoring of food safety (by sensing whether food goes bad) and helping in the early detection of cancer (by sensing the growth of tumors). The rapid advances in and range of sensor technology have the potential to influence the course of every sector. This means that legacy establishments should be on top of the new developments in sensor technology. They should consider monitoring such developments an important aspect of their business environment and an integral part of their strategic planning process.

How to equip products with sensors thus occupies a key place in new product development strategies. Accordingly, legacy firms must expand the goals of their innovation processes beyond offering new product features to offering new data features. Making data-related features compelling is critical to attracting digital customers to use sensor-equipped products. In this endeavor, however, sensors are only a means to an end. The ultimate goal of equipping products with sensors is to collect data on product-user interactions. And this is possible only when firms succeed in acquiring digital customers.

Why Are Digital Customers Different?

At first glance, digital and legacy customers, or the nondigital customers for a legacy firm's prevailing products, may appear to be the same—and

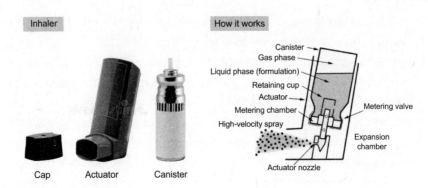

Figure 6.1

The standard inhaler. *Source:* Courtesy of Personal Air Quality Systems Pvt. Ltd.

in fact, they are often the same individuals or corporations. The same legacy customer who uses Nike's standard shoe is also a digital customer when using Nike's sensor-equipped shoe. This customer may purchase both kinds of shoes and use them as alternates. Similarly, British Airways may use GE's standard jet engines in some of its aircraft (in this way remaining a legacy customer) while using its sensor-equipped engines in others (thus becoming a digital customer).[2] A logical question to ask, then, is, Why should digital customers be any different from legacy customers?

The Case of Smart Inhalers

To appreciate why digital customers are different from legacy customers, we can consider the recent introduction of smart inhalers by pharmaceutical companies such as AstraZeneca, GlaxoSmithKline, and Novartis. Inhalers are devices that deliver medication directly to the lungs and respiratory tract in the form of a mist or spray. They are commonly used for such respiratory diseases as chronic obstructive pulmonary disease (COPD) and asthma. In its standard form, the product consists of a canister that holds the medication and a plastic actuator and a cap that enables the inhaler to pressure release the right dosage of the medication (see figure 6.1). A patient inserts the inhaler into his mouth, squeezes the receptacle, and inhales the medication. Customers of these standard products are legacy customers.

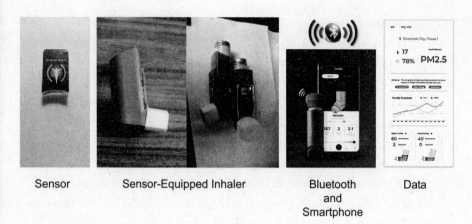

| Sensor | Sensor-Equipped Inhaler | Bluetooth and Smartphone | Data |

Figure 6.2

The sensor-equipped inhaler. *Source:* Courtesy of Personal Air Quality Systems Pvt. Ltd.

A smart inhaler has a sensor, an electronic chip, on the plastic actuator that can collect various kinds of data and can communicate with a mobile phone or a wearable device through Bluetooth connectivity (see figure 6.2). To inhale the medication, the patient uses the smart inhaler in exactly the same way as he would a standard inhaler. Customers for smart inhalers are digital customers.

Collaborations between pharmaceutical and tech companies are behind many of the smart inhalers on the market today. These collaborations are synergistic unions of complementary strengths: the pharmaceutical companies have patented medications, strong brand names, and an established customer base, while the tech companies have the sensor technology know-how and the skills to analyze sensor-generated data. As examples, AstraZeneca has partnered with Adherium, GlaxoSmithKline has partnered with Propeller Health, and Novartis has partnered with Qualcomm Life.[3]

Features of standard inhalers: Consider how a standard inhaler is used to treat asthma, an inflammatory disease of the lungs. The US Centers for Disease Control and Prevention estimates that 25 million people suffer from asthma in the US alone; almost one in twelve children in the US suffer from this disease.[4] Worldwide the numbers are understandably larger, with more than 339 million people living with asthma.[5] Common symptoms include wheezing, shortness of breath, coughing, tightness in the chest, and difficulty talking. Patients experience these symptoms because of inflamed and swollen airways in their lungs, along with a tightening of muscles around the airways, making them narrow. When these symptoms exacerbate, patients can experience an asthma attack and struggle to breathe. Triggers for asthma exacerbation include various allergens and pollutants in the air the patient breathes, such as dust, pollen, pet dander, and mold.

Usually, two kinds of medications are prescribed as treatments (there is no cure). They are dispensed through two kinds of standard inhalers. One class of medications, inhaled corticosteroids, are taken regularly to keep inflammation in check and prevent the airways from swelling; they are prescribed as maintenance or preventative inhalers. Bronchodilators, the other class of medications, are prescribed for rescue purposes when a patient experiences an acute asthma attack to reduce the muscle tightening that the inhaled corticosteroids alone do not adequately control. Patients typically keep both types of medication with them, one for daily prescribed use and the other for whenever they experience an acute asthma attack. Standard inhalers can provide analog data to patients through mechanical counters on the plastic receptacle. The counters reveal the doses a patient has taken and the doses that remain before the canister is empty.

Features of smart inhalers: Smart inhalers generate digital interactive data every time a patient uses them. For instance, they record the time and date, the dose inhaled, and the amount of medication that reaches the lungs (as opposed to, say, sprayed into the mouth) for every use. Sensors capture the angle at which the inhaler is held when the canister releases the medication. If the canister is not held at an angle close to the ideal angle, the smart inhaler infers that the medication was not adequately sprayed into the lungs. Sensors also track the inhaler's location. All such data go into a smartphone app through Bluetooth connectivity. In addition, smart inhalers can collect and use environmental data. They can (through APIs) have access to other IoT devices within the home that detect mold or dust mites. Foobot is one example of such a device.[6] When the user ventures outside (and has engaged location tracking), smart sensors can also pick up data from other environmental data sources. These sources provide real-time updates relevant to the specific location a user may be in, such as pollen and humidity levels, pollution conditions, and other irritants that can cause an asthma attack.

Through such data, smart inhalers can offer a broad range of features to digital customers. A. Vaidyanathan, the founder and managing director of Personal Air Quality Systems (PAQS),[7] a startup in Bangalore that manufactures sensors for smart inhalers, categorized for me these features as "basic and advanced." Basic features include tracking the consumption of preventative doses, reminding users to take preventative doses, tracking when and how often rescue inhalers are used, reminding users to carry inhalers (especially the rescue inhaler) when leaving home, and tracking the location of rescue inhalers during an emergency. A key benefit of these basic features is improved adherence to medication regimes and hence better control of asthma. Studies show that smart inhalers improve asthma control and reduce incidents requiring rescue inhalers.[8] And reminding users to always carry a rescue inhaler, along with the ability to track the location of rescue inhalers during emergencies, can save lives.

The advanced features of smart inhalers are possible through deeper analysis of archived data from large numbers of users. Examples of these advanced features include predicting an acute attack by detecting known irritants (such as dust, pollen, or mold), fine-tuning the predictions by knowing precisely what irritants are more likely to trigger attacks for each individual patient, and tracking the effectiveness of medications, thereby helping physicians fine-tune medication dosages for individual patients. The underlying idea is similar to how Amazon or Netflix, using archived data resources, can predict what an individual user may want from their inventory, as detailed in chapters 1 and 2. Amazon and Netflix use sophisticated algorithms and AI to find correlations between various user behaviors and purchase likelihoods to make their predictions. Smart inhalers similarly can query their data archive to find correlations between the use of rescue inhalers and different environmental triggers to predict asthma attacks.

Most of the smart inhalers on the market today offer the basic features. Smart inhalers were introduced in 2014 and are still in the early phase of adoption; they account for less than 1 percent of the inhaler market.[9] The current market size of smart inhalers is estimated to be around $34 million but is expected to grow to around $1.5 billion by 2025 (the total market for inhalers is around $22 billion).[10] This growth could be far more robust if the producers could harness the full potential of smart inhalers by expanding their basic digital features into more advanced ones. These advanced features could make smart inhalers indispensable to patients as, with repeated use, smart inhalers can learn about each individual patient's unique triggers for asthma attacks and prevent them from happening in the first place. Modern analytics and AI can enable features such as predicting asthma attacks and customizing predictions for each individual user. However, to offer such features reliably, producers need massive amounts of data from smart inhaler usage. For any one individual digital customer to experience the benefits of such advanced features, therefore, thousands of other digital customers are needed.

To understand more about the need for large amounts of sensor data to make products smart, let's consider the IoT thermometer offered by Kinsa Health.[11] This thermometer can track the body temperatures of all its users and detect whether multiple people in an area are getting fevers. This feature can provide early warnings of hot spots for infections (such as COVID-19). However, the value for any individual digital customer materializes only when a majority of people in that user's neighborhood or relevant geographic region adopt the IoT thermometers. Furthermore, if a producer succeeds in gaining large-scale adoption by digital customers, it can expect even more digital customers to flock in, attracted by its now more readily apparent data-driven advantages. These attributes of data-driven features imply that acquiring digital customers may have winner-take-all outcomes, making them different from legacy customers. The potential for digital customers to change the marketplace for an established product like thermometers shows that legacy firms have to rethink their prevailing customer acquisition strategies, designed for legacy customers, when they cater to digital customers.

The Strategic Implications of Digital Customers

The fundamental difference between digital and legacy customers relates to the products they buy and the data they generate. Legacy customers buy standard products and do not provide interactive data on how they use the products. Digital customers, on the other hand, buy sensor-equipped products, generate interactive data, and allow the producer access to that data. Addressing this fundamental difference has many significant implications for legacy firms.

Designing, producing, marketing, and selling sensor-equipped products are not the norm for legacy firms. Similarly, using sensor-equipped products is not the norm for their legacy customers. Catering to digital customers requires changes in the existing business processes of legacy firms. Similarly, to join the ranks of digital customers, legacy customers must change their prevailing expectations from those associated with familiar standard products. The value of new digital features must be appealing. The new benefits offered must be convincing.

The value proposition of sensor-equipped products for digital customers can, however, expand with greater adoption. This is because of network effects. Legacy firms too benefit in new ways because of these network effect advantages made possible by digital customers. To derive these benefits, however, legacy firms must change their prevailing approaches to delivering value propositions to their customers as they move from their long-standing value chains to new digital ecosystems. They also need to modify their long-held premises for revenue and profit generation.

Table 6.1 highlights the key differences between digital and legacy customers and the associated strategic implications. The ensuing discussion elaborates on these points.

Transforming Legacy Business Processes

To start with, as digital customers buy sensor-equipped products, legacy firms need new processes to design products that incorporate sensors. In the case of smart inhalers, pharmaceutical companies formed corporate alliances with tech companies. Not all companies may need such major initiatives; all, however, do need to develop a new understanding of how their products can generate interactive data and fresh capabilities to integrate sensor attributes with their prevailing product features.

Legacy firms also need to establish new processes to harness sensor data to provide new digital services. For smart inhalers, the new processes include establishing fresh APIs that can channel sensor data into individual user profiles; using AI and other analytics to create intelligence that pinpoints asthma attack risks to individual users based on an array of potential environmental irritants; and establishing processes to develop and manage new digital features as customers interact with their products. Chapters 3, 4, and 5 discussed how legacy firms can develop such processes to effectively generate such digital services. Chapter 8, on digital capabilities, elaborates further.

Digital customers also have a deep impact on many prevailing business functions, such as R&D, product development, marketing, sales, and after-sales services. Chapter 4 described how Caterpillar developed new cost-efficient motor graders using data from their digital customers. The company had to change its R&D and product development processes so as to cater to the more refined product-user interactive data offered by their digital customers.

In similar fashion, when engaging with digital customers, legacy firms must change their prevailing marketing, sales, and after-sales service processes. This is because the benefits of the digital services they offer must be established in new ways.

Table 6.1

Differences between legacy and digital customers: Strategic implications

Activity Category	Differences Between Legacy and Digital Customers		Strategic Implications of Digital Customers for Legacy Firms
	Legacy Customers	Digital Customers	
Buying	Buy and use standard products.	Buy and use sensor-equipped products; allow use of interactive data.	*Transforming prevailing business processes*
Customer value proposition at baseline	Enjoy standard product features.	Enjoy both standard product features and features enabled through interactive data.	*Establishing benefits for new digital services*
Benefits of growing customer base for producer	Expanding customer base generates scale advantages for producer.	Expanding customer base generates scale *and* network effects advantages for producer.	*Expanding strategic ways of thinking: from economies of scale to network effects*
Customer value proposition when adoption of product expands	Benefits of standard product features do not change with greater customer adoption.	Benefits of data features improve with greater customer adoption.	*Establishing credibility for future benefits*
Delivering value propositions to the customer	Value chain activities deliver product features.	Value chains continue to deliver standard product features; in addition, digital ecosystems deliver data features that expand customer benefits.	*Transforming prevailing business models: engaging with digital ecosystems*
Revenue and profit generation	Pricing strategies are consistent with value chain business models	Pricing strategies may need to be adapted to platform business models.	*Transforming beliefs about revenue and profit generation*

Establishing Benefits for New Digital Services

Legacy customers understandably are accustomed to the features of the standard products they use. These standard features generate the product's basic value proposition. With inhalers, the core feature is the efficacy of the medication dispensed. Digital features of smart inhalers offer an added and different value proposition, such as reminders to take medications or alerts for possible pending asthma attacks. Establishing the benefits of new digital features and hence the product's new value proposition needs additional effort.

GlaxoSmithKline, one of the producers of smart inhalers, has sponsored studies pointing to evidence that smart inhalers increase adherence to treatments and improve asthma control.[12] Such efforts associate new digital features of the smart inhaler with the product's prevailing medicinal features (that is, smart inhalers help with asthma treatment). With this evidence, a company like GlaxoSmithKline can garner support from insurance companies and physicians to recommend smart inhalers to patients. Producers can also complement such "push" efforts (push from insurance or doctors to patients) with "pull" efforts (pull from patients asking for the product). Creative advertising that raises awareness of the product's special digital features, such as the ability to track rescue inhalers or reminding users to carry them, is one such example. For digital services to succeed, the benefits of new digital features must be thoughtfully established for prospective digital customers. New value propositions must be carefully framed for maximum impact.

Expanding Strategic Mindsets: From Economies of Scale to Network Effects

Because the benefits from digital services improve with greater adoption of sensor-equipped products, expanding a firm's digital customer base generates a network effects advantage. The more digital customers GlaxoSmithKline acquires vis-à-vis its competitors, for example, the larger are its comparative sources of data and greater is the relative power of its analytics. These increases ultimately generate superior digital features. Such superiority in turn attracts more digital customers.

By comparison, increasing a firm's legacy customer base builds advantages of economies of scale. One of these advantages includes lower unit costs of the firm's products. For instance, by attracting more customers for its legacy inhalers, GlaxoSmithKline is able to spread the fixed costs entailed in the development, production, and marketing of its standard inhalers over a larger number of sold inhalers. Consequently, GlaxoSmithKline benefits from lower unit costs for its standard inhalers.

It's essential to note that such scale advantages apply even when a firm is expanding its digital customer base. After all, standard products and smart products share most of the same components. Smart inhalers, for example, have the same components as standard inhalers while including a sensor. Hence an expanding digital customer base reduces the unit costs for smart products, too. In addition, this expanded digital customer base generates network effects. As noted in chapter 1, data- and software-driven exchanges can connect millions of customers in ways that physical products cannot; this is how Netflix became a juggernaut supplier of video content. Digital customers, connected to the company through networks and sensors, allow firms to capitalize on both scale and networks effects advantages. This point is important because it requires legacy firms to change their long-standing premise of scale being the cornerstone of competitive advantage. Instead, they need to recognize how network effects may play an equally important role. A shift in mindset from economies of scale to network effects as the cornerstone of competitive advantage also implies that legacy firms must change their prevailing business models to deliver new value propositions to their digital customers.

Establishing Credibility for Future Benefits

The basic value proposition of standard products for legacy customers does not change with increasing product adoption. The medicinal properties of an inhaler for, instance, remain the same irrespective of the number of users. However, the value propositions realized through the digital features of smart products improve with increased product adoption. The ability of smart inhalers to predict an asthma attack, for instance, improves with growing product adoption. In such situations, the benefits of digital features may have to credibly established *even before they can be demonstrated.*

One approach to doing so involves the concept of outcome-based sales. When GE launched its sensor-equipped products (such as jet engines, locomotives, and turbines), the company adopted this approach to establishing its credibility in delivering new data-driven services derived from its products. Using sensor data generated by GE products, the company expected to offer customers benefits such as better fuel efficiencies, operational efficiencies, and reduced downtimes by predicting component failures before they happened. At the time of the launch, these benefits were just a promise; they were expected to materialize only when adequate data became available. However, GE was convinced that the benefits not only would materialize but would get stronger as more and more GE customers adopted the company's sensor-equipped products and provided access to sensor data. To underscore its confidence, GE transformed its commercial terms, charging customers for products and for the data-driven services derived from the use of these products separately. GE offered its sensor-equipped product at a reduced price, but it made up for the drop in revenues by charging a percentage of what its customers actually saved by using GE's digital services through improved fuel and operational efficiencies. The sale thus was "outcome-based" as GE's revenues depended on the benefits materializing.

It may be pertinent to note that GE's digital initiatives ran into rough times for a multitude of reasons. The current fate of its initiatives should not preclude us from appreciating the underlying strengths of the ideas the company propagated. Indeed, as highlighted in chapter 4, GE's pioneering efforts helped clarify and frame many useful concepts, such as the industrial internet and digital twins. Outcome-based sales is one such concept.

Transforming Prevailing Business Models: Engaging with Digital Ecosystems

What changes when firms offer smart products to digital customers? Offering smart products to digital customers has two parts: one, the foundational product to which the sensor is attached; and two, the data-driven services that the sensor helps generate. For the foundational product, not much changes. A firm's prevailing value chain and its underlying scale advantage remain important and relevant. Glaxo-SmithKline, for instance, needs its value chain to offer the foundational product to its customers. For a firm to offer the smart product's digital services to digital customers, however, its value chain is not enough. Offering digital services requires constructing new digital ecosystems that can effectively harness the potential of data and unleash the power of network effects.

To deliver its digital services, the producer of a smart inhaler needs a production ecosystem to internally channel sensor data and generate digital services, such as tracking rescue inhalers or sending reminders to customers to take their medication. In addition, it needs a consumption ecosystem comprising (among other things) entities that provide real-time data on environmental triggers for asthma such as humidity, mold, pollution, or pollen.

Taken together, production and consumption ecosystems help amplify the value of the inhaler's sensor data. The greater the number of data sources and recipients (such as digital customers and data sources for asthmatic triggers), the more the value of the data is amplified, and hence the stronger the network effects advantage. Just as scale amplifies the power of a standard product through value chains within the product's industry, network effects amplify the power of a smart product's data through that product's digital ecosystems.

When engaging with newly constructed consumption ecosystems, firms also need to extend their value chains into a digital platform, as highlighted in chapter 5. In the case of smart inhalers, for instance, the feature of alerting a digital customer to a potential attack when he enters an area with mold or pollen is possible only through a digital platform that enables data exchanges across different data sources, such as the real-time location of the digital customer and data sources that provide real-time updates on air quality. Adopting digital platforms to serve digital customers changes a company's approaches to prevailing revenue and profit generation.

Transforming Mindsets on Revenue and Profit Generation

For legacy customers served through value chains, revenue and profit margin strategies are usually influenced by how a product crosses break-even levels. A break-even point is reached when a firm makes neither a profit nor a loss. The basic variables for a break-even analysis include a firm's fixed and variable costs and the contribution margins a product generates. A break-even point is formulized as $FC = Q (P - VC)$, where FC is fixed costs, Q is units sold, P is price, and VC is variable costs. Price minus variable costs yields the contribution margins for the product. Fixed and variable costs are usually determined by the product and its technology. With these assumed as given conditions, a firm develops a pricing strategy that influences sales quantities and contribution margins (depending on market conditions) together to generate far more returns than its fixed costs.

On the other hand, recovering fixed costs, though important, is not usually the primary focus with digital platforms. Instead the focus is on generating network effects through greater platform adoption. The premise is personified in what Eric Schmidt of Google meant in chapter 2 by saying "ubiquity first, revenue later," or "URL." Indeed, many digital titans give away the core platform services for free, with a long-term goal of building network effects. To generate revenue, they find other users, or other "sides" of the platform. Facebook and Google make substantial revenues from advertisers, not from the primary users, Facebook friends and Google searchers.

What does this mean for a legacy firm catering to digital customers? It is clearly not practical to give away the product for free. Just as legacy customers are expected to pay for the standard product, it is reasonable to expect digital customers to pay for the foundational product. Key questions for legacy firms are: How should they price their sensor-equipped products? And how should they price their data-driven services?

Consider the approach taken by Samba TV, a TV content recommendation engine and a viewer tracking app maker referred to in chapter 5. Samba TV provides sensors to TV manufacturers such as Sony, TCL, and Sharp, helping them convert their legacy TV customers into digital customers. Interestingly, rather than charging for their sensors, Samba TV *pays* TV manufacturers to equip Samba products with their sensors. To make up for this cost, Samba TV generates revenues from TV content producers and advertisers by offering them benefits from their sensor data (such as who is watching what show). TV manufacturers in turn pass on what they receive from Samba TV to their customers (TV users) through discounts. The objective is to encourage adoption of smart sensor-equipped TVs—to turn legacy customers into digital customers—and to acquire permission to use their viewing data. With greater adoption, TV manufacturers hope to improve the power of data-driven services, such as recommendations for shows on TVs (similar to what Netflix offers), and, in so doing, also build network effects for their brand.

The customer benefits from the discount. In addition, the customer can also expect to get benefits from the TV manufacturer's data-driven services. These data-driven benefits, however, may take time to materialize as their efficacy crucially depends on large amounts of data. The discount is an immediate benefit aimed at accelerating rates of adoption of sensor-equipped TVs and attracting digital customers. And the approach has worked. According to Ashwin Navin, the CEO and cofounder of Samba TV, over 30 million TVs worldwide are equipped with Samba's sensors (the company was founded in 2008 and sold its first TVs in 2011). Also, according to Navin, almost all smart TVs today have some form of sensing ability.

The producers of smart inhalers, by contrast, have opted to take a different tack with their pricing strategy. So far they are charging a premium for their sensor-equipped products. They see their digital services as an added value proposition, for which they expect customers to pay. A consequence of this approach, however, has been a slow rate of adoption of smart inhalers. Their adoption is less than 1 percent, though smart inhalers were introduced in 2014.

Being expected to pay only after the benefits are realized can be a powerful motivator for legacy customers to try unfamiliar digital services. It is one way to get around a catch-22 situation. Producers need legacy customers to become digital customers for the company to establish the benefits of its digital services, while legacy customers need to see these benefits before converting to digital customers. Outcome-based sales in such circumstances can present a win-win scenario. If the digital services do not meet their promise, the customers do not have to pay; if the digital services deliver as promised, producers share the benefits with their customers. The bet that a producer makes is that if it successfully converts legacy customers to digital customers, the data from product-user interactions will deliver promised outcomes. This approach, however, may be more suited for business-to-business transactions, where it may be easier to establish "outcome-based" contracts compared to business-to-consumer transactions. For business-to-consumer transactions, legacy firms must find creative ways to subsidize their new digital value propositions to increase adoption.

Going forward, when catering to digital customers, legacy firms will have to balance competing priorities: between recovering fixed costs, on the one hand, and driving sensor-equipped product adoption to generate network effects on the other. They will have to find creative ways of engaging with their digital customers that not only help build network effects but also generate revenue. In sum, legacy firms must give serious consideration to all the new strategic implications of acquiring digital customers.

Summary: Thoughts on Digital Customers

Digital customers are one of the most significant sources of interactive data. The data acquired from these customers empower legacy firms to expand their value scope from standard product sales to new data-driven digital services. Acquiring digital customers starts with equipping standard products with sensors. Yet this task is not the same as, say, equipping machines in a factory with sensors. Machines do not object to sensors being put on them. Nor do they object to providing sensor data. Customers may need significant inducements to accept sensor-equipped products and allow their data to be captured and used. Migrating a firm's legacy customer base to a digital customer base has both strategic advantages and challenges, as highlighted in this chapter.

While digital customers are a crucial resource for a firm's digital strategy, legacy firms must be careful when incentivizing their legacy customers to provide interactive data. They must ensure that the data are both collected and used ethically. The sharing of interactive data with external entities must be done in ways that do not impinge on the privacy of individual customers. These are significant new challenges, which chapter 9 further expands on.

With legacy customers, a firm differentiates itself through innovative features in its standard products. With digital customers, a firm must differentiate itself through innovative features in its data-driven services. Network effects often drive the power of such data services. It is important to note that not all digital services are associated with network effects. For instance, many of the basic features of smart inhalers, such as sending reminders to users to take preventative doses or tracking the location of rescue inhalers, do not improve with greater adoption rates. With no network effects advantages, however, such features can also easily be imitated by rivals. The more advanced features of smart inhalers are those that improve with greater adoption—and hence are associated with network effects. These features are more difficult to replicate by rivals with smaller digital customer footprints. The smaller rivals do not have comparable volumes of data. Network effects in such cases represent a critical source of competitive advantage.

As one of the most significant sources of interactive data, digital customers represent a critical element of a firm's production and consumption ecosystem infrastructure. Chapters 8 and 10 elaborate on the role of digital customers in helping legacy firms forge new digital capabilities to drive their digital competitive strategies. Digital customers thus are one of the key enablers of a legacy firm's data to digital strategy journey. Chapter 7 turns to another kind of key enabler, the digital competitor.

7 Digital Competitors

Many of us know Alibaba for it is digital e-commerce platforms. Alibaba, in fact, is the world's third largest retailer and e-commerce company by revenue, behind Amazon and Walmart.[1] And since 2017 Alibaba's online profits have surpassed those of Amazon and Walmart.[2] Similarly, many of us know Tencent as one of the world's largest social media companies, dominating the instant messaging space in China. The company's services include online social games, music, movies, and shopping. Its websites are among the top five most visited in the world.[3] Its WeChat multipurpose messaging, social media, and mobile payment app has more than 1.2 billion monthly active users.[4] It is popularly described as a "super app" because of its large array of functionalities.[5] Alibaba and Tencent, digital titans from China, are now among the ranks of the world's largest technology companies.

For a comparison, let's consider three other different but also illustrious companies from China—the Industrial and Commercial Bank of China (ICBC), the Agricultural Bank of China (ABC), and the Bank of China (BoC). ICBC, ABC, and BoC are Chinese state-owned commercial banks, with the Chinese Ministry of Finance providing them their capital. As of 2019, the ICBC ranked as the largest bank in the world in terms of total assets.[6] BoC was ranked fourth largest.[7] In 2020, ABC was ranked fifth in Forbes's annual Global 2000 list of the world's largest public companies.[8]

Until recently, these legacy Chinese banks were a world apart from Alibaba and Tencent in terms of their businesses and customers. Not anymore. Over the last few years, these legacy banks have been on a direct competitive collision course with Alibaba and Tencent in the market for consumer and small and medium-sized enterprise (SME) loans and deposits. Their competitive battle represents the shape of competition facing legacy firms around the world as they confront a new class of digital competitors.

In China, the digital titans Alibaba and Tencent were impossible for established banks to ignore. They first entered the "third-party payment space," which allowed merchants and consumers to bypass the banks for cash requirements when transacting on their platforms. Such payment services were necessary because credit card usage in China was low, making e-commerce transactions difficult. After establishing their dominance in the payment space, Alibaba and Tencent turned their attention to banking. Alibaba (with MYBank) and Tencent (with WeBank) entered the banking space in 2015.[9] By 2018, MYBank had issued more than 1.19 trillion yuan (approximately $177 billion) in loans to nearly 10 million SMEs through its online platform. This was almost 67 percent[10] of the loans issued by ICBC, China's leading SME lender.[11] Tencent's WeBank had issued loans worth 163 billion yuan (approximately $24 billion) in roughly the same period.[12] Also notable is the Chinese digital titans' forays into the deposits business of the legacy banks. By 2017 Alibaba had attracted an estimated 1.7 trillion yuan ($263 billion) in deposits.[13] This amounted to around 12 percent of BoC's deposits for the same year.[14]

How did Alibaba and Tencent achieve such remarkable success in a market dominated by legacy banking incumbents in a span of just a few years? The short answer is through data. Alibaba and Tencent represent a new breed of digital competitors confronting legacy firms in the modern economy. They are digital competitors because they compete primarily with data, not with similar products. Their competitive impact on legacy firms arises from what they can do with data, not what they can do with similar products. We will return to the Alibaba and Tencent story after we set the stage to better understand how the competitive landscape is shifting owing to new digital competitors.

Not all legacy firms may face competitive attacks from digital titans similar to the attacks faced by established banks in China. Yet all legacy firms must be prepared to face digital competitors of varying types. Some digital competitors may be familiar with product rivals while others may not. Some may even be startups. They emerge from more expansive digital ecosystems. Their competitive dynamics overrun prevailing industry boundaries. The old rules of industry-based competition may not adequately apply to them. To effectively compete, legacy firms have to understand their digital competitors' distinctive competitive strengths and their uncommon modus operandi.

This chapter explores the concept of digital competitors and highlights how and why they are different from legacy competitors. The chapter also develops a framework for legacy firms to confront their digital competitive threats.

Competitive Dynamics in Digital Ecosystems

Digital ecosystems expand a legacy firm's value creation scope from its prevailing products to new data-driven services. In its new expanded value space, a legacy firm will also attract new digital competitors. Winning against such new competition demands more than product or product market positioning superiority. It requires superiority in harnessing data. And competitive battles are not just about product features but also about data-driven services. Competitive dynamics in digital ecosystems are thus different from the dynamics that legacy firms experience in their industries.

To appreciate these differences, we begin our discussion with three patterns of competition in digital ecosystems. These patterns also have parallels with industry-based competition. The three patterns introduced here help categorize common competitive scenarios legacy firms may face in the new digital world. Recognizing these competitive patterns also helps delineate different approaches by which legacy firms can confront their digital competitors. Also highlighted are parallels between these new digital competitive patterns and older and more familiar industrial competitive patterns. Recognizing these parallels can help legacy firms better adapt their prevailing approaches for tackling competition to new strategies necessary for competing in the digital world.

Pattern 1: Competitive Equilibrium through Ecosystem Parity

P&G, Philips, and Colgate are legacy rivals for electric toothbrushes. Today, P&G, with Oral-B, Philips, with Sonicare, and Colgate, with Hum, offer competing smart toothbrush brands. These legacy rivals have turned into digital competitors. They compete not just with their products but with the data their products generate.

As of today, each offers similar data-driven features. Sensors on Oral-B's toothbrushes assess the pressure applied during brushing and monitor how long any particular spot is brushed.[15] Algorithms compare actual brushing with desired outcomes and provide a user with feedback through a smartphone app. Philips's Sonicare[16] and Colgate's Hum[17] similarly inform users which spots need more attention and whether they are missing any spots consistently through the sensors integrated into these products, algorithms, and smartphone apps. In their legacy business, these firms compete with symmetric value chain strengths in product development, branding, and distribution networks. In their digital business, Oral-B, Sonicare, and Hum have symmetric digital strengths, each using its data and algorithms to deliver largely comparable data-driven features.

These are early days for smart toothbrushes and smart toothbrush features. Their competitive dynamics will likely evolve into some kind of competitive equilibrium among these brands. For this to happen, each must maintain symmetric strengths in harnessing data. Each must match the others with new smart features. Each must offer similar digital experiences. In other words, they need *ecosystem parity* to remain competitive. Ecosystem parity is when digital competitors maintain symmetric strengths in their production and consumption ecosystems.

Today, each of these digital competitors shows symmetry in its production ecosystems to offer similar smart product features. This is likely to continue. If any of these brands upgrades its algorithms, the others will reciprocate with upgraded algorithms of their own. Any new smart feature introduced by one will likely be matched by the others. A feature that predicts cavities introduced by one, for example, will likely be replicated by the others. To do so they will develop equivalent strengths in their product sensors and their algorithms. Such symmetry in their production ecosystems must also extend into their consumption ecosystems for them to maintain their competitive equilibrium. If Oral-B extends its business model into a tethered digital platform, generating data exchanges among its users and dentists, Hum and Sonicare must follow. They too will have to build a strong platform with equivalent participating dentists. If they do not, the winner-take-all attributes of digital platforms could propel Oral-B into an unassailable competitive position. Ecosystem parity thus allows digital competitors to maintain equivalent data-harnessing strengths and equivalent competitive positions.

Parallels with Industry-Based Competition: Value Chain Parity   A parallel pattern in industry-based competition can be seen with Coca-Cola and PepsiCo in the soft drinks industry. Coca-Cola and PepsiCo maintain competitive equilibrium because of equivalent product strengths achieved through *value chain parity*. Each company owns a unique concentrate formula. Each has comparable bottler networks and similar suppliers (can manufacturers, sugar producers, and artificial sweetener producers). They also employ similar distribution networks, which include major fountains (McDonald's, Burger King, KFC), retailers (grocery stores), and vending machines. Their value chains have parity because of similar strengths all the way from concentrate production to branding and distribution. Both have strong concentrates. Both have similar bargaining power when dealing with a common pool of suppliers. And they match each other with their strengths in distribution and branding.

Coca-Cola's and PepsiCo's competitive battles in advertising and distribution also create barriers around their market positions. Coca-Cola and PepsiCo match each other in branding, each spending around 8 to

10 percent of revenues on advertising. Both also invest heavily in their extensive distribution networks. Consequently, scale in branding and distribution becomes a necessary condition for market viability. This keeps their industry very much to themselves, deterring any new competitor seeking to enter their markets.

P&G's, Philips's and Colgate's competitive battles in developing algorithms and sensors and attracting dentists to their platforms can also generate barriers to new entrants. These barriers to new entrants stem from the network effects generated by the incumbents' data-driven services.

Network Effects and Ecosystem Parity   As P&G (Oral-B), Philips (Sonicare), and Colgate (Hum) battle for more users, they also enhance their direct network effects. Data acquired from increasing numbers of users make their algorithms stronger. Stronger algorithms in turn help improve their data-driven features benefiting each user individually. In other words, each user benefits when a brand has more users. P&G, Philips, and Colgate also build indirect network effects if they extend their products into tethered platforms and attract increasing numbers of platform users. If, for instance, their platforms attract more dentists, users benefit from more choices of dentists. In turn, dentists benefit from having greater access to users. Their platforms may even invite insurance companies willing to offer lower premiums to those with healthier brushing habits. Over time, these network effects become formidable barriers to new entrants wanting to compete in this space. Coca-Cola and PepsiCo preserve their competitive equilibrium with matching value chain strengths. P&G, Philips, and Colgate can achieve similar results with symmetric production and consumption ecosystems strengths—in other words, through ecosystem parity. Figure 7.1 graphically depicts these relationships.

Pattern 2: Competitive Equilibrium through Symmetric Ecosystem Barriers

Hexagon Geosystems is a technology company that digitally surveys and collects topographical data on land surfaces. The company's

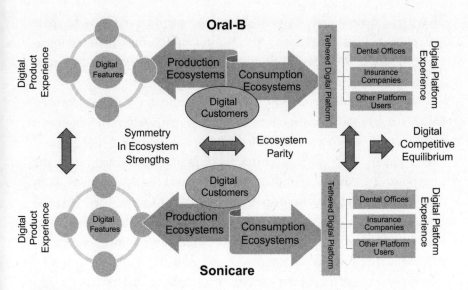

Figure 7.1
Competitive equilibrium through symmetric production and consumption ecosystems.

technology finds useful applications in the construction business. Through geospatial positioning and 3D laser scanning of a construction site, the company's technology can assess optimal ways to dig or move dirt. Through its data, it can also derive an engineering plan that can direct various construction equipment on how to conduct their respective tasks on a project. The technology can, for instance, develop a plan for an excavator on how much earth to move, or for a bulldozer on how much to grade at a project site. The plan also can help contractors find ways to work various construction equipment in tandem. For example, once an excavator has completed its job, it can highlight the next-in-line bulldozer to start grading.

Because these plans are digitally derived and software-driven, they can be uploaded to various construction equipment. Doing so provides real-time guidance to an operator on how to maneuver the equipment. These plans also guide and monitor each machine's progress, alerting operators when the job is done. As Holger Pietzsch, vice president of marketing of Hexagon Geosystems, puts it: "An excavator does not have to dig more than it should, or a bulldozer does not have to grade more than what is necessary. This feature allows construction companies to reduce their prevailing bottlenecks of finding skilled operators, using data to complement their tasks."

Hexagon Geosystems' role in the construction business complements the role of construction equipment manufacturers. Whereas a construction equipment manufacturer like Caterpillar is in the business of producing and selling construction equipment, Hexagon is in the business of helping Caterpillar's customers use their equipment. Both use modern digital technologies, but in different ways. Caterpillar, as described in chapter 4, uses sensor and telematics data for interactive product features and predictive services to reduce product downtimes. Hexagon Geosystems' technology has a different function. It guides Caterpillar's equipment do its job. And through the collection and analysis of data, it also helps connect Caterpillar's equipment to other entities and objects at the construction site to better coordinate their work. These different activities place Caterpillar in the production ecosystems space, while Hexagon Geosystems is in the consumption ecosystems space of the construction equipment business.

Should Caterpillar consider Hexagon a competitor? Yes, if Caterpillar perceives its market as transcending prevailing product sales into data-driven services, if it considers its business scope to go beyond its prevailing industry boundaries into digital ecosystems, and if it plans to expand its strategic scope from its production ecosystems into its consumption ecosystems. Under these circumstances, Hexagon is a digital competitor, competing for a share of Caterpillar's potential data-driven services revenues. Although Hexagon lacks comparable products, it competes for business with data that Caterpillar also has access to.

As of today, Caterpillar, along with its legacy product rivals such as Komatsu and Volvo, has chosen to stay within the realms of its production ecosystems. Hexagon, along with a few other similar players in the digital topography, telematics, and GPS space, such as Trimble and Topcon, has established itself in the corresponding consumption ecosystems space. Key digital competitors have thus opted for a different emphasis on production and consumption ecosystems. Yet they have arrived at a competitive equilibrium because they each face *symmetric ecosystem barriers*.

What Are Ecosystem Barriers? Ecosystem barriers are the difficulties a firm faces when moving from production to consumption ecosystems and vice versa. Let's consider the ecosystems barriers that Hexagon faces. Hexagon does not have the know-how or the competencies to compete with Caterpillar in the manufacturing and sales of construction equipment. It is a data- and software-driven technology company, not a product company. Moving into the production ecosystems space of this business with its own products is understandably hard. It would require building a strong value chain network with foundational strengths in product R&D, product design, large-scale manufacturing, vast dealer networks, and after-sales service—then turning that network into a vibrant production ecosystem.

Moreover, Hexagon's customers—contractors who own and commission construction equipment to execute a project—see value when Hexagon's digital plans to conduct a job can be uploaded to any machine. Pietzsch, the Hexagon executive who also spent twenty-three years at Caterpillar and was one of the key people leading its digital transformation efforts, describes his new company's philosophy: "Most of our customers own a mix of Caterpillar, Komatsu, Volvo and other such equipment. We like to take a neutral approach, emphasizing that our software is compatible with all kinds of equipment." Moving into the production ecosystems space would dilute Hexagon's neutrality. Hexagon lacks the right incentives to enter Caterpillar's production ecosystems space.

Caterpillar too faces ecosystems barriers in moving from its production to consumption ecosystems space. Caterpillar see itself primarily as a product company. It is built around manufacturing scale. Its efficient sales and servicing processes, honed over several decades, are its core competencies. Generating comparable efficiencies and scale in data-driven services is a difficult step. It is not that Caterpillar did not consider entering its consumption ecosystems space. The company has a partnership with Trimble, a competitor with Hexagon in its consumption ecosystems space. Caterpillar could potentially harness Trimble's capabilities and use this partnership to develop a full tethered digital platform and make an emphatic entry into its consumption ecosystems space. It could potentially offer an array of new services coordinating construction work through data sharing among other project participants. It has chosen not to do so. Caterpillar has opted to stay away from its consumption ecosystems and instead develop its strengths within its production ecosystems.

Such a reluctance on Caterpillar's part can also be inferred from its changing strategic vision after Jim Umpleby, Caterpillar's current CEO, replaced Doug Oberhelman. Under Umpleby's leadership, Caterpillar has invested significant resources in retrofitting a million pieces of the Caterpillar equipment operating on various construction sites with sensors and telematics. This is in addition to continuing the practice, started by Oberhelman, of ensuring that all new machines from Caterpillar factories are connected. Data from the field on machine usage and wear and tear inform Caterpillar, among other things, which clients need new equipment or which clients need more service. Caterpillar uses these data to better allocate its sales and service resources and improve its operational efficiencies. In other words, Umpleby's chosen strategy further emphasizes harnessing the value of data from Caterpillar's production ecosystems. The low probabilities of an attack from Caterpillar's consumption ecosystems space (such as from Hexagon) further skews Caterpillar's risk-reward trade-off perceptions in favor of staying within its production ecosystems. The rewards for expanding into its consumption ecosystems, in management's view (as of now), simply do not justify its risks.

Because both Hexagon and Caterpillar face barriers to moving from one ecosystem to another, they face symmetric ecosystem barriers. Hexagon faces barriers moving from consumption to production ecosystems; Caterpillar faces barriers moving from production to consumption ecosystems. Such symmetric ecosystem barriers preserve competitive equilibrium among these digital competitors.

Parallels with Industry-Based Competition: Symmetric Mobility Barriers
The piano makers Steinway and Yamaha have maintained their competitive equilibrium for over a hundred years. Just as Caterpillar and Hexagon differ in their ecosystem positions, Steinway and Yamaha differ in their market positions because of different value chain configurations. And just as Caterpillar and Hexagon face symmetric ecosystem barriers, Steinway and Yamaha face symmetric mobility barriers—or barriers preventing them from moving from one market position to another.[18]

Steinway's grand pianos are the envy of the company's rivals. They are also the top choice for performing pianists. More than 98 percent of concert pianists use Steinway grand pianos for their performances.[19] This is because each Steinway is built uniquely using a manufacturing process that has very little automation. It is because of a highly skilled labor pool that the company can craft such unique pianos. Experienced workers take years to share with less experienced co-workers their tacit insights into choosing and assembling material for high-quality performance. Each piano that comes off the factory floor has a skilled craftsman's stamp on it. Each Steinway grand piano has a unique sound, voice, and feel. Concert pianists are more likely to find among Steinway's offerings a piano that suits their style and turn into natural extensions of their creative minds, hands, and fingers. Their chosen Steinway piano enables them to produce their desired interpretations of a musical score through their performances better than any other piano.

Yamaha, by contrast, is a market and brand leader for upright pianos. Upright pianos have vertically strung strings that make them more compact and occupy less space. They are also much cheaper in price than the grand pianos. Because more people buy upright pianos than grand pianos, uprights are produced and sold in larger volumes. Yamaha also makes grand pianos and competes with Steinway. Unlike Steinway, however, Yamaha emphasizes automation in its operations. As a result, the pianos coming off its shop floors are more likely to be identical. In fact, conformity across all its products is Yamaha's signature quality.

Yamaha's workforce proficiency stems from the company's efficiency in repeating tasks, collective attention to detail in minimizing defects, and following a uniform work pattern that emphasizes conformity.

Steinway and Yamaha face symmetric mobility barriers. Steinway has honed its competencies in making hand-crafted pianos over several decades. It has also groomed several generations of its workforce, enabling them to gain the skills required to master piano making. And it has cultivated close relationships with concert pianists over decades. In other words, Steinway has built its strategic segment over a long period of time. For Yamaha to match Steinway's strengths and find a place in that market would be hard. Similarly, Yamaha has developed its mastery in automation over several decades. It enjoys large volumes of upright sales to reinforce automation's scale-based advantages. Steinway has neither the resources nor the sales volume to generate any scale advantages and move into Yamaha's market position. Both rivals thus maintain their market positions to achieve competitive equilibrium in this industry.

Today, the construction business has attracted different digital competitors in its production and consumption ecosystems. They remain, however, in competitive equilibrium. None has the strengths to overcome its respective ecosystem barriers. Figure 7.2 depicts competitive equilibrium through symmetric ecosystem barriers.

Such an equilibrium may not last, however, when ecosystems barriers are asymmetric and do not hold back digital competitors.

Pattern 3: Digital Disruption through Asymmetric Ecosystem Barriers
Symmetric ecosystem barriers present equivalent hurdles to digital competitors in moving across production and consumption ecosystems. But ecosystem barriers can also be asymmetric. Let's return to the Alibaba and Tencent example that opened this chapter to understand how asymmetric ecosystem barriers influence digital competition.

Alibaba and Tencent have five key interrelated components driving their digital platforms: search, e-commerce, payment services, social networking, and entertainment.[20] Collectively, through these

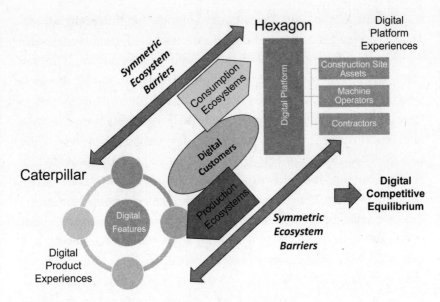

Figure 7.2
Competitive equilibrium through asymmetric production and consumption ecosystems.

components, Alibaba and Tencent extract treasure troves of interactive data about their customers' interests and needs as these consumers use their services. Much of the data is related to these customers' spending needs and activities.

Let's say a person is looking for a car and is seeking recommendations. She is likely to use the search or chat services of one of these digital platforms. This gives Alibaba and Tencent an early signal that this person may need an auto loan. Their e-commerce and payment services platforms add other insights into this person's spending habits, borrowing power, and creditworthiness. Through a history of interactions on their digital platforms, Alibaba and Tencent have precise insights into the needs of hundreds of millions of customers. They know where their customers live, what kind of car they are likely to want, and the auto dealers who could offer them their preferred car at the right price. The same pattern is true for potential home loans, college loans, appliance purchases, and short-term loans for vacations.

For SMEs, Alibaba and Tencent offer, among other things, digital payment processing services and digital storefronts (on their e-commerce platforms), along with digital marketing and logistics services. Through these services the digital titans get similar data on a small business operator's working capital requirements and creditworthiness, just as they do for individual consumers from their digital platforms. Alibaba and Tencent aggressively leverage their data's ability to provide early signals of loan requirements. The data they acquire also provide reliable assessments of creditworthiness so that they can offer competitive and timely loans. Only 1 percent of their loans are nonperforming.[21] Legacy banks, on the other hand, get to know the loan requirements of consumers and SMEs only when they apply for loans. Legacy banks' data processing on a customer's creditworthiness begins only after the loan application has been made and usually after significant paperwork has been gone through. The process not only greatly delays their loan decisions but also generates substantial aggravation for their customers.

Following their success with loans, Alibaba and Tencent soon entered the deposits business. This move further strengthened their loans business: not only did added deposits provide more cash in hand to lend but banking regulations also allowed them to lend multiple times the deposits they had in reserve. In addition, Alibaba and Tencent leveraged their presence in loans to make their deposits business more attractive. Customers using Alibaba and Tencent for most of their day-to-day needs saw an intrinsic convenience in also parking their money deposits with them. Customers spending 80 percent of their money in Alibaba's ecosystem and also making deposits with the company get faster loans through Alibaba. This is because Alibaba uses insights drawn from its customers' transactions in its loans business for faster digital loan processing, using less documentation, and with competitive rates calculated by using smart algorithms. With greater participation in Alibaba and Tencent's digital ecosystems, customers enjoy more data-driven benefits in both loans and deposits.

Alibaba and Tencent have access to data on how consumers use money. Through their platforms offering search, e-commerce, payment services, chat, social networking, and entertainment services, they extract troves of data concerning the consumption of money. Any customer using these services automatically informs the platform owners what he is searching for, what he intends to purchase, and what advice he seeks from friends on the purchase. Alibaba and Tencent thus are at the hub of the banking businesses' consumption ecosystems.

Legacy banks in China, by contrast, are organized primarily around attracting deposits, delivering loans, and dispensing cash. Their business models are anchored on production ecosystems entailing a variety of activities related to managing deposits and loans through their branch offices. Because of their exclusive focus on production ecosystems, they lack the data and the visibility to detect their customers' loan requirements or to know in detail how any of the loans they disburse get consumed. This made legacy banks vulnerable to attacks from Alibaba and Tencent, which could leverage their strong presence in the banks' consumption ecosystems.

In addition, Alibaba and Tencent need not be concerned about ecosystem barriers such as Hexagon faced in its relationship with Caterpillar. The Chinese digital titans could move from their initial presence in the consumption ecosystems of banks to their production ecosystems. After first establishing their strengths in the loans business through data, they quickly expanded into the deposits business. They attracted several small fintechs (firms that operate digital banking processes) as suppliers to their platforms. Such fintechs, contracted by Alibaba and Tencent, execute the back-end production ecosystem processes by digitally managing deposits and loan processing. Legacy banks could neither isolate themselves from these attacks nor match Alibaba and Tencent with equivalent data-derived strengths. This is an important facet of competitive dynamics in digital ecosystems: a competitor can first entrench itself in a legacy firm's consumption ecosystem, then later launch an attack in the legacy firm's production ecosystem. Such a move represents a potent disruptive threat from new digital competitors.

Parallels with Industry-Based Competition: Asymmetric Mobility Barriers
Legacy firms can also expect disruptive threats from digital competitors

that directly attack their production ecosystems. Ever since the arrival of the internet, several fintechs, for example have tried to disrupt legacy banks with digital deposits and loan processing. Such disruptive threats have parallels with industrial competition when incumbents find their established market positions built through their value chains under attack. These attacks are disruptive because legacy firms' prevailing mobility barriers prove to be inadequate defenses. The case of Xerox and Canon is illustrative.

Xerox dominated the photocopier industry until the early 1980s. Xerox established its dominance through patented technologies, branding, formidable after-sales service networks, and strong relationships with large corporate customers. In the early 1980s, however, Japanese companies, most notably Canon, entered the market with small copiers. By then Xerox's patents had expired, which these competitors used as an opportunity to enter the market. They targeted small corporations, such as dentists' or lawyers' offices, that did not need large copiers. Being smaller, they were also more attractively priced than Xerox's large copiers. Furthermore, their products came equipped with basic requisite spare parts and simple instructions enabling their customers to take care of most service problems themselves when needed. This feature eliminated the need for large networks of service centers. All in all, the newcomers found ways to sidestep Xerox's strategic fortress. And they quickly gained traction to significantly expand the copier market and emerge as strong rivals.

Xerox found itself cornered. Its core customers—large corporations—kept asking for large, faster copiers to satisfy large copy volume needs. Yet Canon and other Japanese companies were becoming stronger in the small copier market, which kept growing in size. Staying with its core customers meant Xerox would have to ignore a larger and growing market. Catering to the new market, on the other hand, would have required major reconfigurations of their prevailing value chain strengths. Clayton Christensen's work on disruptive technology characterizes this scenario as an innovator's dilemma.[22] Incumbents in situations similar to those Xerox faced are confronted with comparably tough choices. Staying the course with its core customers could mean Xerox hanging on to a shrinking market. Changing course and addressing the new, larger market, on the other hand, would have required making risky and difficult changes to the company's prevailing practices. In other words, Xerox faced asymmetric mobility barriers. Canon could attack Xerox's established market position. But Xerox could not adequately reciprocate by attacking Canon's new market position.

Why was it hard for Xerox to respond to Canon's competitive attack with small copiers? It is not that Xerox did not understand or know how to make small copiers. The underlying technologies behind large and small copiers are not that different. The critical differences lay in the processes required to produce and sell them—that is, their value chains. Competing with small copiers required Xerox to reconfigure its product development processes, manufacturing, and assembly lines. It also required Xerox to reconfigure how its sales staff catered to its customers because large and small corporations demand different sales approaches. In other words, it required reconfiguring their established value chains. Doing so is not impossible. But it is difficult.

It is difficult because legacy processes and routines in large organizations get ossified over time. Employees get trained in specific ways and get used to prevailing workflows; communication channels among employees and customers get ingrained; and power structures that defend prevailing technologies and processes get established. Organizations consequently get wired to resist any changes to previously ordained rules, particularly when the past has brought them success. Changes that may appear straightforward on paper become arduous to execute in practice.

Rebecca Henderson and Kim Clark describe innovations (such as of small copiers) as architectural innovations.[23] These innovations do not radically change prevailing product technologies; instead, they rearrange how various components of a product are interlinked. The innovations bring about architectural changes in products. Small copiers share the same underlying technology with large copiers but have redesigned components and rearranged interlinkages. Such innovations require incumbents to reconfigure their value chains in order to respond with similar architectural changes in their products. This is something large incumbent corporations find hard to do. The innovation disrupts them.

Most competitive attacks do not require firms to reconfigure their value chains. If they do, though, disruption is a likely outcome. It took several years for Xerox to respond to and recover from the small copier onslaught. Other firms are not that fortunate. Firms like Digital Equipment Corporation, an erstwhile leader in mainframe and minicomputers, never recovered from the competitive impact of desktops in the 1990s. Rigidities in DEC's value chains led to the company's demise.

In the digital world, comparable rigidities manifest when legacy firms fail to change their business processes to elevate their value chain networks into production ecosystems. Legacy firms, in other words, may more likely see parallels in their industrial and digital world disruptive competitive dynamics in their production ecosystems. The dynamics of disruptive competition in their consumption ecosystems, however, are likely to be different and unfamiliar.

Consumption Ecosystems Pose New Kinds of Competitive Threats   Attacks from consumption ecosystems pose a different kind of disruptive threat. As the concept of consumption ecosystems is still new to many legacy businesses, their leaders may not notice new digital competitors establishing a presence in that space. They may not take note as these new digital competitors build asymmetric strengths in consumption ecosystems that allow them subsequently to launch attacks on legacy businesses' production ecosystems. Such attacks can detach or weaken an incumbent's links to its customers. They can overwhelm an incumbent by appealing to its customers with smarter, more prolific, and more personalized services that take advantage of timely and superior data. They can also commoditize the incumbent's legacy offerings by shifting value from products to consumption-based services.

Kodak, an erstwhile legend in cameras, filed for bankruptcy in 2012 and has for all practical purposes exited the camera business.[24]

Its demise can be attributed to powerful new digital competitors rising from its consumption ecosystems that control how pictures are viewed (on screens) and shared (through apps such as Instagram). Players such as Apple, Google, and Facebook dominate this consumption ecosystems space. They have built powerful asymmetric ecosystem barriers, relegating cameras to components in smartphones. Kodak does not have a role even as a supplier to smartphone manufacturers today.

The introduction to this book highlighted similar commoditization threats to legacy automakers with the potential onset of driverless cars. If customers shift their preference from buying cars to purchasing subscription services on car ride platforms, the advantage shifts to those digital competitors that dominate the consumption ecosystems of cars. Such competitors—potentially Google, Apple, or Uber—may have a better understanding of how customers use cars, while legacy automakers know how to produce cars. Google, Apple, and Uber are formidable digital competitors. They can garner data on customer needs for car rides from consumer profiles gleaned from several of their platform interfaces, not just from the smart cars they offer on their platform for rides. Their modus operandi would be similar to Alibaba's and Tencent's with banks. Alibaba and Tencent can collect far more data on the consumption of money from their multifaceted platforms than legacy banks can collect through their individual banking apps. With similar superiority in data acquisition, Google, Apple, or Uber may be better able to understand user requirements. They may enjoy an edge in offering superior digital experiences during rides. Users may consequently care less about what brand of car comes to pick them up than which platform gives them a superior digital experience. In this scenario, cars as products run the risk of being commoditized. Legacy firms must be alert to this kind of competitive threat from digital competitors with asymmetric strengths that allow them to overcome ecosystem barriers. Figure 7.3 depicts digital competitive disruption because of asymmetric ecosystem barriers.

Table 7.1 summarizes the overarching distinctions between legacy and digital competitors.

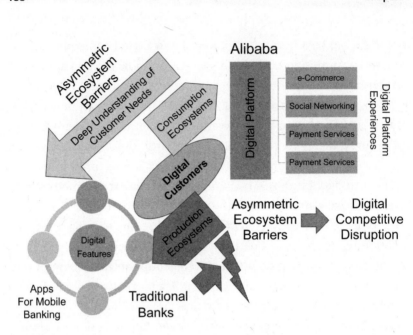

Figure 7.3

Competitive distribution through asymmetric ecosystem barriers.

Table 7.1

Difference between digital and legacy competitors

Competition Attribute	Digital Competitors	Legacy Competitors
Market goal	Build data services market share	Build product market share
Basis of competition	Similar data	Similar products
Competitive thrust	Data-driven service features; digital experiences	Product features
Competitive turf	Digital ecosystems	Industry
Competitive resources	Network effects from production and consumption ecosystems	Scale from value chains
Drivers of competitive equilibrium	Ecosystem parity; ecosystem barriers	Value chain parity; mobility barriers
Drivers of competitive disruption	Asymmetric ecosystem barriers; inability to defend competitive attacks within or from production and consumption ecosystems	Asymmetric mobility barriers; inability to reconfigure value chains in response to innovations or new entrants

A Framework to Compete with Digital Competitors

The three scenarios provided above—consumer goods such as electric toothbrushes, construction equipment, and banking—illustrate competitive dynamics in digital ecosystems and the kinds of moves legacy firms can expect from digital competitors. They also help us compare and contrast prevailing industry competitive dynamics with those of digital ecosystems. The three examples adduced do not necessarily capture all the nuances of digital ecosystem competition. They do draw attention to some new and salient concepts. To recap, these salient concepts are *ecosystems parity* (when digital competitors have symmetric ecosystems and ecosystem strengths), *symmetric ecosystem barriers* (when digital competitors entrenched in production ecosystems find it hard to move into consumption ecosystems, and vice versa), and *asymmetric ecosystem barriers* (when one set of digital competitors faces ecosystem barriers and the other set does not). Using these concepts, legacy firms can find appropriate approaches to reckon with their digital competitors. Figure 7.4 represents such a framework.

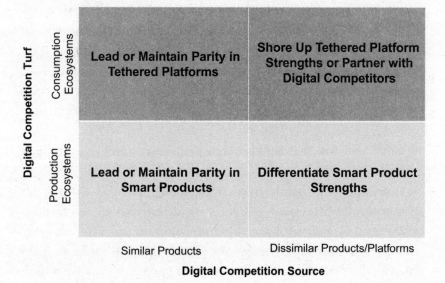

Figure 7.4
A framework for confronting digital competitors.

Legacy firms face likely confrontations from two kinds of digital competitors: those that compete with smart versions of similar products and those that compete with different smart products or digital platforms. P&G's key digital competitors, Colgate and Philips, compete with similar smart products. The legacy banks in China, by contrast, confront digital competitors—Alibaba and Tencent—that operate as e-commerce and social networking platforms, not as banks. Caterpillar not only faces digital competitors with similar smart products (such as Komatsu) but also with software and telematics companies (such as Hexagon).

Legacy firms can also expect their digital competitors to compete on different turfs. Digital competitors can make their presence felt in an incumbent's production ecosystems (Colgate or Philips for Oral-B) and/or in their consumption ecosystems (Alibaba and Tencent for legacy Chinese banks). The framework highlights four broad competitive situations based on these factors. These situations help legacy firms assess when and how to establish leadership or maintain competitive equilibrium. They also help firms become aware of likely digital disruption.

Lead or maintain parity in smart products.   The lower left-hand quadrant of this framework represents the situation in which an incumbent faces digital competitors offering similar smart products and the competition occurs within their production ecosystems. In the example of smart toothbrushes, the digital competitors Oral-B faces are the company's familiar product rivals. In addition, currently production ecosystems represent their competitive turf. To lead in such a situation, an incumbent like Oral-B can exploit first-mover advantages through network effects. This requires aggressively courting digital customers (as highlighted in chapter 6). Gaining a bigger market share yields more customer data, making Oral-B's algorithms smarter and its data-driven features more intricate. A brand with more users consequently attracts even more users because the product features get smarter. To prevent Oral-B from running away with the market, Sonicare and Hum must react. To remain relevant, they must maintain parity with Oral-B in their production ecosystems strengths. This means being equally aggressive in attracting digital customers and matching every smart product feature that Oral-B introduces. This appears to be their modus operandi as of now.

Lead or maintain parity in tethered platforms.   The upper left quadrant of the framework represents competition in the consumption ecosystems space from familiar product rivals. Continuing with the example of smart toothbrushes, for Oral-B to take a lead on this turf requires the company to move first with a tethered digital platform. It must take the lead in connecting its digital customers to dentists or dental insurance companies. Here too, Oral-B can exploit first-mover advantages by fortifying its platform's network effects (through acquiring more data from more digital customers, dentists, and insurance companies). To remain relevant, Sonicare and Hum must match Oral-B with their own equivalent tethered platform and develop equivalent network effects. They must maintain parity in their consumption ecosystems.

Differentiate smart product strengths.   Legacy firms may also confront new digital competitors that do not offer products similar to theirs yet compete in their production ecosystems space. The lower right-hand quadrant represents this context. Most commonly, such digital competitors are software firms that retrofit sensors on incumbents' products. These digital competitors bypass the need to produce and sell products themselves, yet they have access to similar data. Hexagon, for instance, can retrofit sensors on Caterpillar's machines to compete with equivalent predictive maintenance services. Caterpillar's best option in this circumstance is to differentiate itself through its own smart products' strengths. After all, the company knows its product better than anyone else; it should exploit this fact for greater credibility in its products' data-driven services. In other words, Caterpillar must defend its production ecosystems space by shoring up its ecosystem barriers. It can do so by harnessing its value chain strengths for stronger production ecosystems. Caterpillar can do so, for example, by leveraging a superior understanding of product engineering to interpret data from its machines better and develop better data-driven interactive features. The company can also more effectively align new data-driven predictive services for reducing machine downtimes with its legacy capabilities of managing spare parts availability and product maintenance crews. Chapter 8, on digital capabilities, elaborates further on this point.

Shore up tethered platform strengths. Finally, the top right quadrant represents the situation in which legacy firms confront new digital competitors in their consumption ecosystems. Caterpillar encountering Hexagon is one example; Nike confronting Fitbit and Apple Watch is another. This scenario would occur if Fitbit and Apple entered Nike's consumption ecosystems space, such as by connecting communities of runners or athletes with trainers through the respective companies' versions of tethered digital platforms. Fitbit and Apple could then compete with Nike by offering similar platform services without having to produce and sell shoes.

A legacy firm that finds itself in this quadrant has many difficult choices to make. Consumption ecosystems are an unfamiliar competitive turf for most legacy firms. New digital competitors in this space can pose significant threats, yet it is hard to accurately predict their competitive impact. Much depends on the strengths of their ecosystem barriers and the relative powers of digital customers to transcend those barriers. The challenge to legacy firms is to weigh the risk of venturing into an unfamiliar consumption ecosystems space against the risk posed by their digital competitors seeking to commoditize their products. Added to this mix are legacy firms' assessments of the risks and rewards of expanding into their consumption ecosystems space. This topic is discussed further in chapter 10 when we sum up various digital competitive strategy options.

Based on such assessments, one option for a legacy firm is to compete head-to-head by developing and strengthening the strengths of its own tethered platforms. Banks developing apps to get a window into their consumers' spending habits is an example. Alternatively, legacy firms can avoid a direct head-to-head competition by partnering with their new digital competitors in their consumption ecosystems space. Caterpillar's partnership with Trimble is one such example. Either way, legacy firms are better off not ignoring digital competitors in their consumption ecosystems space. Not taking notice of such digital competitors increases the odds of digital disruption.

Digital Competitor Intelligence

Finally, to be on top of digital competition, firms must develop new competitor intelligence. Three questions shape this effort. Who are our likely digital competitors? In which ecosystem will we face them? What is their degree of threat? Let's discuss each of them.

Likely Digital Competitors: Familiar Industry Rivals or New Rivals?

Digital competitors are likely to be familiar industry rivals if sensor and IoT data generation is feasible only from value chain assets, and not from products. Think of the oil and gas business, where embedding sensors on products is impractical. This business, however, has billions of dollars' worth of assets that generate useful data. In oil exploration alone, firms can save up to 50 to 60 percent of their operational costs using modern digital tools such as AI to improve the likelihood of finding reserves (see chapter 10 for more details on the oil and gas business). In such scenarios, when all industry rivals have similar incentives to harness the power of data from their assets, all turn into digital competitors. Firms who do not have access to similar assets are unlikely to emerge as digital competitors.

Digital competitors are also likely to be familiar industry rivals if the data that drives competition is unique to a product category. Oral-B or Sonicare may find their digital competitors restricted to toothbrush makers as data on dental hygene is hard to come by without selling toothbrushes directly to customers.

On the other hand, firms will confront new and unfamiliar rivals if the data they acquire from their products are not unique to their product category. Data on motion that sensor-equipped light bulbs use to enter the security business (by sensing motion in homes supposed to be empty, for example) is available to a host of other products in a home, including camera providers or devices such as Alexa. Digital competitors in such a situation will be an assortment of companies who have access to the same data but do not compete with similar products. Such new digital competitors can also emerge if products can be retrofitted with sensors. Hilti Corporation, an established tool manufacturer, offers data-driven services that help contractors locate appropriate tools for a job in time and avoid work delays. New digital competitors who do not manufacture the tools that Hilti does now offer similar services through tool tracking apps.

Locus of Digital Competition: Production or Consumption Ecosystems?

Production ecosystems become key arenas for competitive battles wherein firms find opportunities to improve operational efficiencies using modern technologies or find ways to offer new data-driven services. In the oil and gas business, Exxon Mobil, Chevron, and British Petroleum, among others, are spending millions to enrich their production ecosystems. They compete for superior efficiencies in oil exploration, better maintenance of their pipelines, and improved safety in their refineries. GE, Pratt and Whitney, and Rolls Royce—key rivals in the jet engine business—have all expanded their competitive scope from their traditionally manufactured products to data-driven services such as predictive maintenance.

Consumption ecosystems become hot arenas for digital competition when there are a growing number of digital complements for a firm's products. Consider the recent advent of 5G technology in telecommunication. 5G cellular networks can transfer large volumes of data at high speeds and with great reliability. This technology hence is well suited for IoT applications where assets share large amounts of data, such as in smart cities or in managing fleets of connected vehicles. Such applications also open new and vibrant consumption ecosystems for telecom providers. Instead of restricting their business models to selling digital connectivity, they can also facilitate and participate in the consumption of digital connectivity. Competition naturally is shifting to this emerging space. Verizon has spent billions in recent acquisitions that include Sensity Systems, which offers IoT platforms for smart city services, and Fleetmatics, which offers fleet management and mobile workforce solutions. Similarly, AT&T has formed a partnership with Synchronos to offer IoT platform services that help office buildings conserve energy. See chapter 10 for more detail on the implications of 5G.

Degree of Threat: Routine or Disruptive?

A critical element of competitive intelligence entails gauging the severity of new competitive threats. Competition cannot be wished away. But they can often be controlled and managed as part of routine business dealings. Paying attention to a firm's ecosystem barriers is an essential requirement to stay on top of managing ongoing digital competitive dynamics. Wherever possible, firms must try to maintain ecosystem parity. They must also keep a close eye on the strength of their ecosystem barriers and invest to shore them up adequately and make them formidable.

Digital competitors may even outdo legacy competitors. Key reasons include the failure of legacy firms to develop adequate ecosystem parity. Peloton, in the stationary bike business, enjoys a sizeable price premium over its legacy competitors by taking the lead in developing its consumption ecosystems, consisting of vibrant communities of Peloton users and trainers. Many of its legacy rivals have thus far opted to continue with their prevailing value chain–based business models. Digital competition can also be disruptive if ecosystem barriers are asymmetric, as we saw with the example of Chinese banks. Also in such circumstances, building adequate ecosystem barriers may not be easy.

Table 7.2 summarizes the discussion on digital competitor intelligence.

Table 7.2

Digital Competitor Intelligence

Who are my digital competitors likely to be?		What is the locus of digital competition?		What is their degree of threat?	
Familiar Industry Rivals	New Competitors	From Production Ecosystems	From Consumption Ecosystems	Low	High
Conditions		*Circumstances*		*Causes*	
• Sensor/IoT data possible only from value chain assets	• Sensor data not unique to a product category	• Rising opportunities for modern technologies to improve operational efficiencies or offer data driven services	• Growing number of digital complements for products	• Ecosystem parity effectively developed	• Ecosystem parity not effectively developed
• Equal incentives for industry rivals to improve asset utilization	• Products able to be retrofitted with sensors			• Ecosystem barriers are formidable	• Ecosystem barriers are difficult to build
• Sensor data unique to a product category					

Summary Thoughts on Digital Competitors

As legacy firms expand their strategic scope from industries to digital ecosystems, they will encounter digital competitors. Some may be their old industry rivals confronting them with symmetric digital strengths. Others may be unfamiliar rivals competing with asymmetric digital strengths and posing unfamiliar threats. The challenges from old and new rivals together will present competitive dynamics that are different from what legacy firms are accustomed to. Competition based on value chain configurations expands into competition based on production and consumption ecosystem strengths that each organization brings.

Legacy firms must understand these new competitive dynamics. At the same time, they must not neglect their legacy strengths in industry competition. After all, their digital ecosystems are built on industry networks. The new strengths they develop to compete in digital ecosystems will depend on their old strengths built when they competed in legacy industries. Even as digital competitors, they must continue drawing on their competitive strengths forged through long-standing industry rivalry. These prevailing strengths empower them to maintain ecosystem parity when confronting digital competitors that were erstwhile legacy rivals. Their old strengths enable them to fortify ecosystem barriers when confronting new digital competitors.

While their old strengths are relevant, legacy firms will also need new strengths. Competing successfully in digital ecosystems requires building new digital capabilities. Chapter 8 discusses what they are and how to build them.

8 Digital Capabilities

A firm's capabilities are an integral element of competitive strategy. They fuel a firm's strategic engine. They make it possible for a firm to achieve its strategic objectives. They also differentiate winners from losers in the marketplace. Digital capabilities likewise are an important aspect of a firm's digital competitive strategy. They make it possible for a firm to effectively unlock the value of data. They determine winners and losers in competitive battles fought through data. This chapter is about digital capabilities: what they are and how legacy firms can build them.

Capabilities, unlike markets, customers, and competitors, are not easy to observe. They are hidden inside the firm. Capability outcomes may be noticeable, but capabilities themselves are hard to spot. An analysis of car breakdowns categorized by manufacturer, for example, may reveal Toyota's superior product reliability capability vis-à-vis its competitors'. But the myriad underlying factors that contribute to that outcome are much harder to observe. Capabilities are tacit. You know they exist, but you cannot directly see them. Their particulars are elusive.

Capabilities stem from a complex combination of resources and processes within firms. They generate value as firms channel their resources and processes toward specific strategic objectives. To continue with the Toyota example, its resources include its assets, operational facilities, R&D know-how, a vast network of experienced suppliers, a knowledgeable workforce, and strong financial reserves. Its processes encompass a myriad of functional and cross-functional activities that effectively utilize its resources toward achieving specific strategic objectives, such as product reliability.

Toyota's key processes for product reliability are shaped by principles such as total quality management (TQM),[1] lean manufacturing,[2] and Six Sigma.[3] TQM helps focus and align all functional activities, including managing supply chains, operations, product design, and customer service, toward the goal of achieving customer satisfaction. Lean manufacturing and Six Sigma are similar cross-functional efforts designed to align a firm's processes to ensure quality. The strength of Toyota's resources, in tandem with such cross-functional alignment of its processes, gives Toyota its competitive edge in product reliability. Many of Toyota's resources, such as its plants, materials, and other assets, may be visible on inspection or inferred from the company's balance sheets. The processes by which those resources are mixed and matched to produce specific capabilities such as product reliability are not.

Digital capabilities, like legacy capabilities, stem from a combination of a firm's resources and processes. Yet digital capabilities differ from the capabilities most legacy firms are familiar with. They are oriented toward achieving different kinds of strategic objectives. Digital capabilities primarily augment the value of data, while legacy capabilities boost the competitive impact of products. For that reason, digital capabilities entail the use of different kinds of resources. They necessitate different kinds of processes. And they generate new kinds of value.

Like legacy capabilities, digital capabilities are difficult to observe. Yet one can infer what they are by comparing them with the more familiar legacy capabilities. By comparing and appreciating their differences, firms are better able to assess how to extend their legacy capabilities into new digital ones. This chapter elaborates on how digital capabilities differ from legacy capabilities. It then uses these distinctions to highlight how legacy firms can expand their legacy capabilities into new digital capabilities.

Understanding Digital Capabilities

Primarily, legacy capabilities help firms improve their competitiveness within their industries. Digital capabilities, on the other hand, enhance

Table 8.1
Key differences between legacy and digital capabilities

Attributes	Legacy Capabilities	Digital Capabilities
Strategic objectives	Enhance product strengths	Enhance data strengths
Resources	Value chain resources	Digital ecosystem resources
Processes	Functional and cross-functional value Chain workflows	Data sharing and integrating API networks
Strategic scope	Corporate scope/Degree of diversification	Breadth of data-driven services

a legacy firm's competitiveness within its digital ecosystems. Four key attributes show the differences and similarities of digital and legacy capabilities. These attributes are strategic objectives, resources, processes, and strategic scope. Table 8.1 highlights the main differences of digital and legacy capabilities along these dimensions.

Let's discuss the importance of each attribute.

Strategic Objectives

Legacy capabilities are geared to maximize what a given firm's products can achieve in the markets in which it competes. They enhance product strengths, which become visible through such traits as product design, product quality, and product availability at a competitive cost. Essentially, capabilities enable legacy firms to produce and sell their products more effectively. Data too play a role, but to support the production and sales of products and value generation from products.

Digital capabilities focus on data. They expand the role of data from one that supports products to one that generates value in parallel with products. A key strategic objective of digital capabilities is to enhance data's strengths in ways that expand the value scope of data. Digital capabilities help legacy firms generate fresh avenues for revenue through data beyond what was traditionally possible through products alone.

Chapter 1 discussed how the digital titans expanded the role of data from one that enabled their early digital platforms to one that is now a core value-generating engine for them. The early role of data in Facebook's social network platform, for example, was to facilitate social interaction without the need for physical proximity. Digital social interaction was the primary intended function of the platform. Over time, this functionality helped Facebook advance its digital capabilities, enabling the company to generate deep insights into users and create powerful user profiles. And as these digital capabilities gained strength, the role of data in Facebook's business models also expanded. In this expanded role, data continued to improve the functioning of the social networking platform, Facebook's primary product, by attracting more users and building strong network effects. In addition, data opened new vistas for value creation, notably advertising. Facebook's data now generate billions of dollars of revenue through digital advertising. Facebook's digital capabilities, in other words, made data a revenue generator. Data went beyond something that initially just supported Facebook's primary product to becoming an equally (or more) important strategic asset.

Digital capabilities facilitate such a strategic shift from products to data for legacy companies, too. They allow a mattress maker like Sleep Number to mass customize its mattresses through smart algorithms and sensor data (as we saw in chapter 4). In doing so, data make Sleep Number's primary products, mattresses, stronger. Data drive Sleep Number's product features, such as the ability of mattress foams to adapt their shape to improve each individual's sleep experience. Digital capabilities enabled by data also expanded Sleep Number's business domain from mattresses to wellness assurance services, opening up new revenue-generating vistas beyond its legacy business of mattress sales.

Similarly, digital capabilities allow State Farm Insurance to track actual driving behaviors of individual customers. The insights garnered from these data enable State Farm to improve the accuracy of a key business practice, estimating individual auto insurance risks, and to customize policies to individual drivers. These digital capabilities also help State Farm influence individuals' driving behaviors through apps that alert drivers when they inadvertently exceed speed limits or drive through a red traffic signal. Such new features, based on real-time driving data, lower State Farm's overall costs of insurance claims by reducing accidents and thus improving policy profitability. These profitability improvements from new digital capabilities reduce risks and supplement what State Farm's legacy actuarial and policy underwriting processes do to predict risks.

New revenue-generating opportunities from data may not be immediately apparent to legacy firms as they begin developing their digital capabilities. Facebook, for instance, did not foresee the billions of dollars in revenue the company receives from digital advertising when it started a social networking platform. Facebook's success, however, exemplifies the untapped potential of data-driven capabilities. Every firm can benefit from extracting data's full value, even if not on a scale similar to Facebook's. Digital capabilities enable achieving such strategic goals.

Resources

Differences in their underlying strategic objectives direct legacy and digital capabilities to draw on different kinds of resources. Legacy capabilities are about enhancing product strengths; hence they draw on value chain resources. Value chain resources comprise all the units, assets, and entities entailed in producing and selling products. For manufacturing firms, they include materials and supply chains. They include a variety of assets that convert materials to products and facilitate sales, such as brands, distribution networks, and after-sales services. They include firms' products and customer bases, which can generate scale-based advantages in their operations. For service firms such as insurance companies, value chain resources include a diverse spread of policyholders, depth in actuarial and underwriting talent, a network of agents to sell policies, and policies that generate revenue streams. Whether part of manufacturing or service firms, all value chains need human resources to manage them. Their resources also include various IT systems embedded in the value chains and designed to support operations to make and sell their offerings.

Digital capabilities, on the other hand, are about enhancing data strengths. Therefore, they draw on digital ecosystem resources. Digital ecosystem resources comprise all the resources that contribute to building and using a legacy firm's production and consumption ecosystems. Production and consumption ecosystems differ in the kinds of resources they draw on. To delve deeper into the nature of their differences, it is useful to discuss two facets of each of these ecosystem resources: *infrastructural resources,* which enrich a legacy firm's production ecosystems and make its consumption ecosystems vibrant, and *data resources,* which production and consumption ecosystems generate, share, and amplify for value.

Production Ecosystem Infrastructural Resources

Production ecosystems, as elaborated in chapters 3 and 4, emerge from value chain networks. A firm's value chain resources also serve as foundational resources for the firm's production ecosystems infrastructure. More specifically, production ecosystem infrastructures emerge when firms' foundational value chain resources, such as their value chain entities, units, and assets, digitally connect to form a network that generates and receives data. In other words, prevailing value chains transform into production ecosystem infrastructures when digital technologies leverage value chains' innate capacities to enhance data connectivity.

Turning Existing Infrastructure into Digital Infrastructure   Such a transformation occurs in several ways. Primarily, it requires a widespread use of sensor-equipped and IoT-enabled entities, units, and assets across value chains. Retrofitting existing value chain assets with sensors and making them IoT-enabled is usually a first step. The example of Elemental Machines and the R&D labs it supplies (discussed in chapter 4) illustrates one such a step. Customary value chain assets within R&D labs, such as centrifuges, deep freezers, and spectrometers, transform into a production ecosystem infrastructure by becoming sensor- and IoT-enabled, and by becoming smart components of a connected network.

Adding New Digital Infrastructure Legacy firms can also replace their unconnected assets with new kinds of digital assets. New Balance, a Boston-based athletic shoe manufacturer, is experimenting with 3D printers that could potentially replace their traditional molds. Molds are scale-intensive assets used to produce shoe soles. They come in pre-specified standard sizes. Once a mold is created for a select shoe size (say, size 7), it can generate soles of that size in scale. A single mold typically needs to produce at least 2,000 soles a month to justify investments in its tooling. Established shoe companies such as New Balance produce much larger volumes than this minimum threshold.

3D printers, in contrast, mass-customize soles based on sensor data. Sensor data include scans of a user's actual foot size and foot contours, along with registration of body weight and walking gait. New Balance has installed such scanners in some of their select retail stores. "3D printers allow for a far more nuanced approach to sole design," says Mark Clinard, senior vice president of global footwear at New Balance. Rather than produce sole sizes in specific increments (such as sizes 7, 7.5, or 8) by using different molds, the same 3D printer can generate a fine-grained continuum of sizes depending on sensor data from any user. 3D printers even provide users with slightly different shoe sizes for the left and right foot. (Apparently many users have minor differences in their left and right feet sizes).

Smart Products and Digital Customers as Digital Infrastructure In addition to the smart assets that produce products, products themselves add to a legacy firm's production ecosystem infrastructure when they are sensor-equipped. So do the digital customers that these sensor-equipped products attract. Smart products and digital customers add to production ecosystem infrastructures by expanding firm capacity to generate data. Sleep Number's capacity to generate product-user interaction data increases with the number of smart mattresses the company sells and the digital customers it engages. Similarly, the greater the number of driver-safety apps that State Farm's customers use, the greater is State Farm's capacities to generate data from its customers. Smart products and digital customers are both part of Sleep Number's and State Farm's production ecosystem infrastructures. They help legacy firms offer more interactive product features.

Expanding IT Systems into New Digital Infrastructure   IT systems embedded within value chains also serve as important foundations for production ecosystem infrastructure. IT systems, such as the enterprise resource planning (ERP) systems highlighted in chapter 3, are usually designed to operate within circumscribed boundaries of data sources and recipients related to specific value chain activities. Consider the ERP system of Fender, a reputed guitar maker. The system may receive data (such as requests to deliver prescribed quantities of different guitar models) from the Guitar Center retail chain (a customer). The system then shares these data across specific various value chain entities, helping Fender automate select facets of its workflows. Guitar Center's order alerts Fender to prepare and supply requisite components, schedules production, notifies pertinent distribution centers to process delivery, generates requisite invoices, and reports payment receipts.

Such a system is a useful foundation for an expanded data integration infrastructure with new kinds of software, machine learning algorithms, and AI. It is important to expand traditional IT into such a new infrastructure because a firm can expect to encounter broader sources of data, emanating from a wider array of sensor- and IoT-enabled assets, as discussed earlier. In addition, firms must also prepare to handle an exponential increase in real-time data streams from their digital customers. Such data can potentially stream from millions of individual digital customers. Imagine all of Fender's guitars being sensor-equipped or all of StateFarm's customers using their driver safety apps. New data sources also include unstructured data, such as from social media. For instance, rock star Bruce Springsteen mentioning Fender's guitar[4] in a concert or in an interview can generate a spike in demand much before Guitar Center places its orders. Interpreting and acting on such data calls for new software, new algorithms, and AI engines—all of which are necessary elements of a firm's production ecosystem infrastructure.

Finally, just as human resources are needed to manage value chains, companies also need talented people to manage production ecosystems. Human resources are thus another important part of a firm's production ecosystem infrastructure. Managing production ecosystems requires people with specialized skills in software and data analytics. We will elaborate more on the new kind of human resources companies need when discussing how to build digital capabilities later in this chapter.

Production Ecosystem Data Resources

Production ecosystem infrastructures help legacy firms generate, share, and process a new kind of data. These data is both quantitatively and qualitatively different from the data traditionally used to support value chain operations. The new kind of data is also an important aspect of a firm's production ecosystem resources.

The data driving production ecosystem resources are quantitatively different from data used for legacy capabilities. This is simply because there is much more data, and the data come from many more sources. In addition, the data is qualitatively different because they are interactive rather than episodic. A message sent when a machine breaks down is an example of episodic data; the continuous monitoring of machines to predict breakdowns before they occur is an example of interactive data use. A sale reported when it occurs is an example of episodic data; real-time streaming of product-user exchanges is an example of interactive data generation. Interactive data also come from pinpointed sources, such as individual customers or individual machine components. As highlighted in chapter 1, using digital titans as examples, interactive data of this kind offer far more potential for value than do episodic data. Interactive data allow various entities (such as suppliers or dealers) and assets (such as machines or robots) to talk to one another in real time. Interactive data generate deep insights from tracking every individual asset or product-user interaction.

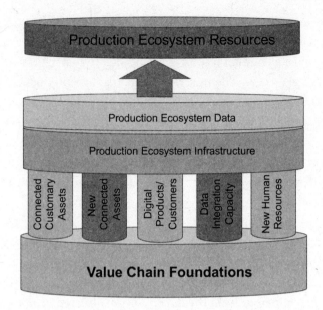

Figure 8.1
Production ecosystem resources.

Such data, in addition to the infrastructure that generates them, represent important ways in which production ecosystem resources differ from prevailing value chain resources. Figure 8.1 summarizes the discussion on production ecosystem resources. As the figure depicts, production ecosystem resources are built on the foundations of various legacy value chain assets, connected assets, and an infrastructure that can generate and share data across these connected assets, along with the data that are generated and shared.

Consumption Ecosystem Infrastructural Resources

Consumption ecosystems, as we know from chapters 3, 4 and 5, are built on complementor networks. Complementor networks are networks of third-party entities that complement a product and its sensor data. Complementors, unlike value chains, have not played any important part in legacy business models. A firm thus needs to look outside its value chains to find support for its consumption ecosystem infrastructure. This infrastructure takes shape when a firm extends its business scope from its value chains into a tethered digital platform. Tethered digital platforms, as discussed in chapter 5, are the primary means by which legacy firms compete in their consumption ecosystems. Tethered digital platforms thus embody a firm's consumption ecosystem infrastructure.

A combination of external and internal inputs contributes to consumption ecosystem infrastructures vis-à-vis a firm's tethered digital platforms. External inputs come from modern technologies that offer an environment of IoT-enabled entities and assets that a firm can connect to. They come from an army of developers who can help connect these entities and assets. Internal inputs include a firm's digital customers, new software assets, and human resources with new skills. Both external and internal inputs are necessary to build strong digital tethered platforms and thereby a robust consumption ecosystem infrastructure.

Oral-B, for instance, benefits from the ubiquity of sensors, proliferation of IoT-enabled assets, widespread acceptance of smartphone apps and the establishment of high speed 5G cellular networks, among others (see chapter 7). These external inputs can help Oral-B construct a tethered digital platform. These external forces can provide connectivity to entities such as dental offices (for dental health services) and insurance companies (for reduced premiums), making them eligible to become Oral-B's digital tethered platform users and offer new data-driven platform services. In addition, Oral-B can rely on a subset of over a million developers with skills to weave their external APIs and connect them to these dental offices' and insurance firms' apps or websites.

Apart from these external inputs, Oral-B also benefits from internal inputs in its efforts to construct a tethered digital platform. Digital customers are their most important internal contributors. Digital customers provide the base to attract other platform users. Oral-B needs digital customers to generate sensor data that can attract connected dental offices and insurance companies to its tethered digital platform. In addition, Oral-B also requires new and more advanced software and data processing capacities that are tailored to manage tethered digital platforms. To build such capacities, legacy firms may require new or additional investments over and above what they may choose to deploy for their production ecosystem infrastructures. And finally, new human resources with experience and skills in managing digital platforms are important internal inputs for consumption ecosystem infrastructures.

Consumption Ecosystem Data Resources
In addition to infrastructure, data play an important part as a consumption ecosystem resource, just as they did for production ecosystems. Here too, data that constitute a consumption ecosystem resource are different from the data that firms use to support their products with their legacy capabilities. Consumption ecosystem data, like production ecosystem data, are interactive rather than episodic. The data come from both a firm's digital customers and external entities that complement these data as platform users. Interactive data are essential to drive exchanges among users of a tethered digital platform. Interactive data generated while a customer is brushing his teeth, for example, when connected to dental offices can lead to better dental health care. The data provide insights into companies about the use of their products and customer behavior and enable them to offer new services to customers in return. Figure 8.2 depicts consumption ecosystem resources. These resources are a combination of various internal and external digital assets, digital platform infrastructure, and the data generated by the digital platform.

Processes

Just as differences in strategic objectives direct legacy and digital capabilities to draw on different kinds of resources, they also direct them to draw on different kinds of processes. The processes that legacy capabilities draw on are geared to enhance product strengths. They take shape in the form of functional and cross-functional workflow routines that manage various value chain activities and their interdependencies.

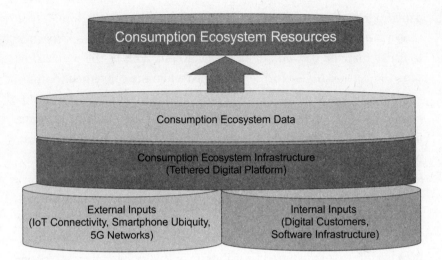

Figure 8.2
Consumption ecosystem resources.

Processes Driving Legacy Capabilities: Functional and Cross-Functional Routines

Functional workflow routines reflect established processes to manage specific functions. They are "routines" because once established, they are repeated many times. Salespeople making sales calls in a prescribed manner are an example of a sales function routine. Cross-functional workflow routines, on the other hand, are prescribed ways to interact across functions. They include practices such as cross-functional product development or customer service team meetings, along with other such customary procedures established to coordinate work across functions. An array of such functional and cross-functional workflow routines within a firm's value chain strengthen legacy capabilities to produce and sell products.

How Routines Drive Legacy Capabilities

Functional and cross-functional workflow routines contribute to legacy capabilities in many ways. Functional workflow routines strengthen functional skills. For example, medical representatives of a pharmaceutical company who periodically engage with physicians and hospitals in a methodical manner strengthen their sales function's skills. Similarly, a routine to vet suppliers and systematically follow scientific approaches to gauge material cost and quality strengthens skills in the purchasing function. Such skills are further amplified when the concerned routines are backed by rich resources. A pharmaceutical company's sales routines, for example, become more effective when supported by a strong brand, high-quality products, and a knowledgeable and motivated team of medical sales representatives. Purchase routines similarly gain strength from operational scale and large volumes of purchase.

Cross-functional routines manage interdependencies across functions and units within firms. They are needed because multiple functions have to come together to manage a firm's value chain. No function is an island. Toyota, referred to at the top of this chapter, needs to coordinate several company functions to deliver reliable products. Toyota achieves its capabilities at product reliability through several cross-functional routines guided by TQM principles that the company has honed over the years.

Cross-functional routines are more complex than functional routines. They are more difficult to establish and manage. Their cause and effects or links to capabilities are also harder to untangle. Strategy literature refers to this difficulty as "causal ambiguity."[5] It is easier to understand links between sales routines and sales capabilities, for example, than to understand the links between TQM routines and product reliability. Causal ambiguity also makes cross-functional routines difficult for rivals to imitate. This is because rivals find it hard to replicate processes they do not fully understand. Cross-functional routines thus not only can strengthen legacy capabilities, they can also help sustain a firm's competitive edge by deterring rivalry.[6]

Routines become stronger over time as firms can incrementally improve on them. Experience also helps strengthen established routines to reinforce prevailing capabilities. In chapter 7, we described how Steinway's capabilities to produce quality pianos improves over time. On the flip side, routines also engender rigidities. Functional and cross-functional routines, once established, are difficult to reconfigure. Such rigidities, as highlighted in chapter 7, are among the prime reasons why firms such as Xerox get disrupted. In fact, the problems associated with the innate rigidities of workflow routines have spawned a massive consulting practice industry anchored on principles such as process reengineering.[7] Process reengineering directs firms to keep evaluating their routines, remove unnecessary ones, reconfigure old ones, and add new ones, all to instill dynamism. Process reengineering, however, is not easy. It is not uncommon for firms to invest millions in their process engineering efforts with little certainty about the returns on those investments.

In sum, legacy capabilities draw on functional and cross-functional routines to manage value chain activities and their interdependencies. They channel disparate value chain resources to deliver better outcomes with respect to producing and selling products. This is in line with the core objectives of legacy capabilities, which are to enhance product strengths.

Processes Driving Digital Capabilities: API Networks

Digital capabilities, on the other hand, draw on processes that channel digital ecosystem resources in order to enhance data strengths. Such processes serve many purposes. Processes channeling production ecosystem resources can deliver improved operational efficiencies. They can also offer new data-driven product features, along with predictive services and innovative approaches for mass customization. Processes channeling consumption ecosystem resources generate new digital platform services. At the core of these processes are data-sharing and data-integration mechanisms made possible by a network of APIs, discussed at length in chapter 2. APIs, as we saw in that chapter, create conduits to connect various data resources through software. API networks thereby power the sharing and integration of data for stronger data outcomes.

Recall the various data-driven initiatives of Caterpillar, highlighted in chapter 4. Equipped with sensors and telematics, every Caterpillar machine is a data resource. These machines generate data on a variety of different operational aspects, such as idle time, fuel efficiency, the amount of dirt moved in a day, its location, and so on. Trimble, Caterpillar's JV partner referred to earlier, helps create an intricate API network for Caterpillar that connects data from each of Caterpillar's machines to a variety of different entities that use the data for different purposes. These entities include customers such as Bechtel, one of the largest engineering and construction companies in the world and owner of thousands of these machines operating worldwide on construction sites. They include around 165 Caterpillar dealers. And Caterpillar itself also receives these data in its various office locations. According to Robert Painter, president and CEO of Trimble, "In the non-consumer world, companies are looking to partner with someone who has the expertise in relevant technology areas and a deep vertical domain knowledge. That, along with an approach to include the entire ecosystem in the process, is what companies are looking for in their digital transformation journey."

Trimble's API network makes the right kind of data available to the right entity in the form that the entity desires. Bechtel may want operational data on its entire fleet. Dealers may want data on which customer's machine requires immediate replenishment of spare parts. Caterpillar may want these data to improve the design of its products, offer predictive maintenance services, or know which customers are likely to need more machines or more services. An API network thus allows Caterpillar to generate value in various ways. It can generate new revenues from customers who benefit from its data-enabled product features and services. It can also improve its own internal operational efficiencies.

The above is an example of how API networks channel production ecosystem resources for data-driven benefits. Chapter 2 described this kind of API network as internally focused and contributing to a legacy firm's intrafirm and supply chain interfaces. In addition, API networks can also channel consumption ecosystem resources for data-driven benefits. An API network that connects Whirlpool's refrigerators and ovens in customer homes with Yummly's recipe apps[8] helps Whirlpool offer its tethered digital platform services (discussed in chapter 5). This kind of API network is externally focused and contributes to a legacy firm's complementor interface. All in all, API networks, whether internal or externally oriented, reflect a blueprint for all the data-sharing and data-integration processes within a firm's production and consumption ecosystems.

Transparency of API Networks

Because API networks are codified through software and have visible blueprints, they make data-sharing and data-integration processes more transparent than cross-functional processes. They also make data integration easier than cross-functional integration. That's because cross-functional integration relies on laying down procedures and expecting people to follow them. Presumably, it is easier to direct software to follow routine instructions, compared to people. On the other hand, the transparency of API networks may also make it easier for competitors to replicate. Amazon's APIs on order fulfillment on their e-commerce platform, for example, can be replicated by others. What is harder to replicate is Amazon's repositories of data and other aspects of its formidable digital ecosystem infrastructure. Ultimately, legacy firms will have to rely on a combination of their digital resources and processes to build and sustain their uniqueness.

Flexibility of API Networks

Data-sharing and data-integration processes driven through API networks are also less rigid than functional and cross-functional routines. They can be reconfigured relatively easily through upgrades in software. In fact, APIs are routinely modified and changed through software upgrades to rearrange internal data flows. The ease of reconfiguring APIs is behind the success of companies such as Twilio, a maker of communications software. Twilio's APIs, highlighted in chapter 2, allow companies to configure their text, voice, and picture messaging capabilities in ways that their business needs dictate.[9] The fact that a wide array of companies, including Uber, Airbnb, Home Depot, and

Walmart, can configure Twilio's offering for their individual require-ments is evidence of the innate flexibility of APIs. API networks can link atomic aspects of various asset or process functionalities. They can be as fine-grained as their software allows them to be. They can create alternative architectures for linking various data sources. They can also reconfigure these architectures through software, making them a tool that generates exceptional flexibility in data-sharing and data-integration processes. For this, API networks have to blend in with leg-acy functional and cross-functional processes.

API Networks Inject Dynamism into Legacy Processes

The innate flexibility of APIs to reconfigure their networks can inject fresh dynamism into legacy processes. An example here is the new product development process for developing an "upper" for a shoe by an athletic shoe company. The upper goes on top of a shoe's sole. Devel-oping an upper requires a keen understanding of fashion trends and the ability to adapt designs to different consumer tastes. It involves cross-functional teams for integrating the different kinds of inputs required to arrive at a few design alternatives that can be used to build proto-types. The designers take inputs from sales and marketing on fashion trends; procurement and supply chain partners offer inputs about the possibility of getting requisite material in time and at a reasonable cost; in-house and offshore operations disclose the feasibility of manufactur-ing the item; finance helps with costing and revealing what kinds of budgets are realistic. The process may take four to five months.

Now let's consider how this legacy product development process changes when infused with API networks. Data on market trends come from several API feeds from companies specialized in tracking them. Some APIs provide data on what shoe colors and fashions are trend-ing in different geographic locales. Others suggest colors trending in adjacent industries, such as cars or apparel. There are APIs that can provide the design team members with data on material properties, reli-able suppliers, likely prices, and delivery expectations for any fabric the design team may consider. These API feeds supplement the activities of the cross-functional teams as they coordinate the steps for developing an upper design. The process is now far more dynamic. The feeds can be reconfigured, with new data sources added and others dropped. A greater variety of options can be considered. Answers to "what if?" scenarios come faster. There are more ideas for designs. Designs can be adapted faster because design teams can now respond faster to changing trends. And better designs can be devised in much shorter times. As Ravi Shankavaram, vice president of Global IT at New Balance, remarks, "Integrating API networks into legacy processes may initially seem to slow things down as they provide far more options, but eventually they can substantially improve speed and agility." The process can be done in days or weeks rather than in months.

There has been considerable interest in the notion of dynamic capabilities in the strategy literature. They are seen as a firm's ability to recombine and reconfigure assets and organizational processes as markets and technologies change.[10] It is hard for legacy capabilities to be dynamic because of the inherent rigidities in legacy firms' processes. It is difficult to keep track of changing market dynamics. Digital capabilities can be far more dynamic because API networks inject more flexibility into firms' underlying processes and because API networks can reconfigure how data assets are generated and shared with greater fluidity.

Strategic Scope

Strategic scope refers to the range of value creation opportunities a firm can engage in. Legacy firms see it reflected in their corporate scope, or the number of industries in which they maintain a presence. Johnson & Johnson's strategic scope, for instance, spans medical devices, pharmaceuticals, and the consumer-packaged goods industries. In theory, as long as a firm has the cash to do so,[11] it can acquire any number of companies and establish presence in any industry of its choice. Received wisdom, however, suggests that firms must not diversify into "unrelated" industries, and that they must remain within the realms of "related" industries to be successful. A substantial body of literature on corporate diversification supports this view.[12]

Related businesses are businesses in which a firm's legacy capabilities find relevance. They are businesses in which a firm can not only contribute with its own capabilities but also strengthen their capabilities in return. This kind of give and take depends on the extent to which the underlying value chain resources driving a firm's legacy capabilities finds synergies with the value chain resources of the other businesses. Disney Corporation's strategic scope, for example, includes businesses such as theme parks, hotels, movie production houses, TV and cable companies, cruise lines, and retail stores. Disney possesses the capabilities to compete in these businesses because of the underlying complementarities and synergies it finds across the resources of these businesses. Guests at Disney hotels get VIP access to Disney's theme parks; the theme parks in return benefit from the hotels attracting loyal customers. Consequently, Disney's hotels in Orlando have higher occupancy rates than its rivals, despite Disney's higher room rates. Similarly, Disney's cruise line business complements its theme park business. Disney's movies also complement the company's theme parks, allowing them to develop popular rides (such as Dumbo or Snow White). Theme parks enhance Disney's family-friendly brand, which in turn powers the popularity of many the company's movies. Such synergies also apply to Disney's TV and cable and Disney store retail businesses.

Some value chain resources are more versatile than others. They find synergies across a wider range of businesses and provide for greater capability bandwidths to compete in them. C. K. Prahalad and Gary Hamel describe such capability bandwidths as core competencies.[13] Disney's resources, for instance, provide the company with broad capabilities to effectively compete across a wide range of industries. Other value chain resources, such as those of airline companies, offer narrower capability bandwidths. The value chain resources of airline companies include their planes, airport hubs, and specialized human resources (such as pilots and aircraft maintenance crews). Such value chain resources are unique to airline businesses and are less likely to find complementary

synergies with other kinds of businesses. Such resources drive narrower strategic scopes. Many such businesses end up as single-industry
businesses. Around half the businesses in the United States are single-
industry businesses for these reasons.[14]

Now think about digital capabilities. The focal resources driving them
are digital ecosystem resources. Just as value chain resources do, digital capabilities influence a legacy firm's strategic scope. They expand a
legacy firm's strategic scope by increasing value-creating opportunities
from products to data-driven services. In this endeavor, production and
consumption ecosystem resources expand strategic scope in their own
unique ways.

Production ecosystem resources expand a legacy firm's strategic
scope from products to data-driven services, largely preserving the
firm's presence in its prevailing business domain. For example, Caterpillar's production ecosystem resources power its expansion into offering new data-driven features and predictive maintenance services for its
construction site machinery. Such an expansion, although broadening
the company's sources of value creation, maintains the company's presence within its prevailing construction equipment business domain.

Consumption ecosystem resources, on the other hand, can broaden
a legacy firm's strategic scope beyond its primary business domain. This
is because consumption ecosystem resources expand revenue-creating
opportunities through digital platform-based services. Depending on
the data and kinds of platform users that the data attract, platform services can expand the scope of products in a variety of directions. A
digital platform tethered to a light bulb and its data takes the light bulb
into home security, warehouse logistics, and street security systems, as
discussed earlier in this book.

Just as with value chain resources, consumption ecosystem resources
also vary in their abilities to expand a legacy firm's strategic scope. Much
depends on the nature of the sensor data generated by the product
when participating in a tethered digital platform (discussed in chapter
5). Digital platforms tethered to toothbrushes and construction equipment may generate new services only within the product's domain.

Digital platforms tethered to light bulbs, on the other hand, generate new services far beyond the primary product's domain.

The potential of consumption ecosystem resources to expand strategic scope has two notable characteristics. One, legacy firms may find more options to expand strategic scope through their consumption ecosystem resources than through their value chain resources. Two, strategic scope expansion through consumption ecosystem resources is less risky than strategic scope expansion through value chain resources. The following examples illustrate these points.

When General Mills was looking to expand its business in Europe, it chose Nestlé to form an alliance, called Cereal Partners Worldwide. Both companies expanded their strategic scope through this alliance, rooting their expansion on the underlying synergies across their value chain resources. General Mills benefits from Nestlé's distribution network in Europe; Nestlé, on the other hand, benefits from adding General Mills brand to its portfolio of consumer packaged goods. General Mills and Nestlé were among only a handful of companies suited for this alliance insofar as only few companies possessed requisite synergies through their brands and distribution networks. And despite these apparent synergies across their value chain resources, their alliance entailed considerable risks owing to the substantial investments it demanded for their respective scope expansions.

Now consider this example of Nestlé expanding its strategic scope using its consumption ecosystem resources.[15] Pertinent consumption ecosystem resources entail digital platforms connecting consumers to various third-party service providers. These third-party service providers include startups or companies that suggest recipes and cuisine preferences; they also include companies that advocate for health consciousness by highlighting food allergies or calorie counts. Like an app economy, not all these partnerships may bear fruit, but a few may become blockbusters. Nestlé can form partnerships with thousands of potential entities (unlike the narrow set of choices available through value chain resources). The company can also shift the business risks of such partnerships to its platform partners. If any particular service fails, the burden is more on the concerned third-party service provider rather than on Nestlé (unlike the more equally shared risks with value chain alliance partners). Nestlé's digital platforms can focus on attracting all kinds of partners without worrying about the risks of revenue generation or the usefulness of the synergies upfront.

Building Digital Capabilities

A legacy firm's digital capabilities do not develop in a vacuum. They arise from the foundations of the firm's legacy capabilities. They emerge when the firm's legacy resources and processes are expanded into new resources and processes tailored for digital capabilities. They gain strength when legacy and digital resources, along with legacy and digital processes, are fused together to deliver new outcomes seamlessly. Just as value chain processes benefit from strong value chain resources, digital ecosystem processes benefit from strong digital ecosystem resources. The more connected entities within a legacy firm, for instance, the more intricate its API network can become, making its data-sharing and data-integration processes even more powerful.

The strength of Caterpillar's digital capabilities at offering data-driven services in predictive maintenance, for instance, builds on such a synthesis. The company needs production ecosystem resources (sensor-equipped machines, the data from those machines);consumption ecosystem resources (IoT connectivity among the company's assets on a construction site); API networks channeling wear-and-tear data from an array of assets to Caterpillar, its dealers, spare part warehouses, and service technicians; and the cross-functional processes (between sales, service, billing units, and dealers) that execute service and repair jobs and collect payments. All such elements of legacy and digital resources and processes have to be synchronized in order to develop strong digital capabilities and achieve better outcomes. Better outcomes in this case include reduced downtimes for Caterpillar's assets on a construction site. Such outcomes are not feasible without new digital capabilities. Figure 8.3 depicts how legacy and digital resources and processes

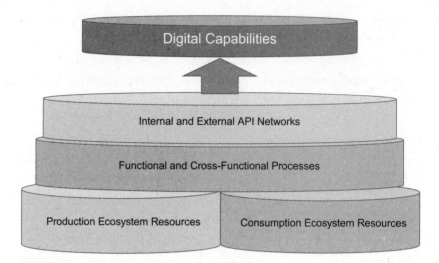

Figure 8.3
Fusing traditional and digital resources and processes.

can be fused to build digital capabilities. Legacy and digital resources blend into production and consumption ecosystem resources; similarly, functional and cross-functional processes (legacy processes) blend into internal and external API networks (digital processes) to generate new digital capabilities.

Developing an Organizational Climate for Digital Capabilities

In addition, to generate value, legacy firms must also channel these new fused resources and processes toward achieving fresh digital strategy objectives. This requires developing an organizational climate in which digital capabilities can sprout and thrive. Three organizational attributes provide an appropriate context for succeeding in these efforts: leadership vision, workforce skills, and workforce buy-in (see figure 8.4).

Leadership Vision

The development of digital capabilities begins with leadership vision. It is through leadership vision that a firm is able to set its new digital

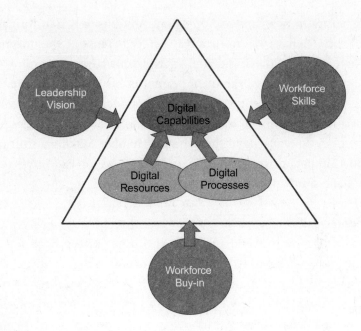

Figure 8.4
Building digital capabilities.

strategy objectives. Leadership vision enables the availability and flow of necessary investments to build new digital ecosystem infrastructures, create capacities to generate new kinds of data, and build the necessary processes for data sharing and integration. Visionary leaders understand that data have untapped value and can perceive the new opportunities data can unlock for them. Visionary leaders illuminate and clarify new strategic goals for the rest of the organization, whether they are limited to enhancing operational efficiencies or venturing into more ambitious strategic scope expansion through new data-driven services. They recognize the need to experiment, given the evolving nature of the digital world. They set a culture for managers to take requisite risks. They are keenly aware of new digital competitors and are prepared to build requisite digital capabilities to counter them.

Building new digital capabilities is a lot of what digital transformation is about. It involves an overhaul of legacy resources and processes and charting a new strategic direction. Any business transformation is difficult. Digital transformation is harder because of the uncertainties involved in achieving digital strategic objectives. According to a McKinsey survey,[16] fewer than 30 percent of business transformations succeed. Only 16 percent of the study's respondents indicated any kind of success in their digital transformation efforts. Such challenges put a bigger onus on leaders and their strategic resolve. Making a shift from products to data places extraordinary burdens on top executives to get their leadership vision right.

Workforce Skills

New digital resources and processes also usher in the need for new workforce skills. Digital ecosystems demand greater digital literacy from the workforce. A part of this digital literacy entails specialized software skills. Software skills allow legacy firms to imbue their workforce outputs with different quality attributes, such as design flexibility, user-friendly interfaces, fast development cycles, and agile and iterative development processes. These attributes complement the more typical legacy workforce skills such as consistency and reliability in their outputs. Skills in software, the ability to design APIs, and the ability to write machine learning and AI algorithms are highly specialized. Legacy firms such as Ford, P&G, and Walmart are finding themselves competing with the digital titans such as Facebook, Google, and Amazon for people with such specialized skills.

Digital literacy is not to the province of just a few specialists, however. As new digital infrastructures replace old ones, all employees need to become familiar with using new digital tools and software. Software and AI are also bound to eliminate the need for many old skills. For instance, smart machines that can talk to one another, direct their own operations, and self-correct mistakes are likely to replace people whose jobs were to perform such tasks manually or to operate machines that were less automated. These machine operators will need new skills that move them from operating machines to making decisions based on interpreting data. The same applies to marketing professionals, who will need to master how to manage social media. Accountants need to be aware of the latest software tools. Almost every function will find old processes intermingling with new digital processes. Without adequate workflow skills, legacy firms will stall in their efforts to build new digital capabilities.

Workforce Buy-In

As new digital winds sweep through a legacy firm, they invariably bring disruptions in old power structures and fresh insecurities in the workforce. Jeff Immelt's signaling GE's shift from an industrial to a software company was rooted in a bold strategic vision. Yet that signal also generated several uncertainties among the workforce and caused many workers to become anxious about what their role in the company would be. A company where engineers ruled the roost for several decades saw software specialists as the new rising elite. Many were unclear as to how their old engineering skills could merge with the new demands for software skills. Sales personnel accustomed to selling products were unsure about how to sell outcomes-based services. Nor were GE's customers easy to convince, in light of the relative difficulty perceiving the benefits of data compared to familiar product features. It may be that GE faced challenges like these because the company was a pioneer among industrial firms, leading the digital charge. Those were early days when the necessary building blocks for a digital strategy were not evident to all. Today things are different. Organizations cannot afford paralysis when building new digital capabilities.

Workforce buy-in is critical to avoid paralysis when trying to merge old legacy capabilities with new ones. Clarity at the top leadership level is a good start. That clarity has to filter down to the rest of the workforce. It is certainly not easy for all in the workforce to be happy or convinced about the necessity for the new required initiatives. Ensuring that most do is an important challenge to overcome when building new digital capabilities. It requires new kinds of training programs and fresh ways of incentivizing and motivating people to work toward new strategic goals.

Summary Thoughts on Digital Capabilities

Digital capabilities are a critical ingredient for legacy firms to compete in the modern digital world. They are new capabilities but can be built on the foundations of old ones. While this chapter highlighted what is different about digital capabilities, in reality such capabilities do not exist in separate buckets within a firm. Resources behind legacy capabilities blend in with new resources required for digital capabilities. Old assets become connected assets. Legacy products become digital products. Legacy customers become digital customers. They coexist. And they feed into each other's strengths.

Similarly, processes associated with legacy capabilities intertwine with new processes empowering digital capabilities. Legacy processes benefit from new API networks. To be successful, legacy firms have to find ways to blend their legacy and digital capabilities in seamless ways.

Finally, digital capabilities can be honed to achieve specific strategic goals. A firm, for example, can focus on excelling at offering interactive product features or data-driven mass customization of its smart products. In this case, the firm will invest in its production ecosystem infrastructure, along with the data resources and internal API networks needed to develop strong digital capabilities for those goals. Or a firm may focus on extending its value chain into a tethered digital platform. In this case, the firm will invest to develop its consumption ecosystem infrastructure, along with data resources and external API networks to develop a different set of digital capabilities. Firms can also do both, balancing how they harness their production and consumption ecosystems with new digital capabilities. Chapter 10 uses these ideas to offer an overarching framework for digital competitive strategy. Before we consider how these ideas shape a legacy firm's digital competitive strategy, however, we must discuss some important issues relating to the ethical use of data. The next chapter does that.

9   Looming Battles around Data

We are almost at the point where we can turn what we know about data into a framework for pursuing a digital competitive strategy. We have absorbed key concepts of digital ecosystems, digital customers, digital competitors, and digital capabilities. These concepts provide critical foundations to appreciate the various contingencies that shape how a legacy firm can unlock value from data to develop new sources of competitive advantage. They give us the necessary tools to construct an overarching framework for crafting a digital competitive strategy. Before we get to that final step, we need to give data, a central reason for this book, one more look. We need to acknowledge and appreciate a different facet of data, a facet of data that is controversial.

Thus far we have viewed data only as a value generator that expands business possibilities into the digital realm. From this positive perspective, data are a new elixir for legacy firms. The primary role of data, from this perspective, is to revive firm fortunes and instill new excitement in strategic goals. That, however, is not the whole story. Not everyone sees data the same way, nor do all people share that excitement. Many believe that the unbridled use of data by corporations can inflict serious damage on society. And indeed, harnessing data for corporate advantage can have several negative effects.

The coming decades will witness mounting battles among various stakeholders, including consumer groups, regulators, and corporations, over who controls data. Competing forces will grapple to find the right balance between the benefits of greater access to data and the need to restrict access to avoid deleterious consequences, including but not limited to the amassing of market power by those who control data and the erosion of personal privacy from the use of those data. It is too early to provide categorical answers to the ongoing debates on these issues and the vexing questions they represent, and this chapter does not take a side in these debates. Instead, it offers a perspective on the issues surrounding data's controversial power and the forces swirling around its proponents and detractors. Legacy firms must be aware of these forces before they embark on their digital initiatives. This chapter is a necessary sojourn before we get to our final destination in our data to digital strategy journey.

To set the context for this chapter, let's discuss the 2020 ballot initiative in Massachusetts called *Question 1*. This ballot initiative is a reflection of the kind of confrontation legacy firms may face in regard to their use of data.

The Massachusetts 2020 Ballot Initiative: Question 1

Do you approve of a law summarized below, on which no vote was taken by the Senate or the House of Representatives on or before May 5, 2020? This proposed law would require that motor vehicle owners and independent repair facilities be provided with expanded access to mechanical data related to vehicle maintenance and repair.

That is how Question 1 was framed. It attracted significant attention in the run-up to the November 2020 election. Millions of dollars' worth of ads promoting both sides of this issue dominated television airwaves for weeks. A yes vote would oblige car manufacturers to open their car components' sensor data to any independent repair facility a consumer chose. It would reinforce a consumer's right to repair the car she owned at a facility of her liking. A no vote, on the other hand, would permit car manufacturers to restrict its sensor data to entities of the manufacturer's choice—usually their own dealers and select repair facilities. It would restrict a consumer's right to repair her car only at select places of the manufacturer's choice. "Right to repair" is a catchall phrase for a series of legislative efforts that have progressively allowed consumers to choose when and where to repair the products they buy.

For consumers voting yes, the argument was simple. They owned the car. Hence they reserved the right to repair it at a place of their liking. Any restrictions on their right to repair would be tantamount to car manufacturers imposing their market powers over them. Having more choices to repair their cars, they reckoned, would also lower their repair costs. Similarly, for independent car repair shops, their choice was fairly straightforward. A yes vote would give them access to the necessary data to repair modern cars. A no vote, on the other hand, would lock them out. Many small and independent repair shops joined together to campaign for a yes vote out of rising fear of losing their livelihoods as cars became increasingly digital.[1] According to the Global Automotive OEM Telematics Market Report, 41 percent of all new motor vehicles sold worldwide in 2018 were equipped with telematics systems (sensors). In North America, the rate was 53 percent.[2]

For car manufacturers, the stakes were clear. A yes vote threatened to weaken important foundations of their digital competitive strategy. A yes vote would create uncertainty about the returns on their investments in sensors and sensor-equipped products. It would challenge a manufacturer's control over sensor data. This is, after all, a notable illustration of the tethered digital platforms discussed this book. Sensor data–enabled car repair is one of the features manufacturers offer through their tethered digital platforms, facilitating data exchanges among car users and select repair shops. From the automakers' standpoint, car repair shops are important platform users that determine the quality of their digitally driven car repair services. Taking away control over who can access their sensor data would take away their right to choose who should complement their data within their platforms and whom to invite as digital platform users. It would take away their independence to shape their products' digital experiences. More fundamentally, a yes vote would question their rights to the data generated by their products.

Among those supporting a no vote on the Massachusetts ballot question were activist groups concerned about cybersecurity threats rising from unfettered access to the car's sensor data. For example, a group called the Coalition for Safe and Secure Data put out an ad during the run-up to the 2020 election showing a man opening the garage door of a home—a home that was not his—with a click. The ad went on to warn how opening sensor data from cars without controls could empower unsavory people to pair that data with garage codes and break into private homes. Similarly, some domestic violence advocacy groups supported a no vote. They raised concerns of stalking and abuse from more open access to a car's sensor data. One TV advertisement claimed that a woman fleeing from an abusive partner was at greater risk if her partner could track her location and even disable her vehicle.

Cybersecurity threats were another issue in the debate over Question 1. Some advocates argued that lax control over data elevated cybersecurity threats. Others insisted those concerns are overblown and pointed to the fact that the ballot initiative was about "mechanical data" and not GPS data or data from connected phones. Moreover, they saw hacking as a perpetual threat, with or without open access to data.[3]

Question 1, like most ballot initiatives, had supporters and detractors. From a consumer's viewpoint, it seems only fair that car companies must make their data available to all repair shops. That way, they can decide where to get their car fixed without limitation. But such a rule also implies removing restrictions on the entities that can complement a car's sensor data. From a manufacturer's viewpoint, preserving control over its products' complements is important. After all, razor manufacturers restrict the blades that can complement their products. Smartphone manufacturers similarly restrict their charging ports' accessibility only to proprietary connectors. Data, from these manufacturers' viewpoint, are no different and should enjoy the same privileges. Having control over data is necessary to monitor product quality and shape user experiences.

Question 1 eventually passed with 75 percent of the vote. Yet the broader issues underlying this debate on the appropriate use of data by corporations are far from settled. This ballot initiative is a harbinger of other controversies and battles looming ahead, shaping the boundaries for acceptable use of data by corporations. The issues underlying Question 1 go far beyond auto companies and Massachusetts. They affect all legacy firms. They have global ramifications. So, what should legacy firms do? Be sensitive to the debate. Be ethical. And find a way to thread the needle between societal concerns, rising regulations, and harnessing data for competitive advantage. Let's expand on two broad forces that legacy firms must keep their eye on, societal apprehensions about the rising use of data and the regulatory forces shaping the role of data.

Societal Apprehensions about the Rising Power of Data

Why should we worry about the untrammeled use of data? Views highlighting the reasons why we should worry abound in newspapers, magazines, and books. A months-long series of stories in the *New York Times* (Fall/Winter of 2019) titled "The Privacy Project" is one example.[4] The newspaper notes in its introduction, *"Companies and governments are gaining new powers to follow people across the internet and around the world, and even to peer into their genomes. The benefits of such advances have been apparent for years; the costs—in anonymity, even autonomy—are now becoming clearer. The boundaries of privacy are in dispute, and its future is in doubt. Citizens, politicians and business leaders are asking if societies are making the wisest tradeoffs."*

One of the stories in this series reports on a scientific conference held in Las Vegas. This conference invited medical technology companies and experts to assess the likelihood of medical products being hacked. The idea was to stress test data security in smart medical technology products within a made-up hospital environment. An interview with one of the lead scientists at the conference, however, saw the discussion veering in a different direction. According to the interviewee, medical devices such as smart pacemakers or ECG machines are not really the main concern for health data security risks. Far bigger concerns come from new techniques, such as digital phenotyping,[5] that help users glean insights into our health from how we interact with a broad array of digital technologies in our daily lives. Phenotypes are observable human traits. Digital phenotyping is about aggregating data on an individual's traits collected through smartphones, wearables, and other connected devices. Such aggregated data can offer robust proxies for human traits with respect to health and disease.

How we type on our keyboards can reveal early signs of Parkinson's disease. What we post on social media platforms can expose depression. Online shopping behavior can reveal whether the shopper is pregnant. The broader digital environment around us threatens to encroach on our private lives. And a large part of that environment is shaped by the digital titans such as Facebook, Google, and Amazon. These digital titans pioneered the unlocking of data's untapped potential at an unprecedented scale. In doing so, their business models amassed massive amounts of personal data. It is hence not surprising that the digital titans are also the prime source of societal apprehensions about data and its role in our day-to-day lives. The apprehensions they generate have ramifications for all legacy firms attempting to generate interactive data through their products. Smart pacemakers and ECG machines generate the same kind of apprehension, even if their impact on privacy maybe minimal. Legacy firms have to reckon with this reality.

The scale of data collected by the digital titans is a big factor behind these apprehensions. Consider Skywalk Labs, part of Alphabet (Google's parent company) and its project to convert a twelve-acre strip of Toronto's waterfront into a smart microcity that resembles something from a sci-fi movie about the future. Plans include high-rise timber towers, heated streets that melt snow, AI-enabled traffic lights, and pneumatic trash collection systems.[6] The widespread use of sensors is a big part of this urban planning initiative, with sensors embedded in the concrete of homes and in streets and sidewalks. The goal is to monitor everything from health care to zoning regulations, greenhouse emissions, and traffic flows.[7] To many, such collaborations between city governments and corporations to collect widespread data on a city's residents and visitors evoke a surveillance state where technology controls how we behave.

Shoshana Zuboff's book, *The Age of Surveillance Capitalism*, gives one perspective on the underlying reasons for such apprehension.[8] Zuboff argues that industrial capitalism relied on exploiting and controlling natural resources. What she describes as surveillance capitalism, by contrast, relies on exploiting and controlling human nature. Much of her analysis draws on the actions of such firms as Facebook and Google. Her thesis is that personal data collected by such powerful digital titans not only can predict our behavior but also can be used to influence and modify it. Such inordinate power, according to her, harms the institutions of democracy, freedom, and human rights.

The plan for the Skywalk project has been shelved for now. This is not necessarily because of privacy concerns but because of the COVID-19 pandemic and its related economic uncertainty in 2020. It is not far-fetched to imagine that such urban planning innovations may become commonplace in the near future. City governments may deem that the benefits of reduced congestion, lower crime rates, and fewer vehicular accidents outweigh the threats to individual privacy. Individuals may not have a choice, just as living without the internet or a smartphone today is not really a choice for most individuals, despite the associated privacy concerns. Individual views may have an impact only through broader social movements. The social mobilization that went into having Question 1 a ballot initiative in Massachusetts is one example. When societal concerns about the role of data gather enough momentum, they end up with governments entering the picture through regulations.

Regulatory Forces Shaping the Role of Data

One of the oldest weapons in the regulatory arsenal of governments entails restricting unfair market power or monopoly power through antitrust laws. In a famous example, antitrust actions in the US broke up Standard Oil in 1911. At the time, Standard Oil dominated oil and kerosene production. The company's monopoly control over such products was deemed dangerous because it meant one company could potentially shut down the government and the military if it chose to by, say, curtailing production and supply. The government also believed that Standard Oil was using its market power to unfairly restrict competition. In this landmark case, the Supreme Court agreed on a "rule of reason"[9] that would go on to shape all antitrust cases. The rule of reason became a guiding principle by which the government could decide on a case-by-case basis whether any firm dominated a market by unfair means. And if it was found to have done so, it was liable to be broken up into smaller companies. Mergers and acquisitions would be disallowed.

Scrutiny of potential anticompetitive practices continues today. Regulators also worry about the likelihood of tacit collusion among firms when a few of them dominate a market. It becomes easier to coordinate "fixing" prices, create artificial shortages, or engage in other anticompetitive behavior when only a few firms control a market. And it's understandable that concerns about the negative impact of market power have shifted from old industrial firms to the digital titans in recent times. Data, of course, as we have argued throughout this book, are the new driver of value. It is hence also the new source for market power.

Consider the US Justice Department's October 2020 lawsuit against Google.[10] The DOJ alleges that Google dominates the US "search market" with a market share of 88 percent. Additionally, 94 percent of mobile searches are made through Google's product. According to the DOJ, Google's massive market share has harmed consumers by reducing their choices in search engines and by hampering innovations for better quality options. Earlier, in 2017, Google was fined $2.7 billion by the European Union for violating antitrust rules. The EU's allegation was that Google unfairly exploits its dominance in search engines and smartphone operating systems to restrict competition in shopping services, ad placement services, and smartphone apps.

Such flashpoints between governments and the digital titans are to be expected. The digital titans, after all, derive their inordinate market power from data. And such power is bound to attract antitrust scrutiny. The dynamics of industrial market power and data-driven market power, however, are not the same.

Determining the anticompetitive effects of industrial monopolies is fairly straightforward. It is evident when industrial monopolies restrict supplies to maximize corporate profits. Their negative impact on consumer welfare becomes even more obvious when they indulge in price gouging. On the other hand, the anticompetitive effects of data-driven monopolies are not as easy to pin down. Google may have a dominant market share in search engines. However, Google also gives out its search engine for free. The question of price gouging does not even arise. Google would even argue that its search engine makes it easier for people to shop, rather than restrict competing shopping services. It may even contend that it enhances consumer welfare.

Moreover, it is not clear whether the DOJ can establish that Google enjoys a position of unfair market power in its search functions, despite its 88 percent market share in the search engines market. People conduct searches through all kinds of ways. Not all entail using search engines. They may, for example, search for news on Twitter or Facebook; search for flights through Expedia; or find restaurants through Open Table.[11] In other words, data-driven positions of unfair market power are hard to establish when competition is spread across several interlocking digital ecosystems.[12] They are unlike industrial market power dominance, which occurs within clearly circumscribed industry boundaries.

Mechanisms to enforce antitrust legislations may also differ between industrial and data-driven market power. Preventing mergers or alliances between firms with dominant market shares is one common approach used to prevent concentration of market power in industries. With data-driven business models, partnerships are also achieved through APIs. The goal of such API partnerships is not necessarily to dominate markets with products as with mergers. Instead, it is about finding ways to maximize how much each firm knows about each consumer. Netflix may have one slice of our persona. Amazon has another. Facebook has yet another. Theoretically, if these companies decide to share these slices of information through APIs, they may jointly create a more composite view of an individual to better predict needs and wants. Each could then use this superior understanding of its customers for its own benefit. The threat of collusion in this case is because of how these firms share APIs, not just because of their market share dominance. Regulating how APIs are shared may become as important as regulating relative market shares of products through mergers. Antitrust policies may soon catch up to these changes. Legacy firms must keep track of such changes and see how they apply to their own evolving business models.

Beyond antitrust, the focus of emergent regulatory forces is also on protecting consumer rights and privacy. Europe has instituted some of the most sweeping changes in how it regulates the use of data by corporations. General Data Protection Regulation, or GDPR, is one such initiative introduced in 2018. The new regulatory framework aims to give individuals control over their personal data. Also, by having common rules across Europe, the GDPR aims to simplify the regulatory environment for millions of firms in EU member states. Some important GDPR provisions include mandating consent from consumers before collecting their data, ensuring consumer anonymity, requiring corporations to report any data breaches, and instituting structural changes within organizations, such as having positions such as data security officers. The rules apply to any entity that conducts business with EU residents, no matter where that business is located.

These regulations, of course, come at some cost to companies. Companies must establish new processes on how they manage their data. They must prepare for noncompliance penalties, which could potentially amount to €20 million or 4 percent of global revenues, whichever is higher. Also, the burdens of such regulations may not fall equally on all firms. Smaller firms may be more affected. Sectors such as banks, with a longer history of data compliance, will likely find it easier to adapt to the new regulations than others.[13]

Information Fiduciaries

A different approach to instituting reforms around the use of data involves casting corporations as "information fiduciaries."[14] Fiduciaries are individuals or businesses entrusted with an obligation to behave in a manner that protects the interests of others. Common examples are doctors, lawyers, and accountants. For example, a doctor is obligated to keep information about patients private. The idea is for corporations to step up as fiduciaries and act as trustworthy agents with respect to consumer data. As Jack Balkin and Jonathan Zittrain note in their article in the *Atlantic*, "Google Maps shouldn't recommend a drive past an IHOP as the 'best route' on the way to a meeting from the airport simply because IHOP gave it $20."[15] The expectation is that such initiatives may be less constraining to businesses compared to more rigid regulations such as the GDPR.

Others have pointed out that fiduciary roles may not apply as easily to data-driven business models as they do with doctors or lawyers.[16] A doctor or a lawyer finds few conflicts of interests in keeping patient information confidential. Their businesses do not obviously or systematically gain by sharing confidential information with third parties. Data-driven business models, in particular digital platforms, have a lot to gain by sharing information. Data sharing with external entities is at the core of their advantage. How effectively they volunteer to faithfully act as fiduciaries remains to be seen. But the idea is gathering interest. Mark Zuckerberg, Facebook's CEO, has apparently expressed his support.[17] Some senators are also involved in passing legislations based on this concept.[18] Legacy firms should watch this space.

What Should Legacy Firms Do?

Market power is an implicit goal and a holy grail for an effective competitive strategy. Having market power does not mean a firm is a monopoly, as in being the sole producer in an industry. Starbucks, Nike, and Coke, for example have formidable market power. They also have strong rivals in Costa Coffee (for Starbucks), Adidas (for Nike), and Pepsi (for Coke). And yet they have the wherewithal to exercise tremendous influence in their industries and earn handsome profits. No firm wishes to be in perfectly competitive industries where its products have no differentiation, profitability is poor, and there are no protective barriers to any market position. But firms have to balance maximizing shareholder wealth (through firms' market power) and looking out for societal welfare.

Legacy firms have learned to do this over the years. They understand antitrust policies within their industries and have instituted practices to manage their businesses within regulatory parameters. They also reckon how important it is for their brand and for their long-term survival to be a good citizen in addition to being profitable.

The digital world is no different in this regard. Legacy firms must learn how to maximize benefits from data and yet be good citizens, all while remaining cognizant of the trade-offs between offering exciting digital experiences and managing societal expectations on privacy. To do so they must inject new skills and expertise into their organizations. They must institute new governance practices within their corporate policies to manage data. Such new practices can include the following:

- Making structural changes in the organization, such as appointing chief data officers and making them responsible for ethical, legal, and security ramifications of data.
- Adopting new processes to gather intelligence about shifting societal expectations on the use of data and impending regulatory shifts.
- Imposing strict "data quality" measures and processes to maintain and deliver strong data encryption, data anonymity, and robust checks and balances to ensure digital customer opt-ins.
- Improving transparency as to what benefits customers can expect from data and how their data will be used for those goals.

Summary Thoughts on Data's "Other" Side

Much of the energy that spurs societal apprehension on the use of data and prompts activities by government regulators is centered on the digital titans. Yet perceptions about the use of data for corporate gains and emerging regulatory changes also affect legacy firms. They too will be drawn into the maelstrom as they venture into the digital world.

Keeping a close eye on societal perceptions and new regulatory frameworks is important. Instituting good data governance is imperative. Legacy firms are on the threshold of the formation of a new social contract between corporations and consumers with regard to data. They must be on the good side of this social contract.

That said, this book is about digital competitive strategy. Its viewpoint thus supports maximizing competitive advantage from data. Yes, approaches taken to maximize data-driven advantages must not cross ethical boundaries or willfully hurt society. At times legacy firms will face difficult trade-offs as they strive to improve their fortunes in the new digital world. There are no easy answers.

For over four decades, we have anchored our understanding of competitive strategy on products and framed our strategic choices within industry structures. Such a product industry perspective of competitive strategy has been immensely useful for legacy firms over the years. Robust economic theories provide its conceptual foundations. Empirical research validates this perspective, establishing how industries and their attributes influence firm performance. Leveraging firm capabilities through products and framing competition within industries have forged a widely accepted mindset for strategic decision-making among legacy firms.

But it is time now for legacy firms to build new mindsets. Strategic thinking anchored on products and industries alone is inadequate to thrive in the new digital world. Thanks to modern digital technologies, data can be used far more expansively than was traditionally possible. As a consequence, the drivers of competitive advantage are unmistakably shifting from products to data. And to fully unlock this expansive value of data, a firm needs to harness its digital ecosystems. Just as industry structures amplify the power of products, digital ecosystems amplify the power of data. A shift in emphasis from products to data also requires a similar shift in strategic emphasis from industries to digital ecosystems. In a world where data can unlock significant new value through digital ecosystems, a firm relying purely on old product-industry mindsets will fall behind. The modern business environment requires a new strategic mindset centered on data. It requires framing competitive strategy within digital ecosystems.

Even as legacy firms adopt such a mindset, they must not ignore or lose their prevailing sources of advantage. A shift to data and digital ecosystems does not mean that products and industries become irrelevant. A modern mindset needs the footings of prevailing products and industries. The ideas explored in this book underscore this point.

Let's review the key concepts introduced in preceding chapters. Digital ecosystems evolve from industry networks but also transform them. Production ecosystems develop from value chain networks, then enrich them in new ways. Consumption ecosystems take advantage of existing complementor networks before enlarging them using advances in connectivity. Digital customers emerge from legacy customers when they provide interactive data; digital customers also rely on a firm's prevailing products to generate new kinds of interactive data. Digital competitors may emulate some industry-based competitive interactions, yet they also introduce new competitive dynamics. Besides, many digital competitors are old industry rivals that now compete in new ways with data. And finally, digital capabilities transpire from prevailing capabilities and present new opportunities. These modern digital capabilities also must be fused with a firm's prevailing capabilities to effectively drive digital competitive strategy.

This final chapter presents a framework for digital competitive strategy using these instrumental concepts. It delineates different strategic options for firms to compete and generate digital competitive advantage. It also discusses the contingencies a legacy firm must consider as it envisions, selects, and executes its digital competitive strategy. This is the last stop and the final destination in our journey from data to digital strategy.

A Framework for Digital Competitive Strategy

A digital competitive strategy emerges when a legacy firm unlocks the value of its data using its production and/or consumption ecosystems. Figure 10.1 depicts a framework for digital competitive strategy, integrating all the ideas and concepts introduced thus far in the previous

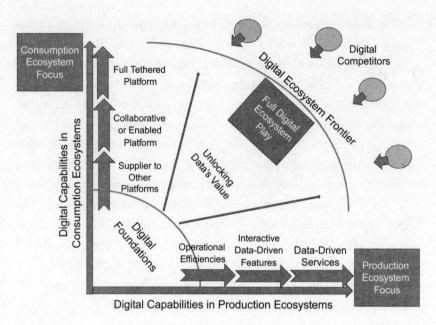

Figure 10.1
A framework for digital competitive strategy.

chapters. It is thus a capstone framework for this book's ideas. Let's discuss its particulars.

The horizontal axis of this framework represents *digital capabilities in production ecosystems*; the vertical axis represents *digital capabilities in consumption ecosystems*. Each of these types of digital capabilities is a combination of resources and processes established to augment the value of data, as elaborated in chapter 8. Digital capabilities in consumption ecosystems harness the value of data to expand a legacy firm's value-creating scope through tethered digital platforms. Value expands on this axis as a firm advances from being just a supplier to other platforms to competing as an enabled or collaborative platform, or competing as a full tethered digital platform (as described in chapter 5). *Digital capabilities in production ecosystems* harness data not only to improve a legacy firm's operational efficiencies but also to further expand its value-creating scope. Such expanded value comes in the form of new revenues derived from interactive data-driven product features and data-driven services (as described in chapter 4).

For a legacy firm to forge its digital capabilities, it first must establish its *digital foundations*. The firm constructs these digital foundations through investing in production and consumption ecosystem infrastructures, investing in data resources, and building API networks. As discussed in chapter 8, this requires assembling a network of connected assets. It requires cultivating digital customers. It entails developing new data resources using these infrastructures. And it requires building vibrancy in the firm's data-sharing and data-integration processes by progressively making its API networks more intricate.

Digital foundations provide the bedrocks for legacy firms to compete with data. As they gain in strength, a firm enhances its digital capabilities in production and/or consumption ecosystems. In doing so, the firm increasingly unlocks data's value, steering toward its *digital ecosystem frontier*. A digital ecosystem frontier represents the maximum value of data a firm can unlock from its digital ecosystems. Two sets of forces shape the arc of a firm's digital ecosystems frontier. One is internal. The stronger a firm's digital capabilities, the more expansive is the arc of its digital ecosystem frontier. The other is external and stems from a firm's competitive environment. The stronger a firm's digital competitors, the less the value of data it may be allowed to unlock for itself and the more limited its digital ecosystem frontier is likely to be. An effective digital competitive strategy is one that maximizes a firm's digital ecosystem frontier. It harnesses a firm's digital capabilities in ways that deliver an advantage over its digital competitors. It also empowers a firm to identify, reach, and operate at an optimal point on its digital ecosystem frontier.

A legacy firm can operate at any point on its digital ecosystem frontier. Each point on the digital ecosystem frontier arc represents a unique digital competitive strategy option. Each point is a distinctive stance that a firm can take to unlock data's full potential and build competitive advantage in so doing. Three generic strategies, each representing a discrete option on a firm's digital ecosystem frontier, serve as key reference points in a continuum of strategic options. They help firms determine how to compete in the digital economy.

The first type of strategy entails a *production ecosystem focus*. With this strategic option, a firm progressively unlocks more value from data as it advances from operational efficiencies to data-driven interactive product features or data-driven services (as detailed in chapter 4). The second option entails a *consumption ecosystems focus*. With this strategic option, a firm progressively enhances the value it unlocks from data by advancing from being a supplier to other platforms to having its own platform, a collaborative, enabled, or full tethered platform (as detailed in chapter 5). And the third option entails a *full digital ecosystem play* that unlocks value from data by harnessing digital capabilities in both production and consumption ecosystems with balanced strengths.

As reference points, these three generic digital competitive strategies help firms understand the trade-offs involved in choosing any one point on the digital ecosystem frontier over another. A firm choosing a point in between a production ecosystem focus and a full digital play, for example, can appreciate the mix of capabilities required to unlock the value of data to compete at that strategic position. It can also assess how its capabilities are likely to fare vis-à-vis the likely competitive threats in that chosen position.

It must be noted that most legacy firms are likely to compete in the spectrum starting from a production ecosystem focus and moving toward a full digital play. After all, most legacy businesses, whether in manufacturing or services, are anchored on value chains. A production ecosystem focus is likely to be their starting point as their preferred digital competitive strategy. A pure consumption ecosystem focus represents a position wherein the primary value of the business comes from a digital platform. Such a focus is unlikely to be as prevalent among legacy firms already anchored on value chains. Even if they extend their value chains into tethered digital platforms, they are likely to be close to a full digital play, and not a pure consumption ecosystem strategy.

A pure consumption ecosystem focus is likely among firms whose business models are based on retrofitted sensors on other firms' products, without actually producing those products themselves. Also, firms that see their value chains getting commoditized, and with little value to extract from their production ecosystems, are likely candidates to adopt a consumption ecosystem focus. For such firms, new value opportunities may come only from tapping into their consumption ecosystems. We discuss this point more later in this chapter.

Several companies discussed in the earlier chapters can be mapped onto each of the three different generic digital strategies. Caterpillar's strategy, for instance, represents a production ecosystem focus. The company provides data-driven interactive features in its products and uses that data to offer predictive services to reduce product downtimes, among other things. Hexagon and Trimble are examples of firms with a consumption ecosystem focus. They operate with retrofitted sensors on construction equipment manufactured by other firms (such as Caterpillar and Komatsu) and offer their own digital platforms to coordinate work on a construction site. Ford is an example of a company choosing to compete with a full digital ecosystem play. The legacy automaker offers data-driven interactive product features using its production ecosystems. The company also operates in its consumption ecosystems through platform services, such as connecting drivers to auto repair shops.

Much of how firms end up in any position in the digital frontier arc depends on the business they are in. Their positions are influenced by how their industries evolve into digital ecosystems. These patterns in their evolution determine where relevant opportunities for unlocking the value of data can come from. Yet firms can also choose their own independent digital destinies. They can chart their own digital trajectories based on how they individually perceive the risks and rewards of pursuing new value-creating opportunities.

The next section spotlights three legacy industries that are morphing into digital ecosystems: oil and gas, telecommunications, and insurance. A variety of forces are causing them to turn them into digital ecosystems. And in each of these emerging digital ecosystems, incumbent firms gravitate toward different generic strategies because of different risk-reward trade-offs.

Forces Shaping Digital Strategies in Emerging Digital Ecosystems

The three industries discussed below represent significant, and different, sectors of the US economy. Analyzing trends across these diverse businesses can help understand how various forces turning them into digital ecosystems shape a firm's options as it seeks an ideal point on its digital ecosystem frontier. An understanding of these forces can also help any firm, irrespective of the nature its business, arrive at an optimal digital competitive strategy for itself. Let us begin with the oil and gas business.

The Oil and Gas Business: Incentives for Operational Efficiencies

The oil and gas business is a \$3.2 trillion business.[1] Companies in this business engage in the exploration of oil and gas reserves. They also manage oil and gas fields to extract, refine, produce, and distribute petroleum products. Their largest-volume products are fuel oil and gasoline. Dominant companies in this sector include ExxonMobil, British Petroleum, and Chevron. China Petroleum & Chemical Corporation (Sinopec) is the largest, with 2019 revenues around \$433 billion.[2] Royal Dutch Shell comes second, with 2019 revenues around \$383 billion.[3]

The oil and gas business has three distinct parts. Its upstream part involves finding wells and drilling for oil and gas. Its midstream part involves transporting the drilled reserves from the wells to the refineries. And its downstream part refines the crude reserves and markets the products, such as gasoline or jet fuel. Some companies in this industry focus on activities in only one part of this stream: upstream, midstream, or downstream. Others, including some of the largest companies in this business, such as Exxon Mobil, operate in all parts of the stream. They run integrated operations. with their own oil wells, pipelines, and refineries.

The oil and gas business is highly capital-intensive.[4] Oil wells, pipelines, and refineries require massive investments running into several billions of dollars. In addition, markets can be volatile, and these investments carry substantial risks. Understandably, improving operational efficiencies is a powerful incentive in this business. Reducing costs wherever feasible and recovering the value of investments as quickly as possible in an uncertain market environment are important objectives. And modern digital technologies, as we now know, offer useful solutions for this purpose.

For example, in exploration activities there are significant costs associated with inaccurate or imprecise projections. Wrong estimates of where to drill or how much to drill can cost millions of dollars. Firms can save up to 50 to 60 percent of their operational costs using modern digital tools such as AI and other modeling techniques to better improve the likelihood of finding reserves.[5]

Pipelines transporting oil and gas are thousands of miles long, often traversing different countries and even continents. Sensor data on soil conditions and the condition of the material flowing within pipelines can help predict where and when in the vast pipeline array corrosion is likely to begin and how it could spread. Using data and analytics to manage corrosion before it damages pipelines can save significant costs.

Most refineries are safe, but even rare accidents carry significant risks. There are strong incentives for automating dangerous jobs and replacing human activity with AI-enabled technology. All aspects of the oil and gas business, whether upstream, midstream, or downstream, use expensive equipment. All of them involve capital-intensive projects. Downtimes are expensive. Using predictive services goes a long way toward reducing downtime and saving operational costs.

Such incentives to improve operational efficiencies, along with the variety of ways by which modern digital technologies can help achieve such objectives, explain why a production ecosystem focus is an attractive option for this sector. And indeed, firms in this business have largely gravitated toward this strategic position. Most of their digital initiatives are geared toward building and channeling digital capabilities to improve their operational efficiencies.

Telecommunications and 5G: Emerging Opportunities in Consumption Ecosystems

The big news in the telecommunications space is the arrival of 5G, or the fifth generation of cellular networks. 5G operates on radio frequencies but includes new spectra that significantly improve its functionality over previous cellular generations. These improvements open up fresh opportunities for carriers such as Verizon, AT&T, and T-Mobile (in the US) and NTT, China Telecom, and Deutsche Telekom (globally) to craft new digital competitive strategies in their evolving digital ecosystems.

Let's consider the impact of 5G cellular networks on the Internet of Things (IoT) applications. The IoT essentially needs various assets to connect to the internet to form a data-sharing network. Wi-Fi is a commonly used protocol for assets to connect to an enterprise network or to the internet, but over short distances. In recent years, IoT-specific protocols such as NB-IoT and LoRa have seen increased use for maintaining connectivity over longer distances. Other approaches include using wireless protocols such as Bluetooth or Zigbee, although their coverage range is even shorter. A 5G cellular network offers several advantages over Wi-Fi and other prevailing protocols for IoT applications.

5G cellular networks transfer large volumes of data at high speeds. Latency, or the lag in data transfer with 5G networks, can be as low as 1 to 2 milliseconds.[6] And the data transfer is far more reliable. This gives the 5G technology a big advantage specifically in those IoT applications where assets not only share large amounts of data but also need quick reaction times. An example is autonomous cars needing to react to avoid potential collisions. Surgeons who use robots for remote surgery need quick reaction times. In one case, a surgeon in China conducted brain surgery remotely for a patient with the help of 5G.[7] Because of the intricacies of such tasks, there are substantial benefits when remote robots react literally in real time. Similarly, in a manufacturing environment, machines detecting defects in their output benefit from instantaneously shifting operations to other machines to limit losses. For these kinds of applications even the milliseconds of latency reductions that 5G offers can make a difference.

Low 5G latency also helps firms engage in edge computing. Edge computing is about doing data computation at the spot (or at the "edge") where data are generated and shared. This could be on a factory floor where multiple machines and robots are conducting interactive tasks and generating large volumes of data in real time. Traditionally, such voluminous data had to be transferred back and forth to centralized servers (or, later, the cloud) for computation, analysis, and recommended actions. This data transfer protocol slows the interactions in interactive tasks among machines and robots. Edge computing is about bringing the cloud closer to the edge, so to speak. The speed, power, and reliability of 5G technology make it possible, while also turbocharging a variety of different IoT applications in the process.

5G offers yet another advantage. Cellular networks have strong radio signals that can travel miles. A cellular tower can provide connectivity to a cell phone up to approximately forty-five miles away.[8] In contrast, Wi-Fi networks have a much lower range, providing coverage up to about hundred feet inside a home, a café, or an office building. Furthermore, the owner of a Wi-Fi network needs to provide access for an external entity to connect to its network. We have all, for instance, provided visitors with our home's Wi-Fi password for them to access the internet. Cellular networks do not need such manual permissions and have their own automated authentication processes instead. As we know, people make cell phone calls for voice and data connectivity from wherever they are using cellular services available through their networks' towers.

Because of these features, 5G networks can offer far greater flexibility in managing IoT networks compared to Wi-Fi. Consider a home visit by a nurse who needs to transfer ECG or blood pressure readings to connected devices in a hospital. The nurse would find it easier to access the internet using a 5G cellular connection. Using a Wi-Fi network instead would require permission from the patient for the nurse to access the internet through the patient's home network. Similarly, Coke's bottlers may find it easier to replenish smart vending machines in various buildings when the company's truck drivers can seamlessly share data with those vending machines. In a Wi-Fi environment, every driver would need special access to vending machines. In a 5G environment they do not face these restrictions and can access the internet to easily link different vending machines to their sensor-enabled devices for their replenishment services. Also, delivery trucks can detect the need for timely replenishments in vending machines even when they are miles away because of the wider range of cellular networks.

The advantages that 5G cellular networks bring with them clearly provide carriers such as Verizon and AT&T many new business opportunities. A most obvious one is that they can sell superior data connectivity services for higher prices to both individual and business customers. They can also sell data connectivity to more customers across a larger slew of applications, including new IoT applications, such as in connected cars, to access remote health services, in smart cities, or for logistical purposes. Such options bring new value. They also reinforce the telecommunication providers' old business models of selling data connectivity. And the value is from doing more of the same.

What could Verizon or AT&T do differently? Rather than focusing on selling data connectivity alone, could they also offer services that their data connectivity stimulates? Consider the following two scenarios. In scenario one, Verizon provides connectivity for medical equipment carried by traveling home nurses for 5G connectivity. Verizon charges a premium for this connectivity. This is based on the fact that its superior coverage more reliably allows the traveling nurse to connect to the internet regardless of location and facilitates data exchanges with connected devices in relevant hospitals. In scenario two, Verizon not only offers connectivity to the devices carried by traveling nurses but also develops a network providing sensors for other complementary assets and entities that can exchange and use the generated data. Furthermore, Verizon could offer a platform that manages and provides a remote health care service entailing traveling nurses, doctors, and hospitals. Such a platform service would allow traveling nurses to take 3D pictures and share them in real time with remote specialists. It would also allow the nurses to see and send high-definition videos for on-the-spot medical guidance. In providing such services, Verizon would also get access to valuable interactive data about how various devices connected through 5G were used.

In scenario one, Verizon remains a pipeline[9] business, selling data connectivity. In the second scenario, Verizon extends its business scope into its consumption ecosystems comprising the traveling nurses, doctors, and hospitals that use Verizon's data connectivity. Verizon thus unlocks more value from the data connectivity that it sells. It also extends its pipeline into a platform. Note that because 5G expands the use of data connectivity in a variety of IoT applications, Verizon and other carriers have the option of expanding into an array of different consumption ecosystems. They can facilitate exchanges for connected cars, for assets and entities within smart cities, for robots within smart factories, and in numerous other such applications.

In the current phase of 5G rollouts, much of focus of the major telecommunication carriers appears to be on strengthening their prevailing role of selling voice and data connectivity over 5G-enabled devices. This concentration is understandable, given the considerable potential for this market. Revenue expansion strategies include finding new areas where 5G provides an advantage and selling attractive cellular plans. One example is through offering 5G wireless "routers" for mobile and fixed applications. Such "5G routers," when placed in fire trucks, police vehicles, and ambulances, for instance, can provide fast and reliable connectivity to first responders. 5G routers in new buildings and manufacturing plants and on construction sites eliminate the need for expensive and time-consuming laying of cables to establish cellular connectivity.

There are also some early signs of alternative strategies. Consider some of Verizon's recent acquisitions. One of them, Sensity Systems, offers IoT platforms for smart city services, among other things.[10] Another acquisition is Fleetmatics (acquired for $ 2.4 billion), which offers fleet management and mobile workforce solutions.[11] These are strong signals of Verizon extending its pipelines into platforms in the IoT solutions space. AT&T is making similar moves.[12] For example, it has formed a partnership with Synchronos to offer IoT platform services that help office buildings conserve energy.

Increased vibrancy in IoT applications will understandably attract many players to offer new platform business models. Verizon's acquisitions of companies like Sensity and Fleetmatics are examples. Time will tell how these acquisitions evolve and how significant an impression carriers like Verizon will make in the IoT platform services space. If their current efforts remain experimental, or if they choose to withdraw from these early moves, they would be opting to play the role of suppliers to third-party platforms. For telecommunication carriers to establish their presence in their consumption ecosystems, particularly across a broad range of IoT applications, requires new capabilities. Elevating their role from being suppliers to platforms to offering their own digital platforms requires strategic vision and resolve. It will ultimately come down to how each carrier views its risk-reward trade-offs. Watch this space to see how it evolves.

The Insurance Business: The Changing Role of Data

Insurance companies have long relied on data. They assess risks and underwrite policies based on analyzing large pools of historical and aggregated data. Using actuarial skills, they discover important parameters that can influence risk. Age, demographics, medical history, residence zip codes, and nature of work are some examples of parameters that help predict risks for, say, life insurance. Insurers use their underwriting skills, honed through years of experience analyzing their proprietary data, to help generate profitable policies. Large capital reserves further allow them to underwrite large pools of risk. These large pools of subscribers also allow them to use low-risk subjects to subsidize high-risk subjects. In addition, they have a deep understanding of complex regulations. All these factors have acted as barriers to entry into the insurance industry and have benefited the incumbents for many decades. Until now.

Modern digital technologies are injecting turbulence into what was a stable and well-protected turf. The prevailing approaches, which use aggregated and historical data, are being challenged by new approaches that use individual-level and real-time data to assess risk. Modern technologies enable close and accurate monitoring of individual subjects' risks in ways that were not possible before. Rather than using age and demographics, parameters inferred from aggregate data, to predict a driver's auto insurance risk, for example, it is possible to do so by directly monitoring the driver. And data on observed driving habits may more accurately predict a driver's auto insurance risk. It is also possible to use these data to influence driving behavior, making it safer and thereby reducing auto insurance risk. Nor is this all: modern digital technologies are changing legacy insurance business practices in a variety of other ways.

Take, for instance, the practice of accepting, processing, and settling claims. Automation in this part of an insurance company's value chain can reduce the costs of the claims process by up to 30 percent.[13] In the event of an auto accident, for example, it is possible to remotely capture details as to where and how the accident happened, along with detailed visuals of vehicle damage. Alibaba's subsidiary Ant Financial has a product called Ding Sun Bao that analyzes such data using AI-driven, deep learning, and image recognition tools that can literally reconstruct the scene of the accident.[14] The technology can give an accurate assessment of the damage within seconds to enable an insurance company to process and settle a claim quickly digitally, without any paperwork. AI-based tools can also detect and help reduce fraudulent claims.

Because risk assessments can be made by real-time monitoring of assets and subjects, a wave of new entrants may soon confront the incumbents in this business. Prevailing industry entry barriers based on the need for large pools of subjects to reduce average risk may no longer act as an effective deterrent. Because access to individual-level data is possible, new entrants can even cherry-pick low-risk subjects. Several sectors of legacy insurance, such as auto and home insurance, may see an onslaught of new digital competitors.

Such competitors could enter through multiple openings. Firms offering sensors designed to collect real-time data about weather and soil conditions to optimize agricultural productivity can also deliver crop insurance to farmers. Their data not only help analyze risk more precisely but also help in expeditiously settling claims when sensors detect damage from pests or bad weather conditions. Similarly, businesses offering sensors in homes to monitor risks of water leaks or fire can also offer home insurance. Telecom carriers with telematics in cars can offer auto insurance. With real-time data and continuous monitoring, these new players not only can predict risks, they can intervene to reduce risks. Sensors detecting burst water pipes in a home, for example, can automatically shut off the water system. A McKinsey study predicts that customers may soon prefer paying premiums not to be compensated for damages but for services that predict and prevent risk.[15] To service such customers, there is a pressing need for insurance companies to revamp how they use data.

Insurance underwriting, like the telecommunication business discussed earlier, has traditionally been a value chain–driven business. The standard business model has been to underwrite and sell policies. Within this legacy business model, modern technologies help unlock more value from data by opening up new opportunities in its production ecosystems. Digitizing their claims processes or introducing advanced analytics to detect and prevent fraud are examples of how insurance companies can improve their operational efficiencies. Individual-level interactive data acquired through apps can also help provide new service features, such as predictive alerts of an impending health risk for a policyholder. In addition, data of this kind can be used to help mass customize policies that incentivize individual consumers with reduced premiums when they act in ways that reduce risk.

Moreover, modern trends in this business may also require prevailing value chains to extend into platforms. Underwriting and selling a policy may no longer be enough. Getting a handle on external factors that influence risk and thereby improve the profitability of a policy is now as important. Life insurance and health insurance, for example, are more profitable for an insurance company if holding the insurance influences the broader lifestyle of a consumer toward a longer and healthier life. To wield such influence may require the insurance company to operate on digital platforms that connect consumers to various health improvement objects, such as wearables, or entities, such as yoga instructors or physical trainers.

In other words, insurance companies may need to also engage with their consumption ecosystems, in addition to embellishing their production ecosystems. We see some firms doing so. Ping An, a Chinese insurance company, offers a variety of apps and platforms in the areas of health care, car sales, and real estate. Through these apps and platforms, Ping An engages in the consumption ecosystems of the company's health, auto, and home insurance businesses. WeChat, Tencent's super app, highlighted in chapter 8, entered the online insurance space in 2017. We saw what this firm achieved by harnessing troves of interactive data through its apps to gain an advantage in the consumption ecosystems of banks. Time will tell if it can do the same in the insurance business.

Picking a Digital Competitive Strategy Option

Three points are notable from the trends across these diverse businesses. First, opportunities for harnessing new value from data can come from both production and consumption ecosystems. Second, how firms react to these new opportunities varies. What may be a risky choice for one firm may seem to be an attractive option for another. As a result, firms are likely to make different bets on the emphasis they place on their digital initiatives. And third, how firms go about making these bets will shape the nature of digital competition and competitive dynamics in different digital ecosystems.

In the oil and gas industry, new opportunities are available predominantly within the businesses' production ecosystems. These opportunities also appear fairly obvious to all incumbents. Most of the competition in oil and gas thus is restricted to companies' production

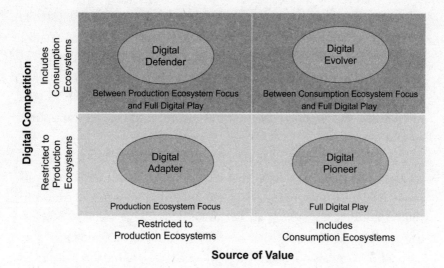

Figure 10.2
Picking a digital competitive strategy.

ecosystems. And it may also remain that way. In telecommunications, are new opportunities are emerging in the carriers' consumption ecosystems. There are early signs of incumbents interested in leveraging these opportunities. How they establish their presence in managing the new IoT applications they facilitate and how they compete with their own platforms and platform services will become clearer over time. In the insurance business, digital competition is gathering strength in both production and consumption ecosystems, with players making different strategic bets. Some are content to use modern digital technologies to improve internal efficiencies. Others are experimenting with more ambitious new business models.

In other words, how firms perceive new value opportunities evolving for them and how competitive pressures develop within their digital ecosystems will shape every individual firm's strategic decisions. Figure 10.2 depicts how individual firms may gravitate to different digital competitive strategy options because of these factors.

The horizontal axis of this matrix represents the source of new value from data that any individual firm perceives to be worth its interest. A firm may see value worth pursuing only in its production ecosystems, especially insofar as most legacy firms are anchored on value chains. Or a firm may see value worth pursuing in its consumption ecosystems as well. The vertical axis of this matrix represents how digital competition is shaping up. Digital competitors may be restricted within a firm's production ecosystems or they may also contest in their consumption ecosystems.

The lower left quadrant is where a firm perceives the value of data that is worth pursuing only within its production ecosystems and finds that its digital competitors also see it the same way. Exxon Mobil in the oil and gas business is an example. It sees new value in increasing operational efficiencies through modern digital technologies, just as most of its rivals do. Such firms will choose a production ecosystem focus. They will invest in new capabilities that enrich their prevailing value chains, turning them into production ecosystems. In doing so, they will also adapt to their new digital reality—recognizing that their prevailing value chains must be adapted to function as production ecosystems. A firm choosing to do so is a *digital adapter*. Most major firms in the oil and gas business are digital adapters.

The lower right quadrant is where a firm perceives new value worth pursuing in its consumption ecosystems, yet most of its competitors do not. Nest, the smart thermometer producer, was the first to recognize value in its consumption ecosystems. It extended its smart thermostat into a platform with connections to cars, home appliances, and security systems as platform users before any of the other thermostat producers did. Similarly, Nike was the first athletic shoe manufacturer to recognize value in its consumption ecosystems space when it introduced the Nike Community Forum to create communities of joggers and athletes.[16] Such a move takes a firm from a production ecosystem focus to a full digital play option. By moving early, Nike was also a *digital pioneer*, venturing into this new strategic position before others opted to do so. Peloton, the smart exercise equipment company that connects users to trainers and engages strong communities of health enthusiasts, is another example of a digital pioneer. Verizon and AT&T may be digital pioneers if they establish their presence in IoT platform services before the other carriers do. Such moves carry more risks. (Nike has since withdrawn its community forum). Yet a firm has to weigh such risks against the benefits of notching up network effects early and creating barriers to entry for rivals.

The upper right quadrant is where there is a growing consensus among firms that there is value worth pursuing in their consumption ecosystems. For example, it is possible that more and more insurance firms will start paying attention to the broader lifestyle of a consumer in order to better understand their policy risks. Or, as the McKinsey study foresees,[17] insurance may not just be about compensating for damages but more about predicting and preventing risk. If such trends gather momentum, all incumbents will be forced pay more attention to their consumption ecosystems. Many firms will extend their businesses into digital platforms. A firm doing so is a *digital evolver*.

It is important to distinguish digital evolvers from digital pioneers and digital adapters. Only a few digital pioneers discover value in their consumption ecosystems; far more do so as digital evolvers. Digital pioneers are exceptions. They see new opportunities before others do and are also prepared to make more risky bets. Digital evolvers make their moves when everyone else does. By the time they make their moves there is far less uncertainty in the consumption ecosystems space. Digital evolvers are also different from digital adapters, who stay within their value chain–based businesses, augmenting them with modern digital technologies. A digital evolver, on the other hand, "evolves" into platforms by extending its prevailing value chains. It evolves from a production ecosystem focus (along with other digital competitors) into a new position between a full digital play and a consumption ecosystem focus.

How close a digital evolver gets to a pure consumption ecosystem focus will depend on the extent to which the value in its business has shifted to its consumption ecosystems and how tenable its old production ecosystems position is. Consider the grocery stores business. Companies such as Instacart have entered its consumption ecosystems space through online grocery delivery services. Instacart shoppers pick groceries from established grocery stores and deliver them to Instacart's customers. All of Instacart's customers are digital customers, engaging with Instacart's apps and its digital platform. These customers thereby provide valuable interactive data on their day-to-day grocery needs. Using this data, Instacart can develop value propositions that predict, recommend, and offer innovative digital experiences related to its customers' grocery needs.

As part of such a value proposition, it is not far-fetched to imagine Instacart using suppliers that offer to stock groceries at inexpensive warehouses. Delivering groceries from such warehouses reduces costs compared to doing so from branded stores located in expensive downtown neighborhoods. Furthermore, if Instacart is able to offer attractive digital experiences in managing grocery needs, its customers may care less about where the groceries are sourced from.

If such trends intensify, they will spell trouble for legacy grocery stores. The value in their business will decline in their production ecosystems while rising in their consumption ecosystems. Along with other incumbents, each firm may evolve into this new space as the business becomes mostly about offering delivery experiences digitally. The more they see the threat of their branded grocery storefront being commoditized, the closer they will move to a pure consumption ecosystems focus.

And finally, the upper left quadrant represents conditions wherein a firm believes that there is value worth pursuing only within its production ecosystems but notices digital competitors in its consumption ecosystems space. Because the firm does not see value worth pursuing in its consumption ecosystems space, its preferred strategic position is to maintain a production ecosystems focus. Yet it may be drawn into its consumption ecosystems space to hedge its competitive bets. Such a firm will likely move to a point on its digital ecosystem frontier that is somewhere between a production ecosystems focus and a full digital play.

Caterpillar's joint venture with Trimble, discussed in chapter 4, is an example. Such a firm is usually testing the waters in its consumption ecosystems space. It may want to estimate the strength of its digital competitors in that space and assess the fortitude of its ecosystem barriers (or the ability of its digital competitors to move into its space and vice versa, discussed in chapter 7). It may also want to gauge how best to defend its position in its production ecosystems space. Its initiatives in its consumption ecosystems space are thus more defensive rather than surefooted offensive moves. Such a firm is a *digital defender*.

A majority of legacy firms employ value chain–based business models. Most of them are likely to initiate their digital transformation efforts as a digital adapter. Developing a production ecosystems focus may appear to them to be a logical first step. Subsequently, the choice to be a digital pioneer, a digital defender or a digital evolver will depend on several factors. These factors include the underlying nature of its business, the dynamics of digital competition in its business, and the firm's own propensity to take risks when seeking new rewards. The matrix in figure 10.2 helps a firm assess its goals and benchmark the thrust of its digital initiatives vis-à-vis its digital competitors. The matrix also helps keep track of the broad digital trends in its business.

Developing an Action Plan

How should a legacy firm use these ideas? It must develop an action plan to forge an effective digital competitive strategy. Firms are familiar with strategic action plans for their legacy businesses. Developing an action plan involves assessing the industry, taking stock of one's resources and capabilities, envisioning the scope of one's products vis-à-vis the competition, and finding the best way to position one's products for competitive advantage. An action plan for a digital competitive strategy has similar outlines, but the specifics are different. The focus is on data and digital ecosystems, as opposed to products and industries. The five steps described below provides a structure to develop an action plan for a digital competitive strategy.

Step 1: Map Your Digital Ecosystem

Just as traditional competitive strategy requires knowing one's industry, a digital competitive strategy requires knowing one's digital ecosystems. This first step is understanding the full scope of your value creating arena in the digital world. This can be broken down into the following set of tasks:

- Create a blueprint of your value chain network. List all the activities, assets, units, and entities that come together for your legacy business model.

- Identify all aspects of that network that can be connected. The more granular your value chain network is in terms of all its components, the more opportunities you will find to connect them.

- Chart a scheme for connecting them to map your production ecosystems. Visualize all physical interdependencies in the business model and see how they can be made to generate and exchange interactive data.

- Develop a plan to equip your products with sensors. Task your R&D division to come up with innovative and creative sensors. Develop processes to keep track of the kinds of sensors startups and tech companies are developing. Recognize the broad possibilities of sensors, including software and app-based ones that can track product-user interactions.

- Create a blueprint of your complementor network. Consider all the assets, units, and entities that can complement your product's sensor data. Start with known complements. These are usually associated with the primary function of a product. For iRobot's vacuum cleaners, some known complements may be replaceable dirt filters or dirt disposal bags that can be replenished using the product's sensor data. Next, set up brainstorming processes to identify new complements. Chapter 6 suggested pest control services as possible new complements for iRobot if its sensor could detect mouse droppings or termites. List all such possible ideas.

- Chart a scheme for connecting complements to map your consumption ecosystems. Visualize the interdependencies of the complements with the product and find ways to make them generate and share data. For example, how could iRobot connect a product's sensor data in a customer's home to the company's warehouse to automate timely deliveries of dirt disposal bags?

- Envisage all the digital technologies required within your mapped production and consumption ecosystems to achieve data generation and sharing within them.

Step 2: Take Stock of Your Digital Foundations

The first step was to understand the boundaries of your digital ecosystem. This second step is to understand where you are with respect to those boundaries. It involves evaluating where you stand vis-a-vis the digital capabilities required to take full advantage of your digital ecosystems. Consider the following activities:

- Assess your production ecosystem infrastructure. How many assets, units and entities in your value chain network, mapped in step 1, are already connected?
- Assess the scope of interactive data generated by your value chain network. What percentage of your assets, units, and entities provide interactive data?
- Estimate how many of your customers are digital customers. Assess the value of the interactive data they provide. How extensively can you track their product-user interactions? How much of these data are you using? For what purposes?
- Assess your consumption ecosystem infrastructure. How many assets, units, and entities in your complementor network, mapped in step 1, are connected? Assess the value of the interactive data they provide. How many complementors are providing data? How much of these data are you using? For what purpose?
- Create a blueprint of your API network. Assess its scope and intricacy. How much of the API network is internal? How much is external? What governance mechanisms do you have in place to use them as data conduits?

Step 3: Envision a Digital Ecosystem Frontier

This step is to visualize the full potential of data that your firm's digital ecosystems can unlock. It is a step to chart the digital goals your firm must strive for. Consider the following tasks:

- Identify all the areas where you can improve efficiencies in your value chain. List all your operational efficiency objectives. Modern technologies will give you a way to improve operational efficiencies as long as you can identify and specify your objectives.

- Envision all the data-driven features and services possible for your digital customers from your products. Consider the example of Caterpillar in chapter 4 (table 4.1 shows an approach to comprehensively listing all possible data-driven features and services). Develop a matrix similar to what is depicted, adapting it to your business.

- Assess what your digital competitors are offering as competing services. What are their strengths vis-à-vis yours? How strong are the network effects in your data-driven services? How much are you able to leverage them vis-à-vis your digital competitors?

- Envision the full potential of your product's sensor data to create a tethered digital platform. Review the discussion in chapter 5 about how to assess the potential of your sensor data through estimating the sensor data's value, uniqueness. and controllability.

- Envision all the data-driven services possible from such a tethered digital platform. For iRobot (per the example provided in step 1), the list of such possible services could include dirt disposal bag replenishment services, pest control services, or any others that they identify through their brainstorming sessions.

- Assess what your digital competitors are offering as competing platform services. What are their strengths vis-à-vis yours?

- Assess the strengths of your ecosystem barriers. How easy is it for a rival to replicate what you do in your production ecosystems? In your consumption ecosystems? What drives your network effects? How can you bolster them?

Step 4: Select a Desired Point to Compete on the Digital Ecosystem Frontier

This step is about arriving at a realistic digital competitive strategy goal. It builds on your assessment of your digital foundations (step 2) and the opportunities you identify in your firm's digital ecosystem frontier (step 3). Consider the following tasks:

- Evaluate what your firm can realistically achieve from all the opportunities in your digital ecosystems and given the strength of your digital competitors. What can you do to improve operational efficiencies? What kind of data-driven features and services can you generate from your production ecosystems? Can your product be extended into a platform? What kind of platform services do you envisage? Can they stand up to what you anticipate your digital customers can offer? Do you have the financial resources to execute those plans?

- Consider your strategic preference: is it to be a digital adapter or a digital pioneer? What is your tolerance for risk? Does your firm desire to be first in a new digital space when outcomes are uncertain? Or would you prefer to watch what your rivals are doing and keep pace with them? How quickly do you want to see a return on your investment?

- Consider the digital forces shaping up in your business. Are all your rivals moving into the consumption ecosystems space of your business? What kinds of ecosystem barriers do you envisage? What makes more sense for you, to be a digital defender or a digital evolver?

- Depending on your risk-reward preferences, pick an optimal point on your digital ecosystem frontier.

Step 5: Build Requisite Digital Capabilities for Your Desired Digital Competitive Strategy

This step is to move toward your strategic goal. It entails developing an approach to advance from where your digital foundations place you and reach the desired point on your digital ecosystem frontier.

- Drive your digital foundations toward the chosen point on your digital ecosystem frontier. Identify the necessary digital capabilities required to do so.
- Build the necessary production and consumption ecosystem infrastructures. Have you adequately connected all the aspects of your value chain and complementor networks identified in step 1?
- Generate requisite data assets. Have you maximized the data-generating potential of your production and consumption ecosystems identified in the earlier steps?
- Expand API networks to leverage data assets and excel at chosen strategic position.
- Reach the desired point on your digital ecosystem frontier. Continue to assess your position. Refine and revise as needed. Strive to maintain high levels of proficiency.

Closing Thoughts

This book is about providing legacy firms with key inputs necessary to compete in the modern digital era. The introduction outlined three specific inputs: first, a new understanding of how digital technologies have transformed prevailing ways of utilizing data; second, a fresh comprehension of business environments as digital ecosystems; and third, adopting a new mindset for a strategy that builds a data-driven advantage when competing in digital ecosystems. Each of the chapters in this book was written to provide these inputs. In doing so, these chapters also took us on a journey from data to a composite framework for digital competitive strategy. It is time now to conclude this journey.

An important aspiration of this book is to expand a legacy firm's strategic vision while helping leaders overcome digital myopia traps. A legacy firm suffers from digital myopia when it continues to rely primarily on a product-industry mindset for competitive advantage. With this kind of mindset, a legacy firm can fall into several digital myopia traps. It will see data's role only as supporting products. It may use data only to improve its operational efficiencies. It will fail to notice the far greater number of benefits that could be derived from interactive data. It will strive to improve only the prevailing features of its products and miss opportunities to offer new digital experiences through its products. It will fail to notice the existence of its consumption ecosystems. It will miss all the opportunities possible from extending its products into digital platforms. The concepts and frameworks introduced in this book are specifically meant to avoid falling into these kinds of digital myopia traps.

Legacy firms must see the coming years as full of exciting new opportunities. These opportunities can help them build new productive relationships with their customers and excite them with innovative digital experiences. These opportunities open new vistas for growth. Firms must seize them. They must adopt the new mindsets, use the strategic frameworks, and build the fresh capabilities outlined in this book. They must strive to be digital companies worthy of the new digital era. The future of competitive strategy has already arrived. It is time now to act.

Acknowledgments

There are many people I would like to thank for this book. To begin with, I would like to thank my brilliant wife, Meera, for patiently reading early drafts and being a terrific soundboard for my ideas; my lovely daughter, Kiran, for always encouraging her dad; and our beloved golden doodle, Raga, who stayed by my side all the time as I was writing. Raga passed away a month after I completed this manuscript, a couple of weeks shy of turning 16.

My thanks to Emily Taber, acquisitions editor at the MIT Press, and Robert Holland and Paul Michelman, series editors for the Management on the Cutting Edge, for seeing the potential in my book proposal early on. Emily's editorial inputs with the manuscript have been outstanding, and she has been a great pleasure to work with. My thanks to Deborah Cantor-Adams and Marjorie Pannell for their excellent editorial help and to the entire team at the MIT Press, including assistant acquisitions editor Laura Keeler, art coordinator Sean Reilly, book designer Emily Gutheinz, production manager Jim Mitchell, and senior publicist Molly Grote.

My thanks to Sandra Waddock, Joe Raelin, Raj Sisodia and Debjani Mukherjee for their feedback and encouragement during the early drafts of the book proposal. My thanks to Michael Goldberg for his excellent editorial help as I crafted each chapter.

Several others have helped me in various ways in creating this manuscript. Some provided their feedback on all or select chapters as they were being written. Others provided their expertise in specific areas or connected me to various subject matter experts and sources of data to help me crystallize my frameworks. My thanks to Anand Bangalore, Ashish Basu, Raj Baxi, John Carpenter, Eileen Daly, Liam Fahey, Ranjan Damodar, Alan Fetherston, Rahoul Ghouse, Rajneesh Gupta, Prakash Iyer, Raj Joshi, Anand Kapai, Mihir Kedia, Ashim Kumar, Neeraj Kumar, Rohit Mehra, Rahul Modi, Yash Modi, Shripad Nadkarni, Vasant Tilak Naik, Holger Pietzch, Rajnikant Rao, Ravi Sankar, Shubhro Sen, Ravi Shankavaram, Adam Syed, A. Vaidyanathan, Dr. A. V. Vedpuriswar, Ankit Vemban, Kumar Vemban, and Tieying Yu.

My thanks to Andy Boynton, Dean of the Carroll School of Management, Boston College, for supporting this book.

I dedicate this book to my late parents, Dr. K. S. Subramaniam and Savitri Subramaniam, both excellent educators and beacons for my life.

Notes

Introduction

1. "The World's Most Valuable Resource Is No Longer Oil, but Data," *Economist*, May 6, 2017, https://www.economist.com/leaders/2017/05/06/the-worlds-most-valuable-resource-is-no-longer-oil-but-data.

2. Jacques Bughin, James Manyika, and Tanguy Catlin, "Twenty-Five Years of Digitization: Ten Insights into How to Play It Right," McKinsey & Co., May 2019, https://www.mckinsey.com/~/media/mckinsey/business%20functions/mckinsey%20digital/our%20insights/twenty-five%20years%20of%20digitization%20ten%20insights%20into%20how%20to%20play%20it%20right/mgi-briefing-note-twenty-five-years-of-digitization-may-2019.ashx.

3. The book uses "products" for both physical products and services.

4. Nicholas Shields, "Ford Is Pouring Billions into Digital Transformation," *Business Insider*, July 27, 2018, https://www.businessinsider.com/ford-corporate-restructuring-digital-transformation-2018-7.

5. "Carmakers Are Collecting Data and Cashing In—and Most Drivers Have No Clue," *CBS News*, November 13, 2018, https://www.cbsnews.com/news/carmakers-are-collecting-your-data-and-selling-it.

6. Taylor Soper, "Starbucks Teams Up with Ford and Amazon to Allow In-Car Orders via Alexa," GeekWire, March 22, 201, https://www.geekwire.com/2017/starbucks-partners-ford-amazon-allow-car-orders-via-alexa.

7. "Smartphones on Wheels," *Economist*, September 4, 2014, https://www.economist.com/technology-quarterly/2014/09/04/smartphones-on-wheels.

8. "Ford Strives for 100% Uptime for Commercial Vehicles with Predictive Usage-Based Maintenance Solution," Field Service Connect UK 2020, March

5, 2020, https://fieldserviceconnecteu.wbresearch.com/blog/ford-strives-for-100 -uptime-for-commercial-vehicles-with-predictive-usage-based-maintenance -solution.

9. Arielle Pardes, "Old-School Mattress Brands Join the Sleep-Tech Gold Rush," *Wired*, July 29, 2019, https://www.wired.com/story/tempur-sealy-sleep-tech.

10. Erik Brynjolfsson and Andrew McAfee, "The Business of Artificial Intelligence," *Harvard Business Review*, July 2017.

11. James Manyika, Michael Chui, Peter Bisson, Jonathan Woetzel, Richard Dobbs, Jacques Bughin, and Dan Aharon, "Unlocking the Potential of the Internet of Things," McKinsey & Co., February 13, 2020, https://www.mckinsey.com /business-functions/mckinsey-digital/our-insights/the-internet-of-things-the -value-of-digitizing-the-physical-world.

12. Mohan Subramaniam, "Digital Ecosystems and Their Implications for Competitive Strategy," *Journal of Organizational Design* 9 (2020): 1–10.

13. John Joseph, "CIMCON Lighting Launches the NearSky Connect Program to Accelerate Smart City Transformations," Cimcon, October 3, 2018, https:// www.cimconlighting.com/en/cimcon-blog/cimcon-lighting-launches-the-nearsky -connect-program-to-accelerate-smart-city-transformations.

14. Mohan Subramaniam and Mikołaj Piskorski, "How Legacy Firms Can Compete in the Sharing Economy," *MIT Sloan Management Review* 61, no. 4 (2020): 31–37.

15. Mohan Subramaniam, "The Four Tiers of Digital Transformation," *Harvard Business Review*, September 21, 2021. https://hbr.org/2021/09/the-4-tiers-of -digital-transformation.

16. Michael Porter, "How Competitive Forces Shape Strategy," *Harvard Business Review* 57, no. 2 (1979): 137–145.

17. Amrita Khalid, "Ford CEO Says the Company 'Overestimated' Self-Driving Cars," Engadget, April 10, 2019, https://www.engadget.com/2019-04-10-ford-ceo -says-the-company-overestimated-self-driving-cars.html.

18. David P. McIntyre and Arati Srinivasan, "Networks, Platforms, and Strategy: Emerging Views and Next Steps," *Strategic Management Journal* 38, no. 1 (2016): 141–160, https://doi.org/10.1002/smj.2596.

19. Paul A. David, "Clio and the Economics of QWERTY," *American Economic Review* 75 (1985): 332–337.

20. David P. McIntyre and Mohan Subramaniam, "Strategy in Network Industries: A Review and Research Agenda," *Journal of Management* 35, no. 6 (2009): 1494–1517.

21. T. R. Eisenmann, "Internet Companies' Growth Strategies: Determinants of Investment Intensity and Long-Term Performance," *Strategic Management Journal* 27, no. 2 (2006): 1183–1204.

22. Ted Levitt, "Marketing Myopia," *Harvard Business Review* 38 (1960): 45–56.

Chapter 1

1. Rupert Neate, "$1tn Is Just the Start: Why Tech Giants Could Double Their Market Valuations," *Guardian*, January 18, 2020, https://www.theguardian.com /technology/2020/jan/18/1-trillion-dollars-just-the-start-alphabet-google-tech -giants-double-market-valuation.

2. "The World's Most Valuable Resource Is No Longer Oil, but Data," *Economist*, May 6, 2017, https://www.economist.com/leaders/2017/05/06/the-worlds -most-valuable-resource-is-no-longer-oil-but-data.

3. Marshall W. Van Alstyne, Geoffrey G. Parker, and Sangeet Paul Choudary, "Pipelines, Platforms and the New Rules of Strategy," *Harvard Business Review*, April 2016.

4. Mikołaj Jan Piskorski, *A Social Strategy: How We Profit from Social Media* (Princeton, NJ: Princeton University Press, 2016).

5. Erik Brynjolfsson, Yu Hu, and Michael Smith, "From Niches to Riches: The Anatomy of the Long Tail," *MIT Sloan Management Review 7*, no. 21 (2006).

6. Chris Anderson, *The Long Tail: Why the Future of Business Is Selling Less of More* (New York: Hachette, 2014).

7. David P. McIntyre and Mohan Subramaniam, "Strategy in Network Industries: A Review and Research Agenda," *Journal of Management* 35, no. 6 (2009): 1494–1517, https://doi.org/10.1177/0149206309346734.

8. Geoffrey Parker, Marshall Van Alstyne, and Sangeet Paul Choudary, *Platform Revolution: How Networked Markets Are Transforming the Economy—and How to Make Them Work for You* (New York: W. W. Norton, 2017).

9. Carl Shapiro and Hal R. Varian, *Information Rules: A Strategic Guide to the Network Economy* (Boston: Harvard Business School Press, 1998).

10. J. Rohlfs, "A Theory of Interdependent Demand for a Communications Service," *Bell Journal of Economics and Management Science* 5 (1974): 16–37.

11. Michael E. Porter, "Strategy and the Internet," *Harvard Business Review*, March 2001, 11.

12. Ingrid Lunden, "Amazon's Share of the US e-Commerce Market Is Now 49%, or 5% of All Retail Spend," TechCrunch, July 13, 2018, https://tech crunch.com/2018/07/13/amazons-share-of-the-us-e-commerce-market-is-now -49-or-5-of-all-retail-spend.

13. George Carey-Simos, "How Much Data Is Generated Every Minute on Social Media?," WeRSM, August 19, 2015, https://wersm.com/how-much-data -is-generated-every-minute-on-social-media.

14. Rose Leadem, "The Insane Amounts of Data We're Using Every Minute (Infographic)," *Entrepreneur*, June 10, 2018, https://www.entrepreneur.com /article/314672.

15. Simon Kemp, "Digital Trends 2019: Every Single Stat You Need to Know about the Internet," The Next Web, March 4, 2019, https://thenextweb.com /contributors/2019/01/30/digital-trends-2019-every-single-stat-you-need-to -know-about-the-internet.

16. Bernard Marr, "How Much Data Do We Create Every Day? The Mind-Blowing Stats Everyone Should Read," *Forbes*, September 5, 2019, https://www .forbes.com/sites/bernardmarr/2018/05/21/how-much-data-do-we-create-every -day-the-mind-blowing-stats-everyone-should-read.

17. Josh Constine, "How Big Is Facebook's Data? 2.5 Billion Pieces of Content and 500+ Terabytes Ingested Every Day," TechCrunch, August 22, 2012, https:// techcrunch.com/2012/08/22/how-big-is-facebooks-data-2-5-billion-pieces-of -content-and-500-terabytes-ingested-every-day.

18. Breanna Draxler, "Facebook Algorithm Predicts If Your Relationship Will Fail," *Discover*, November 20, 2019, https://www.discovermagazine.com/the -sciences/facebook-algorithm-predicts-if-your-relationship-will-fail.

19. "Google and Facebook Tighten Grip on US Digital Ad Market," eMarketer, September 21, 2017. https://www.emarketer.com/Article/Google-Facebook -Tighten-Grip-on-US-Digital-Ad-Market/1016494.

20. Mohan Subramaniam and Bala Iyer, "The Strategic Value of APIs," *Harvard Business Review*, January 7, 2015, https://hbr.org/2015/01/the-strategic-value-of -apis.

21. Carlos A. Gomez-Uribe and Neil Hunt, "The Netflix Recommender System: Algorithms, Business Value, and Innovation," *ACM Transactions on Management Information Systems* 6, no. 4 (December 2015).

22. Kartik Hosanagar, *A Human's Guide to Machine Intelligence: How Algorithms Are Shaping Our Lives and What We Can Do to Control Them* (New York: Viking, 2019).

Chapter 2

1. Bala Iyer and Mohan Subramaniam, "Corporate Alliances Matter Less Thanks to APIs," *Harvard Business Review*, June 8, 2015, https://hbr.org/2015/06/corporate-alliances-matter-less-thanks-to-apis.

2. Bala Iyer, Nalin Kulatilaka, and Mohan Subramaniam, "The Power of Connecting in the Digital World: Understanding the Capabilities of APIs," Working Paper, May 2016.

3. Matt Murphy and Steve Sloane, "The Rise of APIs," TechCrunch, May 22, 2016, https://techcrunch.com/2016/05/21/the-rise-of-apis.

4. Daniel Jacobson, Greg Brail, and Dan Woods, *APIs: A Strategy Guide* (Cambridge, MA: O'Reilly Media, 2011).

5. Shanhong Liu, "Microsoft Corporation's Search Advertising Revenue in Fiscal Years 2016 to 2020," Statista, August 12, 2020, https://www.statista.com/statistics/725388/microsoft-corporation-ad-revenue.

6. Mohan Subramaniam, Bala Iyer, and Gerald C. Kane, "Mass Customization and the Do-It-Yourself Supply Chain," *MIT Sloan Management Review*, April 5, 2016, https://sloanreview.mit.edu/article/mass-customization-and-the-do-it-your self-supply-chain.

7. Bala Iyer and Thomas H. Davenport, "Reverse Engineering Google's Innovation Machine," *Harvard Business Review*, April 2008, https://hbr.org/2008/04/reverse-engineering-googles-innovation-machine.

8. Jeff Dunn, "Here's How Huge Netflix Has Gotten in the Past Decade," *Business Insider*, January 19, 2017, https://www.businessinsider.com/netflix-subscribers-chart-2017-1.

9. Shanhong Liu, "Slack—Total and Paying User Count 2019," Statista, March 17, 2020, https://www.statista.com/statistics/652779/worldwide-slack-users-total-vs-paid.

10. Salesforce bought Slack for $27.7 billion in December 2020.

11. Matthew Panzarino, "Apple and Google Are Launching a Joint COVID-19 Tracing Tool for IOS and Android," TechCrunch, April 10, 2020, https://techcrunch.com/2020/04/10/apple-and-google-are-launching-a-joint-covid-19-tracing-tool.

12. Mishaal Rahman, "Here Are the Countries Using Google and Apple's COVID-19 Contact Tracing API," xda, February 25, 2021, https://www.xda-developers.com/google-apple-covid-19-contact-tracing-exposure-notifications-api-app-list-countries.

13. Geoffrey Fowler, "Perspective: Alexa Has Been Eavesdropping on You This Whole Time," *Washington Post*, May 8, 2019, https://www.washingtonpost.com/technology/2019/05/06/alexa-has-been-eavesdropping-you-this-whole-time.

14. Jonny Evans, "How to See Everything Apple Knows about You (u)," *Computerworld*, April 30, 2018, https://www.computerworld.com/article/3269234/how-to-see-everything-apple-knows-about-you-u.html.

15. Bala Iyer, Mohan Subramaniam, and U. Srinivasa Rangan, "The Next Battle in Antitrust Will Be about Whether One Company Knows Everything about You," *Harvard Business Review*, July 6, 2017, https://hbr.org/2017/07/the-next-battle-in-antitrust-will-be-about-whether-one-company-knows-everything-about-you.

Chapter 3

1. Michael E. Porter, *Competitive Strategy: Techniques for Analyzing Industries and Competitors* (New York: Free Press, 1980).

2. Mohan Subramaniam, Bala Iyer, and Venkat Venkatraman, "Competing in Digital Ecosystems," *Business Horizons* 62, no. 1 (2019): 83–94, https://doi.org/10.1016/j.bushor.2018.08.013.

3. See, for instance, Richard P. Rumelt, "How Much Does Industry Matter?," *Strategic Management Journal* 12, no. 3 (1991): 167–185, http://www.jstor.org/stable/2486591; and Anita M. Mcgahan and Michael E. Porter, "The Emergence and Sustainability of Abnormal Profits," *Strategic Organization* 1, no. 1 (2003): 79–108, https://doi.org/10.1177/1476127003001001219.

4. Joe Staten Bain, *Industrial Organization: A Treatise* (New York: Wiley, 1959).

5. Michael E. Porter, "How Competitive Forces Shape Strategy," *Harvard Business Review*, March 1979.

6. Michael E. Porter, *Competitive Advantage: Creating and Sustaining Superior Performance* (New York: Free Press, 1985).

7. Many studies have framed industries as ecosystems because they both are built on interdependencies. For a review, see Mohan Subramaniam, "Digital Ecosystems and Their Implications for Competitive Strategy," *Journal of Organization Design* 9, no. 1 (2020), https://doi.org/10.1186/s41469-020-00073-0.

8. Peter Campbell, "Ford and Volkswagen Unveil 'Global Alliance,'" *Financial Times*, January 15, 2019, https://www.ft.com/content/40d67c72-18c9-11e9 -9e64-d150b3105d21.

9. See, for example, Ming-Jer Chen and Danny Miller, "Competitive Attack, Retaliation and Performance: An Expectancy-Valence Framework," *Strategic Management Journal* 15, no. 2 (1994): 85–102, http://www.jstor.org/stable /2486865.

10. A substantial body of empirical work drawn from economic theories such as game theory support the notion that industry rivals are part of a network of interdependent competitive actions. See, for example, Adam Brandenburgerand Barry Nalebuff, "The Right Game: Use Game Theory to Shape Strategy," *Harvard Business Review*, 1995.

11. Tieying Yu, Mohan Subramaniam, and Albert A Cannella Jr., "Competing Globally, Allying Locally: Alliances between Global Rivals and Host-Country Factors," *Journal of International Business Studies* 44, no. 2 (2013): 117–137, https://doi.org/10.1057/jibs.2012.37.

12. Tieying Yu, Mohan Subramaniam, and Albert A. Cannella, "Rivalry Deterrence in International Markets: Contingencies Governing the Mutual Forbearance Hypothesis," *Academy of Management Journal* 52, no. 1 (2009): 127–147, https://doi.org/10.5465/amj.2009.36461986.

13. Thomas H. Davenport, *The AI Advantage: How to Put the Artificial Intelligence Revolution to Work* (Cambridge, MA: MIT Press, 2019).

14. Sara Zaske, "Germany's Vision for Industrie 4.0: The Revolution Will Be Digitised," ZDNet, February 23, 2015, https://www.zdnet.com/article/germanys -vision-for-industrie-4-0-the-revolution-will-be-digitised.

Chapter 4

1. Mohan Subramaniam, "The Four Tiers of Digital Transformation," *Harvard Business Review*, September 21, 2021, https://hbr.org/2021/09/the-4-tiers-of -digital-transformation.

2. Hau L. Lee, V. Padmanabhan, and Seungjin Whang, "The Bullwhip Effect in Supply Chains," *Sloan Management Review* 38, no. 3 (1997).

3. "Average Research & Development Costs for Pharmaceutical Companies," Investopedia, September 16, 2020, https://www.investopedia.com/ask/answers /060115/how-much-drug-companys-spending-allocated-research-and-develop ment-average.asp.

4. Leonard P. Freedman, Iain M. Cockburn, and Timothy S. Simcoe, "The Economics of Reproducibility in Preclinical Research," *PLOS Biology* 13, no. 6 (June 9, 2015), https://journals.plos.org/plosbiology/article?id=10.1371%2Fjournal .pbio.1002165.

5. "Caterpillar and Trimble Form New Joint Venture to Improve Customer Productivity and Lower Costs on the Construction Site," Trimble, October 5, 2008, https://investor.trimble.com/news-releases/news-release-details/caterpillar-and -trimble-form-new-joint-venture-improve-customer.

6. "Caterpillar and Uptake to Create Analytics Solutions," Caterpillar, March 5, 2015, https://www.caterpillar.com/en/news/corporate-press-releases/h/caterpil lar-and-uptake-to-create-analytics-solutions.html. This was a three-year experiment that has since ended and was only marginally successful. Caterpillar, however, continues to develop internal predictive capabilities, as well as work with third parties.

7. "About Us," Sleep Number Corporation, http://newsroom.sleepnumber.com /about-us.

8. "Leading Tools Manufacturer Transforms Operations with IoT," Cisco, https://www.cisco.com/c/dam/en_us/solutions/industries/docs/manufacturing /c36-732293-00-stanley-cs.pdf.

9. Chet Namboodri, "Digital Transformation: Sub-Zero Innovates with the Internet of Everything," Cisco, September 18, 21014, https://blogs.cisco.com/digital /sub-zero-innovates-with-the-internet-of-everything?dtid=osscdc000283.

10. "Industry 4.0: Capturing Value at Scale in Discrete Manufacturing," McKinsey & Co., https://www.mckinsey.com/~/media/mckinsey/industries/advanced %20electronics/our%20insights/capturing%20value%20at%20scale%20in%20 discrete%20manufacturing%20with%20industry%204%200/industry-4-0-cap turing-value-at-scale-in-discrete-manufacturing-vf.pdf.

Chapter 5

1. Mohan Subramaniam and Mikołaj Jan Piskorski, "How Legacy Firms Can Compete in the Sharing Economy," *MIT Sloan Management Review* 61, no. 4 (June 9, 2020): 31–37.

2. The tethered digital platform framework appeared in the summer 2020 issue of the MIT Sloan Management Review in a paper titled "How Legacy Firms Can Compete in the New Sharing Economy." I acknowledge the contributions of my co-author of that paper, Mikołaj Jan Piskorski, in shaping the ideas behind this framework. I also thank *MIT Sloan Management Review* for publishing that paper.

3. Mark Raskino and Graham Waller, *Digital to the Core: Remastering Leadership for Your Industry, Your Enterprise, and Yourself* (Boston: Gartner, 2015).

4. Steven Kutz, "What It's Like to Play Tennis with a 'Smart' Racket That Sends You Data," MarketWatch, September 4, 2015, https://www.marketwatch.com /story/what-its-like-to-play-with-a-smart-tennis-racket-2015-09-03.

5. Stuart Miller, "Turning Tennis Rackets into Data Centers," *New York Times*, December 23, 2013.

6. "FDA Approves Pill with Sensor That Digitally Tracks If Patients Have Ingested Their Medication," US Food and Drug Administration, November 13, 2017, https://www.fda.gov/news-events/press-announcements/fda-approves-pill -sensor-digitally-tracks-if-patients-have-ingested-their-medication.

7. For how Alibaba and Tencent hold a sensor data advantage over Chinese banks, see Mohan Subramaniam and Raj Rajgopal, "Learning from China's Digital Disrupters," *MIT Sloan Management Review*, January 16, 2019, https:// sloanreview.mit.edu/article/learning-from-chinas-digital-disrupters.

8. Bon-Gang Hwang, Stephen R. Thomas, Carl T. Haas, and Carlos H. Caldas, "Measuring the Impact of Rework on Construction Cost Performance," *Journal of Construction Engineering and Management* 135, no. 3 (2009): 187–198, https:// doi.org/10.1061/(asce)0733-9364(2009)135:3(187).

9. See Subramaniam and Rajgopal, "Learning from China's Digital Disrupters," for a discussion of how traditional banking services are being affected by platform-based business models.

10. Jacob Kastrenakes, "Alexa Will Soon Be Able to Directly Control Ovens and Microwaves," The Verge, January 4, 2018, https://www.theverge.com/2018 /1/4/16849306/alexa-microwave-oven-controls-added-ge-kenmore-lg-samsung -amazon.

11. "Yummly® Guided Cooking Is Here!," Whirlpool Corporation, December 13, 2018, https://www.whirlpoolcorp.com/yummly-guided-cooking-here.

12. Natt Garun, "Whirlpool's New Smart Oven Works with Alexa and Yummly to Help You Avoid Burning Down Your Kitchen," The Verge, January 8, 2018, https://www.theverge.com/ces/2018/1/8/16862504/whirlpool-smart-oven -range-microwave-yummly-alexa-google-assistant-ces-2018.

13. Andrei Hagiu and Elizabeth J. Altman, "Intuit QuickBooks: From Product to Platform," Harvard Business School Case 714–433, October 2013 (revised December 2013).

14. Mike Murphy, "More Than Just Vacuums: IRobot Is Building the Platform for the Robots of the Future," Protocol, August 25, 2020, https://www.protocol .com/irobot-builds-platform-for-future-robots.

15. Arielle Pardes, "Old-School Mattress Brands Join the Sleep-Tech Gold Rush," Wired, July 29, 2019, https://www.wired.com/story/tempur-sealy-sleep-tech.

16. Benjamin Edelman, "How to Launch Your Digital Platform," Harvard Business Review, April 2015, 90–97.

17. For a discussion of how product firms can learn from the digital titans about the use of APIs, see Bala Iyer and Mohan Subramaniam, "The Strategic Value of APIs," Harvard Business Review, January 7, 2015, https://hbr.org/2015/01/the -strategic-value-of-apis; and Bala Iyerand Mohan Subramaniam, "Are You Using APIs to Gain Competitive Advantage?," Harvard Business Review, August 3, 2015, https://hbr.org/2015/04/are-you-using-apis-to-gain-competitive-advantage.

18. See, for example, Bala Iyer and Mohan Subramaniam, "Corporate Alliances Matter Less Thanks to APIs," Harvard Business Review, June 8, 2015, https://hbr .org/2015/06/corporate-alliances-matter-less-thanks-to-apis.

Chapter 6

1. Victoria Dmitruczyk, "Nanotechnology and Nanosensors—Our Future as a Society?," Medium, March 31, 2019, https://medium.com/@12vgt2003/nanote chnology-and-nanosensors-our-future-as-a-society-33522e84c202.

2. P. K. Kopalle, V. Kumar, and M. Subramaniam, "How Legacy Firms Can Embrace the Digital Ecosystem via Digital Customer Orientation," Journal of the Academy of Marketing Science 48 (2020): 114–131, https://doi.org/10.1007/s11747 -019-00694-2.

3. Stacy Lawrence, "Startup Partners with AstraZeneca on Smart Inhalers Ahead of Aussie IPO," FierceBiotech, July 23, 2015, https://www.fiercebiotech.com /medical-devices/startup-partners-astrazeneca-smart-inhalers-ahead-aussie-ipo; Carly Helfand, "Novartis Matches Respiratory Rivals with 'Smart Inhaler' Collab- oration," FiercePharma, January 6, 2016, https://www.fiercepharma.com/sales -and-marketing/novartis-matches-respiratory-rivals-smart-inhaler-collaboration.

4. "What Do You Want to Know about Asthma?," Healthline, https://www .healthline.com/health/asthma.

5. "Chronic Respiratory Diseases: Asthma," World Health Organization, https:// www.who.int/news-room/q-a-detail/asthma.

6. Sandra Vogel, "Foobot—The Smart Indoor Air Quality Monitor," Internet of Business, May 5, 2017, https://internetofbusiness.com/foobot-smart-indoor-air -quality-monitor.

7. "My Air My Health," PAQS, http://www.paqs.biz.

8. Dara Mohammadi, "Smart Inhalers: Will They Help to Improve Asthma Care?," *Pharmaceutical Journal*, April 7, 2017, https://www.pharmaceutical-journal .com/news-and-analysis/features/smart-inhalers-will-they-help-to-improve -asthma-care/20202556.article.

9. Sumant Ugalmugle, "Smart Inhalers Market Share Analysis 2019: Projec- tions Report 2025," Global Market Insights, Inc., September 2019, https://www .gminsights.com/industry-analysis/smart-inhalers-market.

10. Tenzin Kunsel and Dheeraj Pandey, "Smart Inhalers Market by Product (Inhalers and Nebulizers), Indication (Asthma and COPD), and Distribution Channel (Hospital Pharmacies, Retail Pharmacies, and Online Pharmacies): Global Opportunity Analysis and Industry Forecast, 2019–2026," Smart Inhal- ers Market Size Analysis & Industry Forecast 2019–2026, June 2019, https:// www.alliedmarketresearch.com/smart-inhalers-market#:~:text=The%20global %20smart%20inhalers%20market,58.4%25%20from%202019%20to%202026.

11. Donald G. McNeil Jr., "Can Smart Thermometers Track the Spread of the Coronavirus?," *New York Times*, March 18, 2020, https://www.nytimes.com/2020 /03/18/health/coronavirus-fever-thermometers.html.

12. "How Smart Is Your Inhaler?," GlaxoSmithKline, November 8, 2016, https:// www.gsk.com/en-gb/behind-the-science/innovation/how-smart-is-your-inhaler.

Chapter 7

1. Lauren Debter, "Amazon Surpasses Walmart as the World's Largest Retailer," *Forbes*, May 25, 2019, https://www.forbes.com/sites/laurendebter/2019/05/15/worlds-largest-retailers-2019-amazon-walmart-alibaba.

2. Trefis Team, "Amazon vs Alibaba—One Big Difference," *Forbes*, May 22, 2020, https://www.forbes.com/sites/greatspeculations/2020/05/22/amazon-vs-alibaba--one-big-difference.

3. "Qq.com Competitive Analysis, Marketing Mix and Traffic," Alexa, https://www.alexa.com/siteinfo/qq.com.

4. "Tencent Announces 2020 Second Quarter and Interim Results," Tencent, August 12, 2020, https://static.www.tencent.com/uploads/2020/08/12/00e999c23314aa085c0b48c533d4d393.pdf.

5. Bani Sapra, "This Chinese Super-App Is Apple's Biggest Threat in China and Could Be a Blueprint for Facebook's Future. Here's What It's like to Use WeChat, Which Helps a Billion Users Order Food and Hail Rides," *Business Insider*, December 21, 2019, https://www.businessinsider.com/chinese-superapp-wechat-best-feature-walkthrough-2019-12.

6. Zarmina Ali, "The World's 100 Largest Banks, 2020," S&P Global Market Intelligence, April 7, 2020, https://www.spglobal.com/marketintelligence/en/news-insights/latest-news-headlines/the-world-s-100-largest-banks-2020-57854079.

7. Ali, "The World's 100 Largest Banks, 2020."

8. Andrea Murphy, Hank Tucker, Marley Coyne, and Halah Touryalai, "Global 2000—The World's Largest Public Companies 2020," *Forbes*, May 13, 2020, https://www.forbes.com/global2000.

9. Jon Russell, "Alibaba's Digital Bank Comes Online to Serve 'The Little Guys' in China," TechCrunch, June 26, 2015, https://techcrunch.com/2015/06/25/alibaba-digital-bank-mybank/; Catherine Shu, "Tencent Launches China's First Private Online Bank." TechCrunch, January 5, 2015, https://techcrunch.com/2015/01/04/tencent-webank.

10. "ICBC Releases 2018 Annual Results," ICBC China, March 28, 2019, https://www.icbc.com.cn/icbc/en/newsupdates/icbc%20news/ICBCReleases2018AnnualResults.htm#:~:text=As%20at%20the%20end%20of,balance%20of%20loan%20was%20RMB1.

11. "ICBC Releases 2018 Annual Results."

12. Qing Lan, "Tencent's WeBank: A Tech-Driven Bank or a Licensed Fintech?," EqualOcean, August 4, 2020, https://equalocean.com/analysis/2020080414410.

13. Stella Yifan Xie, "Jack Ma's Giant Financial Startup Is Shaking the Chinese Banking System," *Wall Street Journal*, July 29, 2018, https://www.wsj.com /articles/jack-mas-giant-financial-startup-is-shaking-the-chinese-banking-system -1532885367.

14. "Bank of China Limited 2017 Annual Report," April 2018, https://pic .bankofchina.com/bocappd/report/201803/P020180329593657417394.pdf.

15. Jay Peters, "Oral-B's New $220 Toothbrush Has AI to Tell You When You're Brushing Poorly." The Verge, October 25, 2019. https://www.theverge.com /circuitbreaker/2019/10/25/20932250/oral-b-genius-x-connected-toothbrush-ai -artificial-intelligence.

16. Alessandra Potenza, "This New Bluetooth-Connected Toothbrush Brings a Dentist into Your Bathroom," The Verge, June 9, 2016, https://www.theverge .com/circuitbreaker/2016/6/9/11877586/phillips-sonicare-connected-tooth brush-dentist-app.

17. Medea Giordano, "Colgate's Smart Toothbrush Finally Nails App-Guided Brushing," *Wired*, August 25, 2020, https://www.wired.com/review/colgate-hum -smart-toothbrush.

18. R. E. Caves and M. E. Porter, "From Entry Barriers to Mobility Barriers: Conjectural Decisions and Contrived Deterrence to New Competition, *Quarterly Journal of Economics* 91, no. 2 (May 1977): 241–261.

19. Anne Midgette, "Pianos: Beyond the Steinway Monoculture," *Washington Post*, September 5, 2015, https://www.washingtonpost.com/entertainment/music /the-piano-keys-of-the-future/2015/09/03/9bbbbfee-354c-11e5-94ce-834ad8f5 c50e_story.html.

20. Mohan Subramaniam and Raj Rajgopal, "Learning from China's Digital Disrupters," *MIT Sloan Management Review*, January 16, 2019, https://sloanre view.mit.edu/article/learning-from-chinas-digital-disrupters.

21. Evelyn Cheng, "China Wants to Boost Loans to Small Businesses: Tech Companies May Be the Answer," CNBC, January 29, 2019, https://www.cnbc .com/2019/01/29/chinese-fintech-companies-find-new-opportunities-in-business -loans.html.

22. Clayton M. Christensen, *The Innovator's Dilemma: When New Technologies Cause Great Firms to Fail* (Boston: Harvard Business School Press, 1997).

23. R. M. Henderson and K. B. Clark, "Architectural Innovation: The Reconfiguration of Existing Product Technologies and the Failure of Established Firms," *Administrative Science Quarterly* 35, no. 1 (March 1990): 9–30.

24. Ron Adner, *Winning the Right Game* (Cambridge MA: MIT Press, 2021).

Chapter 8

1. Nikolaos Logothetis, *Managing for Total Quality: from Deming to Taguchi and SPC* (New Delhi: Prentice Hall, 1992).

2. Jeffrey K. Liker and James K. Franz, *The Toyota Way to Continuous Improvement: Linking Strategy and Operational Excellence to Achieve Superior Performance* (New York: McGraw-Hill, 2011).

3. Michael Hammer, "Process Management and the Future of Six Sigma," *MIT Sloan Management Review* 43, no. 2 (2002).

4. Will Levith, "Get to Know Bruce Springsteen's One-of-a-Kind Fender Guitar," InsideHook, May 26, 2020, https://www.insidehook.com/article/music/get-to-know-bruce-springsteens-one-of-a-kind-fender-guitar.

5. Ingemar Dierickx and Karel Cool, "Asset Stock Accumulation and the Sustainability of Competitive Advantage," *Management Science* 35, no. 12 (1989): 1504–1511.

6. Jay Barney, "Firm Resources and Sustained Competitive Advantage," *Journal of Management* 17, no. 1 (1991): 99–120, https://doi.org/10.1177/014920639101700108.

7. Michael Hammer, "Reengineering Work: Don't Automate, Obliterate," *Harvard Business Review*, July–August 1990.

8. "Whirlpool Corporation Announces Planned Acquisition of Yummly," Whirlpool Corporation, May 2, 2017, https://whirlpoolcorp.com/whirlpool-corporation-announces-planned-acquisition-of-yummly.

9. Bala Iyer and Mohan Subramaniam, "Corporate Alliances Matter Less Thanks to APIs," *Harvard Business Review*, June 8, 2015, https://hbr.org/2015/06/corporate-alliances-matter-less-thanks-to-apis.

10. D. J. Teece, "Explicating Dynamic Capabilities: The Nature and Microfoundations of (Sustainable) Enterprise Performance," *Strategic Management Journal* 28, no. 13 (December 2007): 1319–1350, at 1335.

11. The Boston Consulting Group, for example, had introduced a popular strategic tool called the BCG matrix, proposing how a corporation could leverage its divisions enjoying high market shares in low-growth industries as "cash cows" to acquire new businesses in high-growth industries.

12. Constantinos C. Markides, "Diversification, Restructuring and Economic Performance," *Strategic Management Journal* 16, no. 2 (February 1995): 101–118.

13. C. K. Prahalad and Gary Hamel, "The Core Competence of the Corporation," *Harvard Business Review*, May–June 1990.

14. Anita M. McGahan and Michael E. Porter, "How Much Does Industry Matter, Really?," *Strategic Management Journal* 18 (July 1997): 15–30.

15. Iyer and Subramaniam, "Corporate Alliances Matter Less Thanks to APIs."

16. Hortense de la Boutetière, Alberto Montagner, and Angelika Reich, "Unlocking Success in Digital Transformations," McKinsey & Company, January 24, 2020, https://www.mckinsey.com/business-functions/organization/our-insights/unlocking-success-in-digital-transformations.

Chapter 9

1. Steph Solis, "Massachusetts Question 1: Right to Repair Ballot Initiative Explained," masslive, September 26, 2020, https://www.masslive.com/politics/2020/09/massachusetts-question-1-right-to-repair-ballot-initiative-will-determine-who-can-access-car-mechanical-data.html.

2. "Massachusetts Question 1, 'Right to Repair Law' Vehicle Data Access Requirement Initiative (2020)," Ballotpedia, https://ballotpedia.org/Massachusetts_Question_1,_"Right_to_Repair_Law"_Vehicle_Data_Access_Requirement_Initiative_(2020).

3. Matt Stout, "Mass. Has Been Pummeled by Ads on Question 1. They Veer into Exaggeration and 'Fearmongering,' Experts Say—*The Boston Globe*," *Boston Globe*, September 21, 2020, https://www.bostonglobe.com/2020/09/21/metro/massachusetts-has-been-pummeled-by-ads-about-question-1-they-veer-into-exaggeration-fear-mongering-experts-say.

4. "The Privacy Project," *New York Times*, April 11, 2019, https://www.nytimes
.com/interactive/2019/opinion/internet-privacy-project.html?searchResult
Position=1.

5. Kit Huckvale, Svetha Venkatesh, and Helen Christensen, "Toward Clinical
Digital Phenotyping: A Timely Opportunity to Consider Purpose, Quality, and
Safety," *npj Digital Medicine* 88 (September 6, 2019).

6. Alissa Walker, "Why Sidewalk Labs' 'Smart' City Was Destined to Fail,"
Curbed, May 7, 2020, https://archive.curbed.com/2020/5/7/21250678/sidewalk
-labs-toronto-smart-city-fail.

7. Sidney Fussell, "The City of the Future Is a Data-Collection Machine,"
Atlantic, November 21, 2018, https://www.theatlantic.com/technology/archive
/2018/11/google-sidewalk-labs/575551.

8. Shoshana Zuboff, *The Age of Surveillance Capitalism: The Fight for Human
Future at the New Frontier of Power* (London: Profile Books, 2019).

9. Alan J. Meese, "Price Theory, Competition, and the Rule of Reason," *University of Illinois Law Review*77 (December 31, 2002).

10. Lauren Feiner, "Google Sued by DOJ in Antitrust Case over Search
Dominance," CNBC, October 20, 2020, https://www.cnbc.com/2020/10/20/doj
-antitrust-lawsuit-against-google.html.

11. A deeply flawed lawsuit that would do nothing to help consumers.

12. Bala Iyer, Mohan Subramaniam, and U. Srinivasa Rangan, "The Next Battle
in Antitrust Will Be about Whether One Company Knows Everything about
You," *Harvard Business Review*, July 6, 2017, https://hbr.org/2017/07/the-next
-battle-in-antitrust-will-be-about-whether-one-company-knows-everything
-about-you.

13. Maya Goethals and Michael Imeson, "How Financial Services Are Taking
a Sustainable Approach to GDPR Compliance in a New Era for Privacy, One
Year On," Deloitte, 2019, https://www2.deloitte.com/content/dam/Deloitte/uk
/Documents/risk/deloitte-uk-the-impact-of-gdpr-on-the-financial-services.pdf.

14. Jack M. Balkin and Jonathan Zittrain, "A Grand Bargain to Make Tech Companies Trustworthy," *Atlantic*, October 3, 2016, https://www.theatlantic.com
/technology/archive/2016/10/information-fiduciary/502346.

15. Balkin and Zittrain, "A Grand Bargain to Make Tech Companies
Trustworthy."

16. David E. Pozen and Lina M. Khan, "A Skeptical View of Information Fiduciaries," *Harvard Law Review*, December 10, 2019, https://harvardlawreview.org/2019/12/a-skeptical-view-of-information-fiduciaries.

17. Russell Brandom, "This Plan Would Regulate Facebook without Going through Congress," The Verge, April 12, 2018, https://www.theverge.com/2018/4/12/17229258/facebook-regulation-fiduciary-rule-data-proposal-balkin.

18. "Democratic Senators Introduce Privacy Bill Seeking to Impose 'Fiduciary' Duties on Online Providers," Inside Privacy, December 21, 2018, https://www.insideprivacy.com/data-privacy/democratic-senators-introduce-privacy-bill-seeking-to-impose-fiduciary-duties-on-online-providers.

Chapter 10

1. "Industry Market Research, Reports, and Statistics," IBISWorld, February 16, 2020, https://www.ibisworld.com/global/market-size/global-oil-gas-exploration-production.

2. Katharina Buchholz, "The Biggest Oil and Gas Companies in the World," Statista Infographics, January 10, 2020, https://www.statista.com/chart/17930/the-biggest-oil-and-gas-companies-in-the-world.

3. Buchholz, "The Biggest Oil and Gas Companies in the World."

4. Kathy Hipple, Tom Sanzillo, and Clark Williams-Derry, "IEEFA Brief: Oil Majors' Shrinking Capital Expenditures (Capex) Signal Ongoing Decline of Sector," Institute for Energy Economics & Financial Analysis, February 26, 2020, https://ieefa.org/ieefa-brief-oil-majors-shrinking-capital-expenditures-capex-signal-ongoing-decline-of-sector.

5. Ben Samoun, Marie-Helene, Havard Holmas, Sylvain Santamarta, and J. T. Clark, "Going Digital Is Hard for Oil and Gas Companies—but the Payoff Is Worth It," BCG Global, March 12, 2019, https://www.bcg.com/publications/2019/digital-value-oil-gas.

6. Stephen Shankland, "5G's Fast Responsiveness Is the Real Reason It'll Be Revolutionary," CNET, December 8, 2018, https://www.cnet.com/news/how-5g-aims-to-end-network-latency-response-time.

7. Julie Song, "Council Post: Why Low Latency (Not Speed) Makes 5G A World-Changing Technology." *Forbes*, February 6, 2020, https://www.forbes.com/sites/forbestechcouncil/2020/02/06/why-low-latency-not-speed-makes-5g-a-world-changing-technology/?sh=126229592141.

8. Bert Markgraf, "How Far Can a Cell Tower Be for a Cellphone to Pick Up the Signal?," Chron, October 26, 2016, https://smallbusiness.chron.com/far-can-cell-tower-cellphone-pick-up-signal-32124.html.

9. Marshall W. Van Alstyne, Marshall Geoffrey G. Parker, and Sangeet Paul Choudary, "Pipelines, Platforms and the New Rules of Strategy," *Harvard Business Review*, April 2016.

10. Ingrid Lunden, "Verizon Acquires Sensity Systems to Add LED Light Control to Its IoT Platform," TechCrunch, September 12, 2016, https://techcrunch.com/2016/09/12/verizon-acquires-sensity-systems-to-add-led-light-control-to-its-iot-platform.

11. Ingrid Lunden, "Verizon Buys Fleetmatics for $2.4B in Cash to Step up in Telematics," TechCrunch, August 1, 2016, https://techcrunch.com/2016/08/01/verizon-buys-fleetmatics-for-2-4b-in-cash-to-step-up-in-telematics/?_ga=2.35330721.1433828888.1607712936-763817211.1607712936.

12. Peggy Smedley, "AT&T Is All-In with IoT." Connected World, October 1, 2018, https://connectedworld.com/att-is-all-in-with-iot.

13. Tanguy Catlin and Johannes-Tobias Lorenz, "Digital Disruption in Insurance: Cutting through the Noise," McKinsey & Co., March 2017, https://www.mckinsey.com/~/media/mckinsey/industries/financial%20services/our%20insights/time%20for%20insurance%20companies%20to%20face%20digital%20reality/digital-disruption-in-insurance.ashx.

14. Tjun Tang, Michelle Hu, and Angelo Candreia, "Why Chinese Insurers Lead the Way in Digital Innovation," BCG Global, February 27, 2018, https://www.bcg.com/publications/2018/chinese-insurers-digital-innovation.

15. Catlin and Lorenz, "Digital Disruption in Insurance."

16. Sarah Judd Welch, "Nike's Forum Shows the Promise and Peril of Community," *Harvard Business Review*, March 25, 2014, https://hbr.org/2014/03/nikes-forum-shows-the-promise-and-peril-of-community?ab=at_articlepage_whattoreadnext.

17. Catlin and Lorenz, "Digital Disruption in Insurance."

Index